BREAK-UP

AUTHORS' NOTE

Break-Up is the culmination of three years of work by two journalists. It is the story of twenty years in the lives and careers of
two politicians. It was prompted by the plight of two female civil
servants repeatedly abandoned by institutions that should have
protected them.

Alex Salmond was acquitted of thirteen counts of sexual assault
on 23 March 2020 after a two-week trial in Edinburgh. More than
a year earlier, Nicola Sturgeon's Scottish government had admitted
its internal investigation into sexual harassment claims against him
was unlawful, unfair and 'tainted by apparent bias'.

This book is not an attempt to retry the case against the former
First Minister. Nor does it shy away from exploring his behaviour
or the culture at the heart of his government. Its intention is to
document as fully as possible what happened, why it happened and
what it means.

Salmond and Sturgeon are two of Scotland's most familiar faces.
To all but their closest friends and family, Ms A and Ms B are
faceless.

The two women who originally came forward to share their
experiences of Salmond have been failed at every turn. By a civil
service that turned a blind eye to misbehaviour at the time and

botched an investigation into it years later; by a legal system that struggled to preserve their anonymity in an age of hyper-partisan social media; by a parliamentary inquiry that spent more time pursuing party political advantage than searching for the truth; and by a political climate that saw them as mere pawns in a wider constitutional battle.

This book does not claim to redress the balance or even seek to take sides. We are not a court of law or a Scottish Parliament committee. Our ambition is to give the fullest possible account of what took place.

The political consequences of this ugly chapter in Scottish public life are impossible to ignore. Salmond's reputation has been damaged beyond repair and he now cuts a lonely figure as he continues to undermine his former protégée. Sturgeon may have survived a finding by the Holyrood inquiry into her conduct that she misled Parliament, but she clearly still bears the emotional scars as she contemplates a final push towards independence.

Salmond and Sturgeon were brought together by a shared dream of breaking up the United Kingdom. We will soon find out what the severing of their relationship means for that continuing ambition.

But some things are more important than Scotland's constitutional future. The fallout from the saga has set the #MeToo movement in Scotland back immeasurably: who now would want to speak out about the misbehaviour of powerful men, particularly in politics, if this is the result?

Break-Up was motivated by our shared frustration that despite all the time and energy eaten up by the controversy this aspect was almost completely ignored. The false conspiracy theories, deliberate disinformation and misogynistic tropes that proliferated in online discussion strengthened our resolve to contribute an accurate take on what happened.

The material that follows draws on more than 100 interviews with politicians, special advisers, civil servants and others involved in the events discussed. Some sources had to remain anonymous because of the jobs they do or the fear of recriminations if they spoke publicly. We are deeply indebted to everyone who gave up their time and insight.

Safeguards rightly imposed during the criminal proceedings to protect the identities of the women who accused Salmond of sexual assault mean the locations, precise details and people involved in some of our narrative have had to be removed or redacted. It also means there are some parts of the story we cannot tell as fully as we would like. These omissions were beyond our control. Any errors were not.

The prologue is told in the first person due to the direct involvement of one of the authors. The rest of the book is the combined effort of two long-term friends collaborating professionally for the first time. It was produced in the face of legal restrictions, defamation threats and online smears.

Journalism is meant to give a voice to the voiceless. We've tried.

David Clegg and Kieran Andrews
Dundee, 7 July 2021

KEY CHARACTERS

THE GOVERNMENT

Alex Salmond: First Minister of Scotland (2007–14)

Nicola Sturgeon: First Minister of Scotland (2014–), Deputy First Minister (2007–14)

John Swinney: Deputy First Minister of Scotland (2014–), Finance Secretary (2007–16)

Kenny MacAskill: Scottish Justice Secretary (2007–14)

Alex Neil: Social Justice Secretary (2014–16), Scottish Health Secretary (2012–14)

Michael Russell: Scottish Constitution Secretary (2018–21), Education Secretary (2009–14)

THE ADVISERS

Peter Murrell: chief executive of the SNP, husband of Nicola Sturgeon

Elizabeth (Liz) Lloyd: chief of staff to Nicola Sturgeon

Geoff Aberdein: chief of staff to Alex Salmond

Kevin Pringle: special adviser to Alex Salmond

Campbell Gunn: special adviser to Alex Salmond and Nicola Sturgeon

Noel Dolan: special adviser to Nicola Sturgeon

Susan (Sue) Ruddick: chief operating officer of the SNP

THE CIVIL SERVANTS

Sir John Elvidge: Permanent Secretary to the Scottish government (2003–10)

Sir Peter Housden: Permanent Secretary to the Scottish government (2010–15)

Leslie Evans: Permanent Secretary to the Scottish government (2015–21)

Joe Griffin: principal private secretary to Alex Salmond

Michael McElhinney: private secretary to Alex Salmond

Chris Birt: private secretary to Alex Salmond

Judith Mackinnon: head of people advice

Nicola Richards: director of people

Gillian Russell: director of health workforce

John Somers: principal private secretary to Nicola Sturgeon

Donald Cameron: principal private secretary to Leslie Evans

THE WOMEN

Woman A: a senior official in the Scottish government

Woman B: a civil servant in the Scottish government

Woman C: an SNP politician

Woman D: a civil servant in the Scottish government

Woman E: a civil servant in the Scottish government

Woman F/Ms A: a civil servant in the Scottish government

Woman G: a Scottish government official

Woman H: a former Scottish government official

Woman J: an SNP party worker

Woman K/Ms B: a former civil servant in the Scottish government

THE LAWYERS

James Wolffe: Lord Advocate (2016–21)

Roddy Dunlop QC: represented the Scottish government in judicial review

Christine O'Neill QC: represented the Scottish government in judicial review

Ronnie Clancy QC: represented Salmond in judicial review

Gordon Jackson QC: led Salmond's defence in criminal trial

Shelagh McCall QC: co-counsel in Salmond's defence team

Alex Prentice QC: led prosecution against Salmond in criminal trial

David McKie: legal representative for Salmond

Callum Anderson: legal representative for Salmond

Duncan Hamilton: legal adviser to Alex Salmond

THE SCOTTISH PARLIAMENT COMMITTEE

Linda Fabiani (convener, SNP)

Margaret Mitchell (deputy convener, Conservative)

Murdo Fraser (Conservative)

Jackie Baillie (Labour)

Alex Cole-Hamilton (Lib Dem)

Maureen Watt (SNP)

Stuart McMillan (SNP)

Andy Wightman (Independent)

PROLOGUE

FOR THE RECORD

BY DAVID CLEGG

23 AUGUST 2018, 2.30 P.M.

I was working in a quiet corner of a Dundee coffee shop when I received the most memorable email of my life. It was from the *Daily Record*'s head of news, Kevin Mansi, and contained just five words and a picture.

'Anon letter that's come in.' The unremarkable introduction meant I nearly spat out my coffee when my phone loaded the attachment, a scanned copy of a 100-word document which had arrived at the newspaper's Glasgow office that morning. The contents, headlined SCOTTISH GOVERNMENT REPORTS SALMOND TO POLICE, were absolutely incendiary.

An anonymous whistleblower was claiming that two women had made sexual misconduct complaints against the former First Minister. The government had investigated the allegations before passing them to the police.

A summary of the most serious charge was also included:

During the week commencing 2 December 2013 late in the evening when Ms A was alone in FFM's company on official

xix

business, and when FM had been drinking alcohol, FFM instructed her to move from a public room to FM's bedroom; repeatedly offered her alcohol; which she declined; instructed her
to take off her boots; instructed her to lie on the bed; lay on top
of her in the bed; kissed her; touched her sexually on her breasts
and bottom through her clothes; continued this conduct for several minutes and only stopped when asked repeatedly by her to
do so.

The claims were so extraordinary that Mansi's initial reaction had
been to dismiss them as the work of a crank. 'Surely it's got to be
shite,' as he put it in a subsequent phone call. Yet on an initial reading my instinct was that several elements of the document seemed
authentic. The dry language used to summarise alleged behaviour
that would ultimately become a criminal charge of sexual assault
with intent to rape could only have been penned by a civil servant.
The small details also felt right – in particular the use of the three
letters FFM to describe Salmond. It was an abbreviation for former
First Minister that would mean nothing to the general public but
which I had heard many times in political circles. On balance, my
judgement was that it was entirely plausible that the account was
genuine.

It was also safe to assume that if it wasn't a hoax then we were
in a race against time to break the story. If this information had
reached us, it would not be long until other media organisations
also got wind of it. The document had arrived through the post in a
standard envelope addressed to the *Daily Record* news desk. For all
we knew, a similar package could have arrived at the office of every
newspaper in the country that morning. We had to proceed with
speed, caution and care. I immediately left the cafe and sprinted
the half-mile back to my house.

This was not the first occasion during my time as political editor of the *Record* that I had been given cause to suspect Salmond could be a potential subject of harassment complaints. I'd been covering the Scottish Parliament for seven years when the #MeToo movement erupted in the autumn of 2017 and sparked a wave of intense scrutiny of the behaviour of powerful men. It was during efforts to establish the accuracy of rumours circulating about SNP minister Mark McDonald that I had a conversation with a Scottish government official that would set the course for what followed. The well-placed figure insisted he had heard nothing unsettling about McDonald's conduct before adding dramatically: 'Everyone working in government knows that if a Harvey Weinstein scandal is going to emerge in Scotland, it will be about Alex Salmond.' Stunned by this comment from a normally level-headed contact, I immediately rang my editor, Murray Foote, to discuss what to do. It was decided that I should drop all other stories and spend the next few weeks digging into Salmond.

I began contacting civil servants, SNP staffers and government employees I knew had worked closely with the former First Minister in the previous two decades. A pattern quickly emerged. Salmond was described as a ferocious boss and hard taskmaster who was prone to shouting and swearing at staff. The word 'bully' cropped up again and again. Several sources also claimed the Scottish government had implemented a secret policy prior to the independence referendum to ensure the safety of female employees working at close quarters with Salmond. Yet it was also evident the former First Minister was an extremely talented and charismatic leader who inspired feelings of loyalty and devotion in subordinates – even those he mistreated. The picture was of a powerful man with a quick temper who had presided over a toxic culture that saw his erratic behaviour indulged and covered up by the civil service.

On 31 October 2017, I submitted a series of questions to the

Scottish government asking if any complaints had been made about Salmond during his time as First Minister. In a separate media enquiry, I also asked if a policy had been put in place to stop women working alone late at night with him. The government insisted there had been no policy and no complaints. Despite continuing whispers at Holyrood about Salmond having skeletons in his closet, none of the claims could be corroborated with sufficient certainty to allow publication. The news agenda moved on, but the gossip in Scottish political circles continued to focus on Salmond's past behaviour.

The anonymous letter that had arrived at *Record* HQ almost a year later suggested there was now something concrete to report on and we would have to move fast. Given the sensitivities involved, it was decided that only three journalists would be made privy to what was going on: Mansi, myself and the new editor, David Dick. Meanwhile, the *Record*'s senior lawyer, Campbell Deane, was traced to a holiday resort and politely asked to stay out of the pub as his services were likely to be required.

I contacted the Scottish government and asked for a comment shortly before 4 p.m., while Mansi made a similar call to Police Scotland for information on the status of their investigation. The reaction from both organisations was bizarre and panicked – giving us renewed confidence in the accuracy of our information.

The Scottish government press office did not deny the substance of what was put to them but would not be drawn on the details. After several frustrating phone calls, I sent an email to the organisation's head of news at 7.06 p.m. highlighting First Minister Nicola Sturgeon's repeated public commitments to transparency in dealing with any alleged cases of harassment and demanding that her words were translated into action.

In a bluff aimed at forcing the issue, I added:

I can confirm that we are proceeding with this story and I will need a response by 7.30 p.m. I also should inform you that it is likely the Scottish Government's stonewalling of legitimate press inquiries on this matter may form a part of the story if a comment is not forthcoming.

I strongly suspected Sturgeon's administration could be trying to cover up the existence of the complaints to protect Salmond and the wider SNP. Ironically, the subsequent Scottish Parliament inquiry would instead focus on whether senior officials had improperly released the information after Salmond pointed the finger at the First Minister's office for leaking it.

The Scottish government replied at 7.19 p.m. with a short and puzzling statement saying they couldn't 'currently' comment on the situation for 'legal reasons'. The police response was even more unusual. It said the force 'would not comment on whether' they were investigating. The responses were significant for two reasons: they effectively confirmed the existence of some kind of complaint against Salmond, but they also suggested the former First Minister was locked in a legal dispute with the Scottish government over the issue. A scenario that would have seemed impossible only that morning began to emerge. Could Alex Salmond really be at war with the government led by his protégée Nicola Sturgeon?

The race was now on to verify the accuracy of the information independently so we could publish regardless of on-the-record confirmation. All the journalists involved were acutely aware that the slightest inaccuracy in any subsequent story could have disastrous consequences. I began methodically recontacting sources who had been useful in recent months in the hope they could provide further corroboration. Tellingly, I found I was unable to get any senior Scottish government special adviser to answer their phone.

Meanwhile, Mansi worked his extensive police contacts. It was not until 8 p.m. that – after consultation with Campbell Deane – we had enough confidence in our information to contact Salmond directly to give him the opportunity to present his version of events.

I was in my small home office when I dialled his mobile number and heard that distinctive voice click onto the line. I had last seen the former First Minister the previous year when I took him for a long lunch in Glasgow two weeks after he lost his Westminster seat. His tone was much colder on this occasion.

'Yes, David, what can I do for you?' he asked.

My heart was pounding as I replied: 'We're doing a story on the allegation the police are looking at. Should I be speaking to a lawyer, or is there a comment I should take from you?'

There was a long pause.

'And which allegation is this, David?'

'The one from December 2013 at Bute House.'

'And what's the detail of it, sorry, David?'

'That a staff member at Bute House was harassed or assaulted after a function.'

In the terse three-minute conversation that followed, Salmond avoided being drawn on the substance of the complaints and focused on fishing for more information on the status of the police investigation and enquiring into who was the source of the story. He also asked for the allegations to be put to him in writing, a request I duly obliged.

With the *Record*'s print deadline looming, an urgent conference call was convened to discuss whether to publish in the event of no substantive response to the details of the allegations being received from the Scottish government, Police Scotland or the former First Minister. This was a big call for David Dick, who had been in the editor's chair for only a few months and was now dealing with the biggest story any Scottish newspaper had tackled in living memory.

After a brief discussion, he decided he was happy for us to proceed and I began writing.

Then, at 9.32 p.m., an emailed response from Salmond's lawyer, David McKie of Levy & McRae, dropped into my inbox. Its contents were breathtaking.

He did not dispute the existence of the allegations or even make a threat of defamation action. Instead, he warned that publication would be a breach of privacy and cited the recent high-profile finding against the BBC regarding coverage of the police investigation into pop legend Sir Cliff Richard.

An accompanying statement from Salmond confirmed he was taking the Scottish government to court over their handling of sexual harassment complaints. The former First Minister also insisted he was completely innocent of any wrongdoing and would fight to clear his name. In an attempt to spoil the *Record* story shortly before publication, the statement was also distributed to a bewildered Scottish press pack at 10 p.m. It was an implicit acknowledgement that the striking headline about to roll off the *Record*'s printing presses on the south side of Glasgow was accurate: SALMOND REPORTED TO COPS OVER SEX ATTACK CLAIMS.

The shocking sexual misconduct allegations against Alex Salmond were finally out in the open, but the fallout was only just beginning.

CHAPTER 1

THE FRIENDSHIP

'If someone asked me if I was a groper I'd say "No". Why can't you say "No", Alex?'

Alex Salmond had endured many uncomfortable moments at the hands of the Scottish media over the previous three decades, but the hastily arranged press conference at the Champany Inn was excruciating.

He had summoned the country's shellshocked political journalists to one of his favourite haunts – a rustic, well-regarded restaurant outside Linlithgow, the town of his birth – within hours of the *Daily Record* revealing he was facing two allegations of sexual misconduct dating back to his time as First Minister. Hard-bitten hacks who had covered the rough and tumble of Scottish politics for years struggled to process the magnitude of the story that had erupted overnight. The most famous Scottish nationalist of the past century, and the man who had taken the country to the brink of independence, had been accused of committing sexual assault in his official residence, Bute House, and was now taking his successor, Nicola Sturgeon, to court over how her government had conducted their investigation into the claims. It was the Scottish equivalent of learning David Cameron had been accused of committing a sex attack in Downing Street and had responded by launching legal action against Theresa May.

The bombshell spawned a host of questions: had Sturgeon known about his alleged behaviour? Had it been covered up at the time? Would the claims end up in a criminal court? What would happen to the women who had come forward? What did it mean for the future of the SNP and Scottish independence?

Despite being a stone's throw from the M9, the motorway which cuts across Scotland's central belt, the Champany Inn is a secluded, stone-built venue set in West Lothian farmland. Cars and broadcast vans from Glasgow and Edinburgh were soon lined up along the narrow track to the restaurant, set back from the road amongst low, white-washed and pantiled buildings. A sunlit court-yard became the impromptu waiting pen for dozens of journalists, leaving diners bemused at the sight of the massed ranks of report-ers, photographers and camera crews.

When the press conference finally got under way shortly after 4 p.m., the throng moved to what appeared at first glance to be a jarringly inappropriate venue. Salmond sat at the head of a narrow wooden table in what would often be used as a wedding marquee – a light, airy canopy with boxes of champagne stacked at the side. The fabric-covered chairs, normally draped in ribbons, were hud-dled tight so the reporters could lean in.

Scotland's longest-serving First Minister, dressed in an unre-markable navy suit and blue tie, was sombre and composed as he made a short opening statement. The questions, starting four min-utes later, took a lot longer and were significantly more animated. The overwhelmingly male composition of Scotland's political press pack meant pictures of the event would give the impression of a chummy old boys' reunion, but the line of questioning pursued by the journalists was far from friendly.

Salmond acknowledged he had made mistakes but insisted he

had never harassed anyone and was innocent of any crime. 'I'm no saint. I've made mistakes politically, I've made mistakes personally, but I refute the complaints that have been made against me and I absolutely deny any semblance of criminality,' he said in a statement that would mirror his attitude to more than a dozen allegations which would emerge in the coming months. He expressed no ill will towards the complainants, who he said had a 'perfect right' to raise their concerns, but was fierce in his criticism of Leslie Evans, Scotland's most senior civil servant. 'For whatever reason, the Permanent Secretary has decided to mount a process against me using an unlawful procedure which she herself introduced,' he said. 'I will let a real court decide whether it was lawful for her to do so.'

Veteran journalists noted that Salmond looked tired and had aged visibly in the four years since stepping down as First Minister. Another significant difference from his time in office was that there were now no government officials on hand to control the press pack and rule difficult questions out of bounds. Reporters took full advantage of the unfettered access and lack of referee. The old Salmond swagger seemed gone as he fended off repeated attempts to tease out salacious details by answering in short, softly spoken sentences with only the hum of the motorway traffic in the background. His responses were calm but rarely forthcoming. 'If I'm wrong, and I fall in the Court of Session, then I've got no alternative [but] to answer the complaints openly and publicly, which I will,' he said. 'But if I'm right, and this process is fundamentally flawed, then those at the top of the administration of the Scottish government – and I am talking about the administration, not politicians, the Permanent Secretary at the top of the administration, will have the most serious questions to answer.'

The journalists in the marquee were less interested in the technical details of the Scottish government's disputed process for investigating the harassment complaints than they were in the nature of the allegations now facing the former First Minister. Citing the pending legal action, Salmond refused to confirm the details that had appeared in the *Record* that morning or give any further information. Asked if there had been any sexual indiscretions, he responded: 'No – I'm not going to give you a list of the mistakes I think I've made.' Other questions included: do you think you used to drink too much as FM? Are your memories sharp? Are you sorry if you made any of the women you worked with uncomfortable? Are you a groper? Have you done anything that would warrant an apology to your wife?

It was an unrelenting barrage that lasted just over forty minutes.

On the final point, Salmond's response was non-committal: 'One thing that's so encouraged me is that friends and family today, and in the case of Moira the last few months, have been incredibly supportive. I've had lots and lots of messages today and I'm grateful for them.'

He also refused to comment on whether he had asked Sturgeon to intervene in the government harassment inquiry and make it go away. He did admit speaking to his former protégée on several occasions about the case but added: 'I'm not going to say what a private conversation between myself and Nicola Sturgeon was.'

His insistence on the confidentiality of those discussions would not last long: he would later accuse the First Minister of breaching the Scottish government's ministerial code of conduct by failing to intervene on his behalf. But while many more months would pass until the full extent of the rift between the pair became apparent, Salmond's cold tone did little to conceal the fact that he was disappointed in the woman who had served as his deputy for ten years, including seven in government.

A few miles away in Edinburgh, Sturgeon was also breaking her silence on the scandal in an extraordinary interview with the BBC.

Her face etched with anguish, the First Minister confirmed that two women had made complaints against Salmond in January and an investigation had been conducted under a new procedure covering ministers and former ministers which she had signed off the previous month at the height of the #MeToo campaign that followed the Harvey Weinstein sexual harassment scandal. 'Although I have been aware for some time of the fact of the investigation – initially from Alex Salmond – I have had no role in the process, and to have referred to it before now would have compromised the integrity of the internal investigation, which I was not prepared to do,' she insisted.

Sturgeon also confirmed she had been told by Evans earlier that week that the investigation was complete and that she intended to make the complaints public. On legal advice, Sturgeon withheld the fact that Salmond had faced eleven separate complaints from the two women, of which five had been upheld by the Permanent Secretary as 'well founded'.

'Alex Salmond is now challenging the Scottish government's procedure in court. The Scottish government refutes his criticisms of its process and will defend its position vigorously,' she added.

Sturgeon's words impressed upon the viewer that she was a politician facing an unenviable dilemma in which she had been forced to choose between loyalty to her mentor and her responsibility as First Minister to ensure all allegations raised with the government were dealt with properly. 'This will be extremely upsetting to members of the SNP up and down the country,' she said. 'It's a difficult situation, but what is important is that complaints are treated seriously, regardless of who the person complained about is.'

Sturgeon would also have recognised the bitter irony of Salmond selecting the Champany Inn as the venue to symbolically sever their friendship by announcing his legal battle against her government. It was the very spot where fourteen years earlier the

most successful partnership in the history of Scottish politics had
been forged.

*　　*　　*

In the summer of 2004, the Scottish National Party was in crisis.
Alex Salmond was a backbench MP whose best days were widely
thought to be behind him, while Nicola Sturgeon was heading
for an embarrassing defeat in the party's leadership contest. Three
years later, the SNP was in government, Salmond was First Minister and Sturgeon was his deputy. The rapid change in fortunes can
be traced back to a steak dinner the two politicians shared at the
Champany Inn on Saturday 10 July 2004.

John Swinney had resigned as SNP leader on 22 June in the wake
of a disastrous showing in the European Parliament elections. The
studious if unflashy North Tayside MSP had been in the party's
top job for four years but struggled to match the media profile Salmond had built up during his first tenure in charge between 1990
and 2000.

Public anger at Tony Blair over the invasion of Iraq should have
provided fertile ground for Scottish nationalist support, as voters
protesting UK foreign policy looked for a new home. Swinney had
been at the forefront of Scottish opposition to the war, joining
large-scale marches in Glasgow and leading debates on the issue
at the Scottish Parliament – but the party's vote share under his
leadership consistently went backwards.

Salmond had been spinning his wheels as the leader of the SNP's
small group of five MPs at Westminster and initially dismissed any
notion that he would return to Edinburgh to resume the leadership. In one interview, he even notoriously declared: 'If nominated
I'll decline, if drafted I'll defer and if elected I'll resign.' He was in-
voking Union Army General William Sherman's response to being

asked to run for US President, but that didn't stop the formulation being wheeled out ironically many times in the years that followed.

With Salmond out of the picture, the contest originally shaped up as a three-way battle between Sturgeon, who was still only thirty-three years old, the Perth MSP Roseanna Cunningham, who had served as Swinney's deputy for the previous four years, and Michael Russell, the former SNP chief executive who had lost his seat in the Scottish Parliament election the previous year. Salmond, who had not yet turned fifty, had been politically close to all three at different times. While publicly backing Sturgeon, he initially seemed content to let the contest run its course without his direct involvement.

That changed on 15 July when, not for the first or the last time, Salmond shocked the Scottish political world by announcing he was launching an audacious comeback bid. There had been a concerted campaign to convince him to enter the race from senior party figures, including the Moray MP Angus Robertson and influential former MSP Andrew Wilson, which only intensified following a car-crash performance from Cunningham, the frontrunner, on the BBC's *Question Time* on 1 July. Nevertheless, the U-turn still came as a major surprise to all but Salmond's closest allies.

Campbell Gunn, then political editor of the *Sunday Post*, recalls a chance encounter with Salmond in London the day before his entry into the race. The legendary journalist, who a decade later would work for Salmond as a media adviser, had been in the House of Commons for the publication of the long-awaited Butler Report into the invasion of Iraq the previous year. The fallout from the inquiry, which determined that the intelligence used by the Blair administration to convince MPs to vote in favour of the conflict had been unreliable, was a piece of parliamentary theatre that Salmond simply could not miss.

Once the drama concluded in the Commons, the two men

happened upon each other at Westminster Tube Station on their way home to Scotland and fell into a lengthy conversation about the ongoing leadership contest. The strengths and weaknesses of the various candidates were discussed without Salmond giving any indication that he was poised to throw his hat into the ring.

Gunn was back home in Glasgow the next morning when his alarm went off as usual to the BBC's flagship *Good Morning Scotland* programme. He picks up the story in his unpublished memoirs:

> The lead item was that in a remarkable about-turn Alex Salmond had announced he was to enter the SNP leadership contest. I dozed off back to sleep, I'd met Alex the previous evening, and we'd been talking about the contest – I was obviously dreaming. Then I jolted awake. No. I had actually heard that on the radio! I jumped out of bed, listened to the remainder of the news programme which confirmed that he would be making an official announcement later that day in Aberdeen. I immediately made plans to head north instead of going through to the Holyrood parliament.

When he arrived at the venue for the press conference – the Marcliffe at Pitfodels, another of Salmond's favourite hotels – Gunn found the politician apologetic for his lack of candour the evening before and strongly hinting that his wife, Moira, may have been behind the sudden twist in the leadership contest. Gunn explains: 'I asked what had been behind his change of heart. Had he seen Roseanna's poor performance on *Question Time*? "No," he said, "but Moira saw it." Mrs Salmond had told her husband he had to stand for the sake of the party.'

Those who are close to the couple all attest to Moira's influence over Salmond, and she was the first name on his nomination papers, so Gunn's theory that she may have been behind her husband's decision to stand is credible. The couple met in the 1970s when Salmond was an assistant economist in the Scottish Office and the then Moira French McGlashan, who is seventeen years his senior, was his boss. They married in the summer of 1981 and Moira, the daughter of a car mechanic from Peebles, taught him how to drive and refined his image. She is often the inspiration behind Salmond's on-again off-again diets, keeping a careful eye on what he eats and drinks, and is studious about his appearance to the point that he has admitted always checking that the flaps of his suit pockets are untucked before going on television to save himself from a row later.

Whatever the motivation behind it, there is no dispute about how Salmond's spectacular entry into the leadership race unfolded. With his mind made up, he got in touch with Sturgeon's team and asked for an urgent meeting. The Champany Inn was already one of Salmond's favourite restaurants and he had formed a close personal friendship with the owners, Clive and Anne Davidson. Its secluded location, away from the prying eyes of the political bubble in Edinburgh, made it an ideal spot for mapping out the future of the party.

Sturgeon arrived with no inkling that her mentor had undergone a change of heart and was about to propose the equivalent of the famous Granita pact between Tony Blair and Gordon Brown. Then, in a move which closely mirrored the deal brokered by the Labour heavyweights, Salmond asked her to withdraw from the contest and instead back him for leader and serve as his deputy. It was an audacious move even for Salmond, who had already developed a reputation for bold and unexpected plays which caught the political establishment off-guard.

Sturgeon asked for forty-eight hours to think about it but agreed within a day. 'He told me straight what he was considering, why he was considering it, and what he thought we should do together as a team,' Sturgeon would later recall to the BBC. 'But he said to me very, very frankly that if I didn't want to do that and I wanted to [continue] as [a candidate for] leader then that was fine, he would perfectly happily back me in doing that. He gave me a veto on it.'

She ultimately calculated that Salmond assuming command with her as deputy would be the best move for the party. Given she was widely expected to fall short in the leadership contest, it could be argued that the move also progressed her personal ambitions.

The main casualty of the arrangement was Kenny MacAskill, who had been seeking the deputy leader role after backing Sturgeon for the top post. On learning of the development, the Lothians MSP agreed to withdraw from the race and give his backing to the Salmond–Sturgeon partnership. It was not the last time MacAskill would find himself at the centre of drama involving the pair. As Scottish Justice Secretary in 2009 he would precipitate the SNP government's first real crisis by approving the release of the man convicted of the Lockerbie bombing, Abdelbaset al-Megrahi, on compassionate grounds. Later still, he would defect from the SNP to the Alba Party ahead of the 2021 Scottish Parliament election, after siding with Salmond over Sturgeon in the feud which had cleaved through the nationalist movement. In 2004, however, MacAskill played a key role in cementing the pair's close political relationship by agreeing to bow out of the deputy leadership contest and give them a clear run. 'My ambition is for the future of the SNP and the future of Scotland,' he said at the time. 'I believe the Salmond–Sturgeon team is the best to unite the party and take the SNP forward.'

The Herald newspaper broke the news of the agreement a few days later in a front-page report which opened by referencing the significance of the restaurant: 'Champany Inn in Linlithgow will now be etched in the annals of SNP history as the place where

Alex Salmond persuaded Nicola Sturgeon to step aside and let the king return from across the water.'

When the votes were counted on 3 September, the king was comfortably returned to his throne. Salmond won the support of 75.8 per cent of SNP members who voted, compared to Cunningham's 14.6 per cent and Russell's 9.7 per cent. It was a resounding victory – 'Mike and I got well stuffed,' was how Cunningham put it – that left no doubt over the future direction of the party. Sturgeon also achieved a handsome mandate for the deputy position, hoovering up 53.9 per cent of the vote. The joint ticket had ensured the Salmond–Sturgeon alliance was now firmly in control.

The pair had been presented very much as a team during the contest, with Salmond telling members that between them they had 'what it takes to appeal to all of Scotland – north and south, male and female, youth and experience'. It was a sales pitch he repeated to the wider public in an interview with the BBC's *Breakfast with Frost* programme two days after the results were announced. Salmond said he had been attracted back to frontline politics because the SNP was now under a 'team leadership'. 'This time I am back and I am back as a team player,' he added. 'It is a novelty for me, but it will be even better.'

In a keynote speech to the SNP conference in Inverness three weeks later, Salmond sketched out the party's main goals over the coming years. He pledged to take the SNP to power at Holyrood in the 2007 election, ensure Tony Blair was 'drummed from office' over the Iraq War and convince Scots that independence represented their best hope for the future. He also stressed that Sturgeon would play a crucial role in achieving these ambitions: 'Nicola and I campaigned as a team, we will lead as a team and we will win as a team.'

Some within the SNP harboured deep scepticism over whether Salmond had really embraced a more consensual approach to internal party politics or had merely identified Sturgeon as a useful asset that complemented his strengths while glossing over his weaknesses. Party strategists certainly hoped that having a young woman from Ayrshire in a prominent position would help them appeal to parts of Scotland they had traditionally struggled to reach. One key adviser at the time says:

> Alex had always been very respectful of Nicola – he made her a member of his shadow Cabinet in the first Scottish parliamentary term – but at this point it wasn't the tight-knit duo it became. He obviously could see the advantages of making her deputy and that all came out of the meeting at Champany. He had to somehow account for the fact it was all a bit Back to the Future – he had already been leader, he'd had a ten-year stint, so it needed that extra element. Nicola gave the whole thing a fresh coat of paint.

The pair had been close for many years, with Salmond an influential presence in Sturgeon's life since she was eighteen. Three years later he had encouraged her to stand as a parliamentary candidate in the 1992 general election, a fact Sturgeon later said showed 'he believed in me long before I believed in myself'. However, their relationship was always primarily political – a situation reinforced by their very different personalities. Sturgeon was a generation younger, more reserved and the pair did not tend to mix in the same circles. Indeed, while Salmond was extremely sociable and enjoyed long boozy lunches and dinners with colleagues, Sturgeon was more comfortable at home with a book when not working or campaigning. 'I wouldn't describe the relationship as deeply warm at that point but clearly there was a lot of respect there,' says Andrew Wilson, the former SNP MSP who also worked for Salmond for a time. 'She learned a lot from being his deputy because the one thing about Nicola at that time was she was absolutely determined to improve herself.'

Salmond's absence from the Scottish Parliament – he had stepped down from Holyrood three years earlier – gave Sturgeon a major opportunity for personal development, as it was her job to lead the SNP at Holyrood and take the fight to the governing Labour–Lib Dem coalition. Her weekly jousts with Jack McConnell at First Minister's Questions (FMQs) thrust her into the media spotlight and bolstered her reputation as an impressive parliamentary performer – a status confirmed when she won Donald Dewar Debater of the Year at the 2004 Scottish Politician of the Year awards ceremony.

It was also at this time that Sturgeon began to work with the man who would become her closest adviser for the next decade. Noel Dolan was a former TV journalist who had worked briefly as Salmond's chief of staff at Holyrood. It was on his former boss's recommendation that Sturgeon brought him in to oversee FMQs. 'We worked very well together,' he recalls.

> It is the only time in the week that you have equal time with the First Minister and so my ambition every week was to get on telly and she was, we were, quite good at doing that. So she got on telly and she got a pretty good profile during those two and a half years, she became kind of well known.

In contrast, Salmond initially struggled to make much of an impression in his first year back in charge. He was being overshadowed at Westminster by Charles Kennedy, the Liberal Democrat leader, who was enjoying success criticising New Labour from the centre left. The Highlander had been an MP since 1983, enjoyed a huge media profile and had successfully positioned his party as the main parliamentary voice of opposition to the war in Iraq. His dominating presence on the UK stage gave Salmond little room for manoeuvre.

The 2005 general election was a disappointment for the SNP. It brought little change in Scotland's political make-up despite a reduction in the number of seats following devolution. The SNP went from five MPs to six but, in terms of vote share, finished five points behind the Lib Dems and only two ahead of the Tories.

However, circumstances changed significantly in Salmond's favour in early January 2006 when Kennedy quit the Lib Dem leadership after admitting seeking help for an alcohol problem. Salmond was soon able to position himself as the foremost Westminster critic of the Labour government over the unfolding disaster in Iraq. Two months later the SNP also managed to seize the UK domestic agenda when their Western Isles MP, Angus MacNeil, reported the 'cash for honours' scandal to the Metropolitan Police. The subsequent sixteen-month investigation into the connections between political donations and the awarding of life peerages kept the spectre of Labour corruption – and the profile of Salmond and the SNP – in national headlines all the way to the Scottish Parliament election in May 2007.

McConnell, who had been First Minister since 2001, enjoyed a reasonably warm personal relationship with Sturgeon, but his team soon realised she added an extra weapon to the SNP's arsenal. Labour's private opinion polling and focus groups had shown that Salmond enjoyed very high levels of popularity with men but was struggling to convince women. There was something about his abrasive and belligerent debating style that was causing a significant gender gap in his approval ratings. It was a trend also picked up by the SNP's internal research; their answer was to give Sturgeon a more prominent role.

'Salmond was beating Jack consistently amongst male voters by this point, but Jack was beating him consistently amongst female voters,' says a source close to McConnell.

> And then from the start of the autumn of 2006 there was a distinct shift and they started running all the adverts of Alex and Nicola as a duo. She was used consistently for the twelve months running up to the 2007 election, for softening up his image and making him more presentable – especially to women.

Sturgeon was very much a woman used to operating in a man's world. The SNP of the early 1990s was a macho environment and she inevitably found herself surrounded by mainly male role models, of whom Salmond was the most important. She spoke candidly about how this climate formed her early approach to politics in an interview with *The Herald* to mark International Women's Day in 2018. 'Most of the people I was surrounded with were men,' she told the journalist Marianne Taylor.

> I have gained more understanding of this by looking back, but I know that influenced how I behaved as a politician when I was younger. You start to adopt – unconsciously – behaviours, the stance, the approach. In politics it leads you to be more adversarial and aggressive in your approach and as a young woman, behaving like the men behave inevitably leads to people seeing you as taking yourself far too seriously. It's a no-win situation and you quickly realise this. If you behave in the way people expect women to behave, the danger is you are treated as not being serious enough. If you emulate the behaviours of the men around you, you are accused of not being feminine.

In retrospect, the timing of the article's publication on 8 March

2018 is noteworthy. It came two days after Salmond had been told the Scottish government had launched a secret probe into sexual harassment allegations against him. Sturgeon insists she knew nothing of the investigation until the following month. While the comments were very much in tune with the public mood at the time, her efforts to distance herself from the often aggressive and abrasive behaviour of her predecessor is striking given what followed in the months and years to come. 'In my early days in politics I probably did subconsciously emulate male behaviour too much,' she said in the same interview. 'A lot of the stuff written about me in my younger days was all about how I was adversarial and never smiled – stuff that would never be said about a man.'

Salmond's 'adversarial' nature had already been well-documented by the time of his second tenure as SNP leader. He was renowned for having a quick temper with staff and vicious debating style with opponents. Yet he also had a personal warmth and charisma that could inspire extraordinary loyalty amongst even those on the receiving end of his tantrums. A number of impressive individuals who worked for Salmond as young men struggled to detach themselves from his orbit as their careers progressed. Kevin Pringle, for years Salmond's chief spin doctor, is probably the best example of someone who left for the private sector on more than one occasion but could never quite sever ties with the man who was frequently called 'the boss' by his staff. Other examples include MSP turned barrister Duncan Hamilton, long-serving chief of staff Geoff Aberdein and digital guru Kirk Torrance. With the exception of Sturgeon, examples of female colleagues who have enjoyed such lengthy associations with Salmond are harder to come by.

Another faithful adviser from his early days, Stephen Noon, captured the essence of Salmond's leadership style in a 1998 article for *The Independent*. Written the year before the Scottish Parliament was set up, Salmond was at that stage just a small fish in the Westminster pond. But the basic description outlined by Noon, who subsequently worked in various roles for the SNP and Yes Scotland before emigrating to Canada to become a Jesuit priest in 2017, would be echoed by many staff over the years. 'Alex is a great motivator because you know however hard you work, he is working harder. He will blaze at you for two minutes if you have done something wrong, but then it's forgotten,' he said.

> He also has a way of finding out what's going on in the office by leaving pauses which he knows you will fill. In your anxiety to fill the silence you can end up confessing everything, but I'm wise to this trick now. He has another annoying habit of asking a question he knows that you don't have the answer to; but he also encourages you to challenge him.

Noon also referenced Salmond's easy rapport with the general public and love of shooting the breeze with strangers – a skill that would be put to great use during the independence referendum campaign in 2014. 'He loves hearing other people's opinions, and during a shopping trip with his wife, for example, he may spend two hours speaking to people in the streets,' Noon added. 'He's able to dominate every room he walks into and he has great personal charisma.'

Salmond's ability to charm had always been a feature of his political campaigning, but if the SNP hoped to ascend to government in 2007, they knew they needed to soften his image and expand his appeal. They also realised this would take more than adding Sturgeon to their campaign posters.

The roadmap for this new direction was devised on the banks of the Spey, in Moray, just two months after the disappointment of the 2005 general election. The party's most influential figures gathered at the Craigellachie Hotel that July, amongst them Noon,

Robertson, Pringle, MacNeil and the SNP's chief executive and Sturgeon's then partner and future husband, Peter Murrell. Alasdair Allan, the national secretary, who had worked in Salmond's Peterhead office and would later represent the SNP on the Holyrood committee inquiry into the government's handling of the harassment complaints, was also in attendance.

The meeting has subsequently gained legendary status in the minds of supporters as the moment the SNP made the switch from being a party of opposition to a party of power, declaring they would be 'ready for government before May 3, 2007, and in government thereafter'.

SNP researcher John Fellows recalled in a 2017 blog the shift in presentation that followed:

> Over the next two years we went from employing a sniping, angry tone across our communications and media work to become the positive, aspirational force in Scottish politics. We honed our message down to two key messages: that the Scottish Parliament election in 2007 was a straight fight between the SNP and Labour, and between Jack McConnell and Alex Salmond to be Scotland's First Minister.

Around this time the SNP was introduced to 'life coach' Claire Howell, who stressed the need for upbeat, optimistic language in political campaigning. Her philosophy was based on the idea that a positive message always beats a negative message. Taking her advice to heart, Salmond took significant steps to be less combative in public as part of continuing efforts to soften his image.

'I would call this Salmond mark two,' says SNP veteran Alex Neil.

He had learned some of the lessons of the mistakes he had

made during his first ten years in the top job. He came back with a much clearer sense of purpose about what he was trying to achieve. He was much more disciplined. He was much more insistent on a more disciplined approach. He had a much clearer strategy. He was much more single-minded about winning the election.

The 2007 manifesto, 'A Culture of Independence', contained populist fare that appealed to the middle-class voters who decide the outcome of all Scottish elections. It pledged to scrap council tax, cancel student debt, support small business and boost the number of frontline police officers.

It also cemented the idea of Salmond and Sturgeon as a team. The pair were pictured together and a foreword by Salmond concluded:

> We are working hard to earn the trust and support of the people of Scotland and we will trust Scots to take the decision on Scotland's future in an independence referendum. The choice will be yours. That is the fair and democratic way. It's time for a Scottish government that cares about success for our nation. Nicola Sturgeon and I are ready to take Scotland forward.

They would soon take Scotland forward to within touching distance of breaking up the British state.

CHAPTER 2

IN POWER

A lex Salmond declared victory before he was sure it was his.

Votes were still being counted in the 2007 Scottish Parliament election when the SNP leader touched down by helicopter on the grounds of the five-star Prestonfield House on the outskirts of Edinburgh. His party had not technically won yet – several constituencies were still to declare in a neck-and-neck contest marred by delays and an unprecedented number of spoilt ballots – but the uncertainty of the result did not stop Salmond presenting himself as not just a winner but a First Minister.

Accompanied by his future chief of staff Geoff Aberdein and Moray MP Angus Robertson, the 52-year-old seized the initiative with a carefully calibrated televised address in the hotel's extensive gardens. 'It is very clear indeed which party has lost this election and the Labour Party no longer has any moral authority left to govern Scotland,' he said. 'Scotland has changed for good and for ever. There may be Labour governments and First Ministers in decades still to come, but never again will the Labour Party think it has a divine right to government.'

The optics of the moment were reinforced shortly afterwards when Labour leader Jack McConnell gave a downbeat TV interview from a drab roadside location in which he called for a weekend of reflection and no 'snap decisions'. 'The contrast with Alex and the helicopter arrival, the podium on the lawn, the look of Prestonfield, and what he was saying contrasted with Jack McConnell standing in a lane,' recalls an SNP staffer. 'It just looked like: "Hang on, this guy's won and this guy has lost."'

Within a few hours, the SNP would indeed be declared the biggest party at Holyrood, although by the slimmest of possible margins. They took forty-seven seats compared to Labour's forty-six, making Salmond's act of political theatre on the Prestonfield lawn seem a self-fulfilling prophecy.

His core team had gathered at the venue in the hope of a historic result. In addition to Aberdein and Robertson, Nicola Sturgeon had travelled across from Glasgow after a breakthrough victory which removed Labour's sitting MSP, Gordon Jackson, from the Govan constituency. (Jackson, a QC, would return full-time to his law career and eventually lead Salmond's defence in the 2020 criminal trial.)

'It was important for Nicola from her point of view to try and win it,' recalls Sturgeon's adviser Noel Dolan. 'She wasn't necessarily expecting that we'd win the election overall. We were kind of hopeful, but we were hoping we were going to win Govan. That would have been a big success. It was a big success as far as we were concerned.'

Also in attendance at Prestonfield were Sturgeon's husband-to-be and party chief executive Peter Murrell, future SNP MP Stephen Gethins, strategists Kevin Pringle, Colin McAllister, Stephen Noon and Jennifer Dempsie, an adviser who would later marry Robertson. These were the key people who had transformed the SNP from a party that was in crisis just three years earlier to one that was now heading for government. Their unexpected triumph arrived like a bolt from the blue. Labour had not lost an election in Scotland since 1955 and the prospect of any other party gaining control of the devolved Parliament had barely been contemplated in the eight years since its inception. 'You have to remember the shock of what happened,' says then *Scottish Sun* political editor Andrew Nicoll.

> The SNP was a fringe group for decades. They stood in elections for eighty years and never won one and then they did – but just barely. The point about the first term, to my mind, was the fact that it was so clearly not the crest of the wave but just the start.

Journalists who had been following the inner workings of the SNP for years suddenly found themselves in high demand for consultancy work as businesses, charities and other organisations scrambled to gain insight into this once peripheral group now running the country.

The decision to govern alone was equally unchartered territory. The first two Scottish Parliament terms had seen Labour and the Liberal Democrats form a coalition in order to gain the sixty-five seats necessary for a Holyrood majority. As leader of the biggest party, Salmond initially attempted to sound out the Lib Dems about a formal partnership, but his insistence that an independence referendum would have to take place at some point during the four-year parliamentary term meant that an agreement proved impossible to reach. Instead, Salmond decided to go it alone, making history on 17 May by becoming the first nationalist to be elected First Minister of Scotland after defeating McConnell by forty-nine to forty-six at a vote at Holyrood. The Tories and Lib Dems abstained, ensuring the SNP would enter government with the support of the two Green MSPs.

Salmond struck an uncharacteristically consensual tone in a victory speech which reflected the reality of minority government. 'I commit myself to leadership wholly and exclusively in the Scottish national interest,' he said. 'We will appeal for support, policy by policy, across this chamber. That is the parliament the people of Scotland have elected and that is the government that I will be proud to lead.'

MSPs also gave their backing to a new Cabinet. Sturgeon, now officially Deputy First Minister, was given the crucial health brief, while Salmond's predecessor as SNP leader, John Swinney, took charge of finance. Another familiar figure from recent SNP history, Kenny MacAskill, was given justice, Fiona Hyslop headed up education and Richard Lochhead was made Cabinet Secretary for Rural Affairs and the Environment.

With little prospect of an independence referendum due to the parliament's unionist majority, the new government initially focused its efforts on implementing as many of the other manifesto promises as possible. Key pledges included cancelling student debt, abolishing council tax and replacing it with a local income tax, free NHS prescriptions, boosting the number of frontline police officers by 1,000 and scrapping tolls on the Forth and Tay road bridges. Free university tuition for Scottish students, a council tax freeze and the successful delivery of the pledges on free prescriptions, police numbers and bridge tolls would follow over the next four years.

The rigours of minority government also ensured party discipline. 'In that first meeting of the parliamentary group, Alex basically said to us all sitting around the table: "Look, we've got a one-seat advantage: if one of us drops the ball, if one of us lets down the rest, we're out,"' says one MSP present. 'From that day forward our whips, frankly, had nothing to do.' The siege mentality fostered by the parliamentary arithmetic would help create the iron discipline that defined the SNP during Salmond's time as First Minister and then fell apart spectacularly in the wake of his sexual harassment scandal.

* * *

The high stakes of government were brought home to Salmond within a matter of weeks of assuming office when the new First Minister found himself dealing with every politician's worst nightmare – a terrorist attack on home soil.

At 3.11 p.m. on 30 June, Iraqi doctor Bilal Abdulla, aged twenty-seven, and 28-year-old engineer Kafeel Ahmed drove a Jeep Cherokee laden with propane gas cylinders and petrol cans towards the door of Glasgow Airport's departure area. It was the first Saturday of the school summer break and they hoped to kill hundreds of holidaymakers. Their demented plan was only thwarted by a concrete bollard that stopped the vehicle's progress before it managed to crash through to the main terminal building, which had around 4,000 people inside.

When the Jeep failed to explode, Abdulla threw petrol bombs from the passenger seat and Ahmed, who was born in India but grew up in Saudi Arabia, doused himself in petrol and set it alight. Abdulla then got out of the Jeep and attacked a policeman who had appeared on the scene as stunned civilians fled for their lives. He was also tackled by a number of passers-by, including Alex McIlveen, a taxi driver who had stumbled upon the attack after dropping off a fare.

Salmond was in Bute House, the First Minister's official residence in Edinburgh, with James Bond star Sean Connery when he learned of the attack from a senior civil servant at around 3.30 p.m. Connery had been Salmond's guest of honour at the Queen's official opening of the third term of the Scottish Parliament, which had concluded three hours earlier, and was staying with the First Minister overnight. The bedroom the actor slept in was nicknamed 'The Connery Room' by civil servants and was the scene of the alleged attempted rape that Salmond would be acquitted of almost thirteen years later.

Back in 2007, Salmond and his celebrity guest turned on the TV to learn more about the unfolding terrorist attack. Salmond later recalled the events to the *Sunday Mail*:

> There was a Sky newsflash. Sean is usually unflappable with these things – I suppose it must be all these Bond films he's been in – but there was still a fair amount of astonishment. This was the first terrorist incident in Scotland really because there had never, for example, been an IRA terrorist incident here. There was shock that Scotland was regarded as a terrorist target.

Salmond began a series of meetings on security in the Scottish government's nearby headquarters, St Andrew's House, and soon received a call through a secure line from Gordon Brown, who had taken over as UK Prime Minister only three days earlier. It was already clear that the attack was connected to two failed car bomb attempts in London the previous day and coordination between Strathclyde Police and the Met would be vital.

The next day at 4.30 a.m., officers raided the terrorists' unlikely lair – a two-bedroom semi-detached house in Houston, Renfrewshire, a small village seven miles west of the airport. The force's community relations experts were keen to make the public aware that the terrorists were not home-grown in a bid to ward off any ill-feeling towards Scotland's Muslim community. This desire would provide the first example of what would become a recurring trend over the years that followed: tension between Edinburgh and London over the responsibilities of the devolved administration.

Salmond visited the airport on the Sunday afternoon to pay tribute to the emergency services and members of the public who had
tackled the bombers. He also decided to reveal the initial findings
of the police investigation, which suggested the terrorists had not
been in Scotland for long but had recently relocated from England.
He later said: 'This was regarded as a crucial message to get out to
strongly nip in the bud any suggestion that this would be an excuse
for inter-faith tensions.'

But Home Secretary Jacqui Smith tried to block the move when
she got wind of it in London. Salmond was in the car on the way
to the airport when a call came through on his mobile phone from
the Labour minister, who warned that the planned statement
risked giving away confidential information. Salmond replied:
'Well, my intelligence comes from Strathclyde Police and the last
time I checked they were under the First Minister's provenance,
and I think I'll just be going ahead and doing that, Home Secretary. Nice of you to phone.'

Salmond's refusal to bow to the wishes of Westminster Cabinet
ministers was a new phenomenon for the governance of the UK.
Up to that point Labour had been in charge in both Westminster
and Holyrood since the start of devolution in 1999. While there
had been occasional tensions, notably over the immigration re-
moval centre at Dungavel, South Lanarkshire, they had tended to
be kept private. The new SNP administration's appetite for regular
disagreements with the UK government was a new dynamic that
posed particular challenges for the civil service, which in theory
remained a unified, UK-wide, organisation.

Salmond's philosophy towards potential conflicts was similar to
that demonstrated in his early declaration of victory in the election: he attempted to bend reality to his will by force of personality. A typical but revealing example was provided by the very
name of the organisation he was leading. Since 1999 the Holyrood

administration had been called the Scottish Executive, with the title reflecting the precedence of the UK government. Salmond wanted to lead a Scottish government, and rather than bother with protracted arguments with London over nomenclature he merely ordered that all signage in Scottish Executive buildings and all logos on Scottish Executive communications were rebranded. Civil servants working in St Andrew's House in Edinburgh left the office on Friday 31 August 2007 with a large sign saying 'Scottish Executive' on the frontage of the building. When they reported to work the following Monday morning, they found it now read 'Scottish Government'.

'Hardly anyone knew what was happening,' says a senior official from the time. 'Salmond didn't present it as a request: he was in control of the building and he just told them the name was changing and that was it. It happened overnight with only a very small circle of people knowing.' The change wasn't made official until the Scotland Act of 2012, when the UK government caved to the inevitable and gave legal recognition to the name now universally used by the Scottish public and media.

* * *

Nicola Sturgeon was leading Scotland's response to a deadly global pandemic more than a decade before coronavirus was even heard of. In her role as Health Secretary, the Deputy First Minister was front and centre during the swine flu crisis in the summer of 2009. Reports of a new virus emerged from Mexico on 24 April and within days newspapers were full of warnings about a 'killer pig flu' with the potential to sweep the world. A global pandemic was duly declared by the WHO on 11 June and three days later the UK's first fatality was reported in Scotland. Sturgeon led news bulletins around Britain as she announced the death, a 38-year-old woman who had given birth prematurely while being treated at the Royal Alexandra Hospital in Paisley.

Sturgeon also won praise for taking personal charge of the Scottish response and overseeing the distribution of antivirals and a vaccination programme. Dolan, Sturgeon's closest adviser at the time, believes she developed considerably as a politician during this period – particularly in terms of the profile provided by doing a daily press conference with chief medical officer Harry Burns. Taking on the responsibility of handling the crisis also demonstrated her willingness to go toe-to-toe with Salmond when required. 'What happened with swine flu is it was one of the first times that Alex had shown any interest in anything to do with the health service and he was wanting to get involved,' recalls Dolan.

Amazingly, he was one of the world's experts on swine flu very quickly. She was getting a bit pissed off about this, but he was coming in and he was showing up for Cobra meetings. Alex stayed interested for about two weeks and then he just lost interest, he went away and got on with the rest of the stuff he had to do.

Dolan, who has had a strained relationship with Sturgeon since retiring in 2016, also pointed out that Salmond's willingness to trust his Health Secretary to lead the response to swine flu was in contrast to how the Covid pandemic was handled. Sturgeon, who by then was First Minister, led the daily media briefings and was the public face of the government's response to the 2020 emergency. Dolan says: '[Swine flu] was the template for the way in which Covid has been handled, although there are differences. Nicola took over Covid rather than leaving it to the Health Secretary. I mean, Alex could have done that, in theory. That shows how the relationship was.'

Another special adviser from the time says Sturgeon's pivotal role handling swine flu showed the strength of the pair's bond. 'His relationship with Nicola was very good at this stage,' says the key aide.

> They didn't always see eye to eye, but it was very much a strong partnership. Nicola was very focused on the health brief; she didn't really perform a role as Deputy First Minister in many ways. She was extremely focused on making sure the health brief was looked after, which I think she did really well.

That Sturgeon was one of the few people who could challenge Salmond was also spotted by more junior officials. 'She had the ability to hold her ground and influence him in a way that other ministers didn't,' a civil servant told *Scotland on Sunday* in 2014 in an article marking Sturgeon's ascension to First Minister.

> There was one particular issue around swine flu where he was asking officials who had been working for thirty-six hours straight to go and find some information that wouldn't have made much difference. Not in the meeting, but outside of that, I heard her have a conversation with him where she said, 'Look, it's not on. You know that it's not a priority.' And that changed his reaction.

Sturgeon's most dramatic confrontation with Salmond came in the autumn of 2009 at the height of the swine flu crisis. Finance Secretary John Swinney was wrestling with the toughest budget settlement since the start of devolution and had the NHS in his sights for cuts. The impact of the financial crisis of 2007–08 was being felt across the world and the Scottish government was having to shoulder its share of the pain. The 2010/11 budget was the first time a

Holyrood administration had faced a real-terms cut to their overall spending. UK Chancellor Alistair Darling, who would later lead the campaign against Scottish independence, had increased health spending in England, but Swinney had initially suggested cutting the NHS in Scotland and spending the resulting money from the Treasury elsewhere. While the row has never been revealed publicly before, Dolan says Sturgeon demanded a meeting with Salmond over the plan and threatened to quit the government unless the frontline health budget was protected. 'Nicola did threaten to resign over it,' he says.

> She went in because she felt very strongly about protecting the NHS and she felt, we both felt, politically it was mad. It transpired that Alex did side with Nicola and the resource part of the health budget, which is about 90 per cent of the health budget, was protected. We used to say all the time 'frontline spending is protected' because the capital budget was badly affected.

In fact, the capital budget, which funds major one-off infrastructure projects, fell by 17 per cent in real terms. Nevertheless, Sturgeon had won a significant internal battle which proved she was the second most powerful force within the SNP.

Their closest aides can only recall one other notable occasion when Salmond and Sturgeon's political alliance frayed during their first term in power. On 10 February 2010, the Deputy First Minister penned a letter asking for leniency on behalf of a constituent who had stolen £80,000 from the taxpayer. Despite knowing he had previously been jailed for fraud, Sturgeon asked a sheriff to consider 'alternatives' to custody for Abdul Rauf after he admitted fraudulently claiming income support for five years while failing to declare thousands of pounds of rental income from a second property. Sturgeon's letter was read out in court by defence advocate Donald

Findlay, who noted how rare it was for representations to be made by someone holding such a prestigious office. Unsurprisingly, the unusual intervention also sparked the interest of newspaper reporters at Glasgow Sheriff Court. It wasn't long before the details filtered through to their colleagues working at the Scottish Parliament and a feeding frenzy began. Labour leader Iain Gray called for Sturgeon's immediate resignation, amid suspicions that her willingness to stick up for Rauf was motivated by a desire to win favour with the large Asian community in her Glasgow Govan constituency.

The controversy had erupted at the worst possible time for Salmond's administration. The First Minister was already embroiled in a cash-for-access row after auctioning lunches in the Scottish Parliament to raise funds for the SNP, and the UK general election was only a matter of weeks away. This was the first time Sturgeon had caused a political problem for her mentor and the pair also disagreed on how to resolve it. 'The opposition were taking it to extreme lengths, but Nicola was shaken by it and realised she had cocked it up,' says a source close to Sturgeon. 'She wanted to put her hands up and apologise but even though Alex was less than pleased with her he was against her apologising. His view is always that you should never apologise because it only shows weakness and gives your opponents an opening.'

If Salmond was angry behind closed doors, he certainly showed no sign of it in public. He initially gave his deputy his full backing and even told MSPs she had an 'absolute obligation' to stand up for her constituents. 'I think she is a fantastic Deputy First Minister and she has my 110 per cent support,' he said.

The row rumbled on for another two weeks before Sturgeon defied her mentor's advice and managed to successfully draw a line under the matter by making an apology to MSPs during a statement at Holyrood. Ironically, in view of what was to come, she maintained that while she had made mistakes it was her 'duty' to intervene on behalf of people facing legal difficulty 'so long as those representations are reasonable, legitimate and appropriate'. It was a theme she would have plenty of cause to reflect on further when Salmond's legal trouble erupted some eight years later.

*   *   *

Alex Salmond showed absolute loyalty to his SNP colleagues and expected absolute loyalty in return. One recurring feature of his time in power was an extreme reluctance to sacrifice ministers when they were under pressure – even if their continued presence was damaging for the government. There were several occasions during the SNP's first term when Salmond fought to keep a member of his Cabinet when the easier move would have been to cut them loose.

The highest-profile example was his support for Kenny Mac-Askill in the wake of international condemnation and domestic anger over the decision to release the Lockerbie bomber, Abdel-baset al-Megrahi, on compassionate grounds. The 57-year-old was serving a life sentence for bombing Pan Am Flight 103 over the town of Lockerbie in 1988, resulting in the deaths of 270 people, including 189 Americans, when he was freed from Greenock Prison and flown home to Libya on 20 August 2009 to a hero's welcome. He had been diagnosed with terminal prostate cancer but would not die for another two years and nine months. US President Barack Obama led the condemnation of MacAskill's decision, saying: 'We have been in contact with the Scottish government, indicating that we objected to this. We thought it was a mistake.'

SNP advisers were particularly astonished at Salmond's support for MacAskill as he had consulted with very few of his colleagues before making the move. 'How Kenny survived Megrahi, I don't know,' says one source. But Salmond showed no sign of any internal disagreement in public and mounted a robust defence of his Justice Secretary, saying the government had stuck to the 'principles of the Scottish legal system' and made a 'difficult and controversial decision for the right reasons'.

However, just a few months later Salmond was forced to sack one senior government minister amid opposition criticism of her performance. In what was probably the SNP's single biggest setback since coming to power, he demoted Hyslop from Education Secretary to Culture Minister after being threatened with a vote of no confidence in December 2009. He had repeatedly threatened to resign if one of his ministers were to lose such a vote, but opposition parties called his bluff amid increasing discontent over class sizes, teacher numbers and the curriculum. 'He was very loyal to his team,' says Dolan. 'But we just had to get rid of Fiona – she didn't actually leave Cabinet at all, she stayed there – but she stopped being a Cabinet minister because politically we would have been out the door. It was essentially just a political decision.'

Perhaps the most personally painful ministerial resignation for Salmond came when his long-standing friend Stewart Stevenson quit as Transport Minister in December 2010. Stevenson, who had worked in Salmond's office before entering the Parliament, had endured days of criticism after much of central Scotland's road network was brought to a standstill by the most prolonged period of snow Scotland had seen for many years. A heavy blizzard on Monday 6 December caused the closure of the M8, M9 and A80, as well as gridlock on many other routes across the country. Thousands of vehicles ended up abandoned and, more damagingly for the government, hundreds of people were stuck in their cars overnight. The M8 between Edinburgh and Glasgow, Scotland's busiest road, was closed for two days. Stevenson came under particular pressure after an appearance on *Newsnight Scotland* in which he described the government response as 'top class'.

The public mood was captured in a vicious *Daily Record* splash that played on a physical resemblance between Stevenson and the drunken priest Father Jack from popular sitcom *Father Ted*. The memorable front-page design was dreamed up by the newspaper's then deputy editor, Murray Foote, who would later go on to become the SNP's head of communications under Nicola Sturgeon. It presented side-by-side headshots of Stevenson and the fictitious priest with the one-word headline FECKLESS. A subhead at the top of the page told the story: 'Snow wonder we're in the grit, our transport minister is Father Jack.'

The influential tabloid's front page convinced Stevenson his time was up, and he told the First Minister he wanted to resign. But Salmond was adamant his friend should not have to take the blame for a 'once in a generation' weather event and attempted to convince him not to go. He relented under Stevenson's insistence he did not want to become a 'weapon' for the opposition and that people had not been given the information they needed. The episode continued to rankle with Salmond, who would reappoint Stevenson as a government minister just five months later. In an example of his dry sense of humour, the First Minister handed him the climate change brief. The political pressure had lifted following the SNP's historic majority victory in the 2011 Holyrood election, in which the party had defied all expectations by winning sixty-nine seats. The result meant they could finally implement their entire political agenda – including a referendum on Scottish independence.

* * *

Alex Salmond's favourite fable involves a medieval court in which a peasant has been sentenced to death by a tyrannical king. In a desperate bid to save his skin, the peasant offers the king a deal. Spare my life for one year, he begs, and I will teach your favourite

horse to talk. When the king agrees, the peasant reassures his confused friends that he hasn't taken leave of his senses but was simply
buying time. 'I have a year now that I didn't have before and a lot of
things can happen in a year,' he tells them. 'The king could die. The
horse could die. I could die. And, who knows? Maybe the horse
will talk.'

The anecdote struck a chord with Salmond because it perfectly
encapsulated his approach to politics: when under pressure, there's
always a chance a solution will emerge if you do whatever is necessary to fight another day. He repeated the story so frequently that
it became the source of arch in-jokes amongst civil servants. When
the First Minister demanded they kick a difficult decision into the
long grass or made a policy pledge that would be challenging to
implement, senior officials would ironically mutter to each other
that 'the horse could die'.

The white paper on independence, published on 26 November
2013, would have required an equine genocide. The 649-page blueprint for a separate Scotland proposed to negotiate the split from
the UK in eighteen months, keep the pound as Scotland's cur-
rency, retain EU membership, increase public spending, cut taxes,
improve pension provision, massively bolster free nursery care,
remove Trident nuclear weapons from the Clyde by the end of the
first term of the Scottish Parliament following independence and
set up a distinct Scottish army. It also claimed the changes would
make every person in Scotland £600 a year better off.

The launch of the long-awaited document, Scotland's Future,
was another moment of high political drama. It was fronted by
the now familiar pairing of Salmond and Sturgeon and held at
Glasgow Science Centre, a popular visitor attraction in the city's
Pacific Quay. Every detail was meticulously stage-managed and
planned. Even Sturgeon's outfit warranted its own press release,
with journalists informed that the Deputy First Minister would

be wearing a 'black Harris tweed jacket with cuffs of Ayrshire lace' by award-winning Scottish designer Judy R. Clark. 'Judy is one of the country's most exciting and talented young designers and I am really looking forward to wearing one of her designs,' Sturgeon was quoted as saying. 'I only hope I can do it justice.'

Salmond's charcoal suit and navy tie did not merit a media statement.

High-profile journalists including BBC political editor Nick Robinson and Channel 4's Gary Gibbon were amongst the 200 media figures in attendance, although there was perhaps not as much worldwide interest as the organisers had hoped for. ITN News's deputy political editor Chris Ship, more used to covering events at Westminster, was bemused to see he had been issued with an 'international' media pass. 'Perhaps that's jumping the gun a bit,' he noted wryly.

In a reversal of the traditional division of labour between the pairing, Salmond's opening statement focused on the substance of the paper while Sturgeon concentrated on loftier principles. 'This white paper is the most detailed blueprint that any people have ever been offered anywhere in the world as a basis for becoming an independent country,' Salmond insisted. 'It puts beyond doubt that an independent Scotland would start from a position of strength.' Meanwhile, Sturgeon said the white paper's vision was 'built on the simple but powerful belief that decisions about Scotland should be taken by the people who live and work here'.

The document was invariably presented as Salmond's vision of an independent Scotland, but he had actually had almost nothing to do with compiling it. Sturgeon had been moved from Health Secretary to a new role overseeing the referendum in September 2012 and handed almost complete autonomy over its content. Behind the scenes, Salmond's lack of interest in the detail had become a source of tension between the pair. Matters came to a head at the start of November when the First Minister went on a five-day official visit to China – his fourth in six years – just as proof versions of the document were being circulated for final approval. His decision to leave the country at such a crucial point had come as a surprise and Sturgeon's disapproval turned to dismay when Salmond proved extremely difficult to contact during the trip despite having been sent drafts that required his sign-off.

A senior civil servant says Salmond's approach to the white paper was reflective of his wider attitude to the constitutional question:

> Once he had decided there was going to be a referendum on independence, he took virtually nothing to do with that white paper. What he wanted was a referendum. He realised they would need to write all this crap to make it happen, but for him that was the boring part. They ended up with this great tome of 650 pages of what could happen and the options that could be pursued, but if he had actually got what he wanted in terms of a Yes vote he would have entirely ignored that book. He wouldn't have paid the slightest bit of attention to it.

Salmond may not have been too invested in the actual content of the white paper, but its explicitly political nature was causing consternation behind the scenes within the civil service. Many critics – including some internal ones – believed the document was a physical embodiment of how the line between the SNP party machine and the supposedly impartial civil service had been blurred to such an extent that the proper division no longer existed. Several sections outlined policy platforms to be put forward by the SNP in future elections to an independent Scottish Parliament. Yet this was a document that had been drafted by civil servants and funded by the British taxpayer.

The conflict was the subject of heated discussion at the top levels of St Andrew's House. Sir Peter Housden, the Permanent Secretary, had made an early judgement that the civil service would provide logistical and policy support to the campaign for independence as it was government policy. However, the extent to which the civil service was directed towards helping shape public opinion proved extremely controversial. Opposition parties repeatedly accused Sir Peter of having 'gone native' and there was a widely held suspicion that he lacked the strength of character to stand up to Salmond and insist that proper procedures and impartiality were maintained.

He was later criticised by Westminster's Public Administration Select Committee after it conducted an inquiry into civil service impartiality in the referendum campaign, with the publication of the white paper a particular focus of their scorn. 'Civil servants should always advise against the appearance of partisan bias in Government documents – and they should not be required to carry out ministers' wishes, if they are being asked to use public funds to promote the agenda of a political party, as was evident in this case,' the committee concluded. 'At the very least, Sir Peter Housden, Scotland's Permanent Secretary, should have required a letter of direction.' A letter of direction is a civil service protocol used when a minister wants to spend public money that does not meet the usual standards of the civil service and means it is the minister who bears responsibility for that use of the funds.

The committee's conclusion reflected what many within the civil service had been saying at the time in opposition to Sir Peter's decision to side with Salmond and put the full force of the Scottish civil service behind the drive for separation. 'Writing the Scotland's Future white paper – that was effectively their manifesto and some of the civil servants were deeply, deeply uncomfortable about that,' says one official who challenged how the issue was handled.

The civil service was not the vehicle through which the political ambitions of the SNP should be pursued and that was the point at which the fact the civil service had been bent to the will of the SNP went too far and we lost our ability to give them robust advice about what was and wasn't possible and instead thought that our job was to get them what they wanted.

One particularly controversial aspect of the white paper was the inclusion of a high-profile pledge to massively increase free nursery care available to parents in an independent Scotland. At the heart of the document was a commitment to what Salmond later termed a 'childcare revolution' that would see thirty hours of free nursery care per week in term time for all three- and four-year-olds, as well as vulnerable two-year-olds. The policy had been deliberately designed to appeal to women voters, who polling consistently showed were much more sceptical about the potential benefits of independence than men. Critics noted that the inclusion of the pledge meant that a document drawn up by civil servants included an SNP manifesto commitment for a hypothetical future election to an independent Scotland's Parliament. It also raised eyebrows as nursery provision was already a devolved issue which the Scottish government controlled under the current settlement.

Salmond's polling problem with women had dogged his entire career to some extent. When he put Sturgeon in charge of the referendum campaign in 2012, one reason was to close the gap in support for independence amongst women. Better Together, the official campaign group for a No vote, conducted perhaps the most extensive private polling that has ever been carried out on Scottish public opinion. Their findings on female voters' views on Salmond were stark. One senior researcher on the team, who observed numerous focus groups carried out across Scotland in the months running up to the vote, described the reaction of women to

Salmond as 'visceral'. 'Even the women who were supportive of the cause did not react well to him,' the source says.

> We would show them images of him and the women in all categories would physically recoil when you showed them pictures of him. It would be a look in their face, a sitting back, a shake of their head. That was the kind of reaction you got from women. They just didn't like him instinctively. We pushed a few of the groups quite hard to understand why they didn't like him and essentially what it boiled down to was that the women thought he embodied everything that they considered to be a bullying male. All the characteristics of a male bully is what they associate with Alex Salmond.

What Better Together strategists suspected but could not prove was that it wasn't just the participants in their focus groups who were branding Alex Salmond a bully. Civil servants with direct experience of working with him were making exactly the same allegation.

* * *

Concerns over Salmond's 'bullying' of government officials were first raised with trade unions within weeks of him assuming power at Holyrood. The new First Minister's explosive temper had been tolerated by SNP staff for years, but the level of forcefulness was not something that mandarins in Edinburgh had experienced before from someone in the top job.

Former SNP MSP Andrew Wilson believes Salmond could be an inspiring leader of a team but would occasionally engage in unacceptable behaviour. 'Intellectually he was absolutely razor-sharp, so you couldn't produce stuff which wasn't hitting the mark and you had to be on top of issues and the agenda,' he says.

He was really good at energising a team, but as always with anything that is a great strength, if it goes to an extreme it can become the opposite. That is obviously what in more modern and enlightened working environments at its worst can be described as bullying by some people.

Kevin Pringle, perhaps Salmond's closest adviser over the years, also offered a candid assessment of his boss in an article for the *Sunday Times* written in the immediate aftermath of the sexual harassment allegations becoming public.

'When people asked me what he was like, I would mutter something about how he was a hard taskmaster but drove himself hardest,' he wrote on 2 September 2018. 'That's true, but as well as being driven he also has a fierce temper. I suspect the latter flows from the former.'

Pringle also made a point echoed by other sources who worked closely with Salmond: that his temper could actually be at its worst when things were going well. 'He went ballistic when he couldn't get through to me from the campaign helicopter when the SNP's majority was confirmed in the 2011 Holyrood election,' he wrote. 'Ironically, the reason for it was Nicola Sturgeon had told us all to put our phones down while she gave us a pep talk. It stung at the time, but I benefited from Salmond's loyalty when things went wrong and mistakes were made, as have many others.'

Amid the concerns about Salmond in 2008, trade unions explicitly told the SNP administration that there had been a history of bad behaviour from ministers of all political parties over the years and a new approach to dealing with such issues was required. Sir John Elvidge, who served as Permanent Secretary between 2003 and 2010, played a key role in drafting the new complaints procedure, alongside the Prospect, FDA and PCS trade unions. Negotiations to thrash out the details of the Fairness at Work policy, as it would become known, stretched from December 2008 to the autumn of 2010, with what to do about any allegations about the First Minister one of the key issues of debate. Email exchanges and minutes of the protracted meetings to agree the procedure show there was 'particular concern' about how to handle any such situation given the power bestowed by the role. One suggestion from the unions was that Whitehall civil servants could be drafted in to independently examine complaints about Salmond or future First Ministers, but this idea was rejected by the Scottish government. Instead, a process was put in place that would see informal complaints initially examined by the Scottish government's head of HR before being passed to the Permanent Secretary and Deputy First Minister, who at the time was Nicola Sturgeon. The policy was signed off by Salmond and finally implemented towards the end of 2010.

Giving evidence to the Holyrood committee inquiry into the Scottish government's botched handling of harassment complaints against Salmond, Sir Peter Housden admitted he had been aware of continued problems with the First Minister's behaviour. He told MSPs that he 'knew that the First Minister could display bullying and intimidatory behaviour' but was less forthcoming about how he had responded.

Did we talk about that? Yes, we did, and we talked a lot about the measures that would ameliorate it for both the individuals and the First Minister, to smooth things along so that they worked better. I will give you a sense of frequency again. For much of the time, that office, that operation – the whole show – ran really well, with great energy and motivation on both sides. The normal diet was of pace, excitement, things happening, things being fixed – on we go. You are all familiar with how political environments work. They are very energising places to be, but they were punctuated by the kinds of behaviours that were a problem in the way that I have described. Did I know about them? Yes, I did ... I did not have to rely on the rumour mill. It was my daily working life: I was in touch with those people and alert to their concerns.

Sir Peter suggested he could not take action because there was never an official complaint made against Salmond:

Did we get more sensitive to them? Yes, we did, but, again, we were working in an informal environment. We did not have an individual or people collectively coming forward to say, 'Up with this, I will not put. You must do something.' Nor did we have a known egregious act. I am sorry about the vocabulary. I am talking about something that would strike anyone, regardless of what the complainant thought about it, as unacceptable behaviour. In those circumstances, you have something to get hold of. If you have a complaint or a known egregious act, you have something that you can act on. I have tried to describe the kinds of things that I did in the absence of those two conditions.

Sir Peter said he had occasional conversations with senior trade union officials about Salmond's behaviour but added: 'The culture in which we were operating was very much one of informal handling of such situations.'

Trade unions were certainly concerned about the situation. Giving evidence to the same committee, FDA General Secretary Dave Penman said the union had raised the 'culture' in the First Minister's office with successive Permanent Secretaries to no avail: 'Although action was taken and short-term improvements or apologies were made, this did not bring about an overall change in culture. Some civil servants expressed to us that they were operating in a culture of fear and were unable to speak truth unto power and discharge their duties effectively.' He added that union members did not trust the government to handle complaints effectively and feared that formally raising issues would be detrimental to their careers.

Numerous officials who worked for Salmond described his bullying behaviour. One senior civil servant says:

> These are pressurised jobs and there is an understanding that there might be behaviours that would not normally be acceptable in a normal workplace, but Salmond took it to an extreme that was unpleasant. There was all the usual shouting, swearing and kicking the chair and spitting the dummy out. We used to entertain ourselves on a Friday when he was off in his constituency office by swapping war stories.

Another official with direct experience of dealing with Salmond adds:

> It was common knowledge. You didn't have to throw a stone very far into the pond to find people in the civil service who had first-hand experience of the bullying and irascibility of the First Minister. The fact the senior civil service team did nothing about it was a source of disappointment. The organisation didn't tackle it and they should have tackled it.

Former special adviser and SNP MP Stephen Gethins says working for Salmond could also be very rewarding despite his demanding personality:

> For all it was a challenge in terms of all the things that people know about – that he was a very, very, very demanding boss, very

long hours, hard work – it was difficult to spend half an hour in Alex's company and not learn something. You knew you were working with somebody who at the time was smart, on top of their game. And actually in terms of the long hours, you would never work longer hours than he did. So it definitely had its upsides and its downsides.

Several SNP sources believe Salmond's behaviour became more unpredictable after the party's extraordinary 2011 election landslide, which gave them an unprecedented majority at Holyrood and guaranteed that a referendum on independence would finally take place. The electoral system had been designed to prevent any one party having a majority and the prevailing view was that the 2014 referendum would be Scottish nationalists' one opportunity of securing their ultimate aim. These senior SNP figures believe the pressure Salmond was under in the run-up to the historic vote and the adulation he received from members of the public as the campaign gripped Scotland's imagination began to affect how he treated staff in private.

'I think around 2013 is when he started to over-enjoy the life of the First Minister,' says one source hostile to Salmond.

This is when you start to get a bit more of the dinners, the drinking, the late nights, the golf games, the not always bothering with Cabinet meetings. There was also the global travel with the extra bit of largesse added on, so the quality of things got nicer, the entourage got bigger. I would in some ways describe it as an expectation of being served. He had reached a point where it was expected that people would do things for him and that is at any level – from a cup of tea to speaking out on some constitutional matter for him to, well, whatever was going on with women in Bute House. It was all part of the same kind of trajectory.

Salmond himself tacitly acknowledged his rough treatment of civil servants in his referendum diaries. 'Under first John Elvidge and more recently Peter Housden I always enjoyed huge support and effort from officials throughout government,' he wrote. 'They have attempted to carry forward the democratically chosen policy in the best traditions of the service.' Turning to special advisers, he added:

> If civil servants are traduced by Tory ministers then special advisers get traduced by everybody. In fact, led by Geoff Aberdein, they were committed, loyal and insightful. Like my private office team they did not always see the sunniest side of my nature. But unfailingly they responded above and beyond the call of duty.

Nicola Sturgeon was silent on Salmond's bullying during his time in power but later admitted his behaviour had not been acceptable and she should have done more to address it. She told the Holyrood committee:

> He could be very challenging to work for. If Alex was displeased with you, he would make that pretty obvious. There were times when I challenged his behaviour in that respect, when I witnessed situations where I thought that he had crossed a line or was perhaps risking doing so.
>
> One of the things that I have thought about is whether those of us who had worked very closely with Alex for a long time had become a bit inured to that kind of behaviour – I am talking about that and not anything allegedly sexual – and whether we had a higher threshold for that than perhaps people in government in 2007 had. Is that something that I think about and have thought about? Yes.

As the independence referendum approached in the summer of

2014, Sturgeon was well aware of Salmond's abrasive treatment of staff. What she didn't know was that behind closed doors the civil service was concealing even more troubling complaints about his behaviour towards young women.

CHAPTER 3

BUTE HOUSE

28 APRIL 2014, 11.33 A.M.

It had happened again. Michael McElhinney was the senior civil servant in charge of overseeing the staff rota for Alex Salmond's private office and had just received an email from a female official who had previously complained about the First Minister behaving inappropriately towards her.

The woman was accompanying Salmond on a trip to Europe and McElhinney had emailed to check on her welfare: 'Hope all going well over there?'

'All fine,' she replied. 'He's a pig, but he's not an angry pig today. Just a disgusting one.'

'Just keep safe,' said McElhinney. 'And keep away from situations or conversations you may feel uncomfortable about.'

Just ten minutes later, the woman, who would go on to accuse Salmond of two counts of sexual assault, confirmed McElhinney's worst suspicions.

'Too late,' she wrote back. 'Didn't even get through the Eurostar journey without him speaking about having sex with me. To be honest, I think I need to minimise my time with him this week after tomorrow.' She asked for the staff rota to be changed so she did not have face-to-face contact with the First Minister.

'Not good,' said McElhinney. 'And not acceptable. We must deal with this. I'll rework the rota for the rest of the week.'

'Sorry,' the woman replied. 'I just need a break from seeing his fat face and hearing his lewd comments. If it is going to cause a mess then obviously I'm happy to continue as is.'

'Not your problem, so nothing for you to apologise for,' said McElhinney. 'I've reworked the rota so that you are not FM cover for either Wed or Thurs this week.'

*　　*　　*

McElhinney had been employed in the private office of Labour First Minister Jack McConnell a decade earlier but had been tempted back for a more senior job with the SNP administration in October of 2013. He had worked closely with Salmond in a previous role dealing with energy policy, admired the politician's ability and was excited at the prospect of having a front-row seat for the upcoming referendum on Scottish independence. When a former colleague, Joe Griffin, got in touch out of the blue, it was just too good a job offer to refuse.

Every government minister in the UK has a private office. Salmond's was a small team tasked with supporting his work, acting as a communication channel between the First Minister and other officials and organising his diary. It was staffed by civil servants known as private secretaries and led by Griffin, the principal private secretary (PPS).

But within a matter of weeks of starting his new job, McElhinney was faced with a problem he had not encountered in his previous thirty years as a civil servant. Several female members of staff approached him with concerns about what they claimed was Salmond's inappropriate behaviour towards them when they had been working alone late at night.

The first sign of trouble came on 30 October, when a female staff member expressed discomfort after Salmond asked her to watch a film with him in the study of Bute House. She said he had switched the lights off and pushed two chairs together so they were huddled close beside each other. While she stressed 'no inappropriate contact' had taken place, and did not want to make a formal complaint, she was still unsettled enough to share her concerns. Alarmed by what he heard, McElhinney raised the issue with Griffin, the senior manager in the department. The seriousness of the incidents reported to the pair and another of their colleagues, Chris Birt, would escalate alarmingly over the months that followed.

Salmond's abrasive treatment and 'bullying' behaviour towards officials was a widely acknowledged problem within the civil service, but neither McElhinney nor Griffin had previous experience of dealing with potential sexual harassment – especially not when it involved the most powerful man in the country. McElhinney shrewdly kept a written record of the alleged misconduct reported to him over the months that followed. His government-issued diary would eventually catalogue nine separate allegations of sexualised language, unwanted touching and other inappropriate behaviour from the First Minister. It would also document McElhinney's mounting frustration at the civil service's inability to offer his colleagues what he believed to be a safe working environment in which they were protected and respected. In 2018, he handed the journal over to Police Scotland and it became a key part of Operation Diem, the investigation into sexual assault allegations against Salmond. Its contents can now be revealed for the first time.

Most of the alleged incidents reported to McElhinney, a father in his fifties, took place in Bute House. The category A-listed building in Edinburgh's Charlotte Square dates back to the eighteenth century but has been used as the First Minister's official residence in the capital since the creation of the devolved Scottish Parliament in 1999. Its distinctive Georgian facade, a popular tourist landmark, conceals a cavernous five-storey building that incorporates private living quarters for the First Minister, office space for civil servants and an opulent drawing room overlooking the square, decorated with paintings on loan from the National Galleries of Scotland, which is frequently used for entertaining guests or holding press conferences. A secondary drawing room has been converted into a Cabinet room to host the weekly meetings of senior Scottish ministers. The building's basement is used as the main office space for staff, with former pantries and servants' quarters now installed with strip lighting and broadband cables. A lift allows direct access to the second and third floors, which have been converted into a private flat for the First Minister. The facilities include a small private kitchen, living room and four bedrooms.

Salmond's work habits were known to make heavy demands on the civil service. He was not an early riser but often worked late into the night at Bute House and would require officials to remain on the premises until the early hours of the morning to provide support.

The most serious incident reported to McElhinney – the details of which would eventually emerge in the *Daily Record* – took place in December 2013 in the First Minister's Bute House bedroom. McElhinney's diary records that he was first alerted to the issue by Griffin and Birt on 16 December. The female civil servant involved – who would later be referred to as Ms A in the Scottish government's probe into Salmond and Woman F in the criminal trial – was said to have complained of 'heavy fondling and an invitation to lie on [the] bed' from Salmond after working an evening shift.

A fuller account of her version of events was presented in the March 2020 court case. Woman F claimed to have moved to a bedroom on the third floor of Bute House with Salmond after he suggested that the private sitting room they had been using on the floor below was too cold. She alleged that Salmond asked her to remove her boots, which she did as it was a carpeted room. Then, she said, the pair first sat at a small table in the bedroom to go through paperwork before he produced a bottle of the Chinese spirit Maotai, which he proceeded to drink steadily, while she 'wetted her lips'.

The civil servant told the court that she felt 'panicked' when Salmond told her: 'Get on the bed,' as she prepared to leave around 11 p.m. 'This was very much within a working environment and culture where you do whatever the First Minister asks of you,' she said. 'I was sitting very primly on the edge of the bed with rising panic.'

She told the court that what happened next progressed with alarming speed. 'I was lying across the bed and the First Minister was lying on top of me.' She said Salmond first pushed his hands under her dress and ran them over her thighs and bottom, before touching her breasts over her clothing. She told the court that he was kissing her 'sloppily and rather haphazardly', while repeatedly murmuring the phrase 'You're irresistible'.

Asked by prosecutor Alex Prentice QC about how she was feeling at this point, Woman F said: 'A mix of panic and disbelief that this could be happening. I knew that I had to stop this, to get away, but how on earth do you actually achieve that?' She continued: 'It seemed very clear that he wasn't going to stop.' She told the court she feared there was about to be 'aggression', and that Salmond 'was going to try to remove my tights and underwear and that he would be pushing the encounter physically'.

She alleged that as she continued to try to block Salmond's hands, his weight shifted and she was able to get up off the bed and leave the bedroom, after saying goodnight.

After she left Bute House, Woman F told the court, she felt a 'looming horror that this was something sufficiently serious that

I would have to tell somebody but I couldn't imagine doing that, couldn't imagine saying the words'. As she walked home, she said, she texted Birt with the message: 'That's an evening that I'll need to forget.' The following morning, Birt responded with concern, and they met in person shortly afterwards. 'I was finding it extremely difficult to talk about,' said Woman F. 'Part of his response was that it could be a crime.'

Birt told the court he thought Woman F seemed 'traumatised' as she told him what had happened. He said she was normally a confident person, but during the conversation her legs were folded up under a chair she was sitting on. 'The way she was sitting, something very clearly upsetting had happened to her,' he said.

Woman F said she then decided to escalate her concerns, alerting Griffin 'that something more serious had happened than the lower-level behaviour we almost took as a baseline'. At a subsequent meeting with Griffin and Geoff Aberdein, she said: 'I used the phrase "get on the bed" but didn't go into details.'

Griffin corroborated her account of the meeting, telling the court he had discussed the issue with Aberdein before raising it with Salmond at his office in the Scottish Parliament: 'I said to him there was a matter I needed to talk to him about that was very sensitive.' He said he had relayed Woman F's version of events to Salmond, including that the First Minister had 'kissed her, tried to kiss her, put his arms around her and made an invitation to lie down on the bed'.

'He said he had been feeling bad about [Woman F],' Griffin added. 'He said he had been drinking. He acknowledged that something had happened for which he felt remorse.'

During cross-examination of Woman F, defence lawyer Gordon Jackson QC suggested that the encounter amounted to 'a sleepy cuddle' on the bed, and that she had drunk a similar amount of alcohol to Salmond. She replied: 'Absolutely not. I refute any suggestion that I cuddled the First Minister.'

Alex Salmond fiercely disputed the woman's claim she had been sexually assaulted but admitted his conduct on the evening in question had been unacceptable – something he partially put down to the pressure he was under nine months out from the Scottish independence referendum.

He lodged a special defence of consent and told jurors he had 'lapsed into a sleepy cuddle' with Woman F. He said he had gone to give her a kiss goodnight while she was sitting on the bed putting her boots on and ended up 'lying side by side' on his bed with one of his arms under her and the other over her. Salmond denied getting on top of her. Asked by Jackson why it had happened, Salmond replied: 'I don't know. It was a thing that happened when you are tipsy and one should know better.' Jackson continued: 'There was no thought in your mind of having non-consensual sex with her?' To which Salmond replied: 'None whatsoever. I have never attempted to have a non-consensual sexual relationship with anyone in my life.'

Salmond confirmed in court that he had a private meeting with the woman in his Scottish Parliament office several days later and apologised to her, adding: 'I was the First Minister. She was in my bedroom. We were tipsy, it shouldn't have happened.'

McElhinney's diary recorded those events in the following form: 'Joe spoke to FM. He apologised – too much to drink – won't happen again – will apologise to [Woman F]. We will revisit operational impact. Joe will consider who in SG [Scottish government] to informally speak to.'

Meanwhile, in her court evidence, Woman F said:

The First Minister told me he was sorry for what had happened and that it was inappropriate. He said that he had been drinking more than usual, not just that night but in general, due to stress. He said that he respected me and wanted to keep working together. I accepted the apology and confirmed we would keep working together.

The jury ultimately returned a not proven verdict on the charge Salmond had sexually assaulted Woman F on the night in question. The not proven verdict, which is unique to Scotland, has been under increasing scrutiny due to the frequency of its use in sexual assault trials and its lack of a clear legal definition. Famously called 'that bastard verdict' by Sir Walter Scott in 1827, it has the exact same practical effect as not guilty.

* * *

In the wake of the December 2013 incident, Griffin, McElhinney and Birt grappled with what to do about the Salmond situation. In the criminal trial, all three testified that they had put informal procedures in place in a desperate bid to stop any further incidents. McElhinney also revealed that they had discussed 'withdrawing private secretary cover altogether under the circumstances', adding: 'We were concerned about making sure the wellbeing of our staff was protected and looked after.'

They did not withdraw support entirely but decided to change the office rota to ensure that women were never alone with Salmond. They said this policy was not recorded in writing and did not trigger an official investigation or review of procedures.

McElhinney said the 'operational steps' were first introduced after the December 2013 incident. 'We would either double up cover late at night or avoid single female contact with Mr Salmond after certain points of the evening,' he told the court. 'We had in place a number of operational steps to try and manage the risk of recurrence. We had no established official policy for these circumstances.'

It did not take long for further issues of concern to arise. On the very same day the First Minister apologised to Woman F, another female staff member complained about his behaviour. This was the same Scottish government official who would send the April email about her experience on the Eurostar and subsequently become Woman G in the criminal trial.

Salmond had recently lost some weight and was enamoured of his new slimline appearance. In October 2013, he gave an interview to the *Scottish Sun* about the 5:2 diet – also known as the bikini diet – which involves sticking to a strict regime of 600 calories per day two days a week. A normal intake – 2,500 calories for men – is then consumed for the remaining five days. 'It can be a struggle, but I've dropped about two stone and two collar sizes,' he said.

According to McElhinney's diary, Salmond had been boasting to Woman G about the weight loss on the morning of 18 December and made an inappropriate comment involving the words 'Does that mean you would need to see me naked?' At 1.45 p.m. the First Minister then had the private meeting with Woman F to apologise for his previous behaviour in the bedroom of Bute House. Later that day Woman G made another complaint, this time saying that Salmond had referred to her as a 'dominatrix' during a conversation.

The problems continued after Christmas. On 8 January, again according to McElhinney's diary, there was an incident while Woman G was travelling back with Salmond from an event. Salmond was alleged to have 'talked to [Woman G] about ball gags and gimp masks and S&M', the entry reads.

By the time McElhinney was dealing with Woman G's email from the Eurostar on 28 April, she had already informed her managers about a more serious alleged incident. Earlier that month, the official had been at a function with Salmond and he had asked her to accompany him back to Bute House. Woman G would later tell the criminal trial:

> We got the lift up to his private living quarters. I went into the sitting room, where I intended to hand over the papers and depart. I left the papers on the table and asked if there was anything else. He said I wasn't to leave – I was to sit with him and he beckoned for me to sit next to him on the sofa.

She confirmed that she followed the instruction, adding: 'I thought if I sat with him for a couple of minutes then I could just leave.'

Salmond then went to the drinks cabinet before returning to the sofa. Woman G said:

> He took out some glasses and a bottle of Limoncello and poured some into glasses for me to have some shots. He said I wasn't to call him First Minister, I was to call him Alex. I told him I wasn't going to be drinking Limoncello, I didn't like it. I think he had already poured a drink for me by that time. He had sat back down. He put his legs up on the coffee table and kept them there.

At this point, Woman G claimed, Salmond, who was fifty-nine at the time, made a sexualised remark to her, saying: 'What I would do to you if I was twenty-six.'

The comment is also mentioned in McElhinney's 2014 diary. The entry reads: '[Woman G] at dinner. Then Bute. Text 00.03 – Not being alone with him again. Then texts about sexual harassment – locked in a "cuddle". "What he would do to me if he was 26" "Wd not let me leave".'

Asked in court what she thought he had meant by the comment, Woman G replied: 'I thought it meant he'd try to have sex with me, have sexual relations with me. He put his arm around me and at that point I started to feel panicked. He leaned in to kiss me.'

She stressed she hadn't given the First Minister permission to kiss her and she felt 'frightened'. 'It was at that moment I thought if I didn't get out that something really serious was about to happen,' she said.

Woman G said she then managed to get to the door and get away. Asked how Salmond responded to her exit, she said: 'He was frustrated and somewhat almost defeated and I said something along the lines of, "I've got to go." I was extremely embarrassed. I felt confused because I hated him for what he had just done.'

Salmond denied making sexual remarks or trying to kiss her. He said she had been upset over a work issue and he had 'put my left arm around her to get her to tell me what was wrong'. He added that he was trying to 'comfort' her. The jury found him not guilty of a charge of sexually assaulting the official on the night in question.

In court, Woman G also claimed that Salmond had smacked her on the bottom in a restaurant while his wife Moira was present in an incident two years earlier. She said it happened in the Ubiquitous Chip in Glasgow's West End in spring 2012 after a dinner. 'We had a few courses,' she told the court.

> It would not have been that late in the evening. Mr Salmond ushered people out and I was standing behind him. He gestured for me to go ahead of him. As he did that he smacked my buttocks. He touched me on my buttocks and carried on leaving the restaurant. I was shocked – it had not happened before.

Woman G said she had told a friend about the incident immediately afterwards but took it no further. 'There was nobody I could conceive of who I could report something to,' she said. 'He was the most powerful man in the country.'

Salmond denied the incident took place and said he had instead put his hand on her 'lower back' to hurry her up with a 'gentle shove'. He said there was 'no sign she took any exception' and it had been 'totally and absolutely harmless'.

Salmond's defence lawyer said such behaviour was considered to be 'nothing' at the time but it had somehow now come to be considered criminal.

The jury again found Salmond not guilty of a sexual assault.

* * *

Woman G's informal complaint about Salmond in April 2014 had sparked increasing panic within the management team at Bute House. McElhinney's diary entries for 23 and 24 April detail a series of fraught discussions with Griffin and Birt about what to do. They all agreed the First Minister's conduct had been 'not acceptable' and must be addressed but were unsure how to proceed in light of the lack of a formal complaint. Woman G was said to be 'very upset' when assured she would be supported through any process and said: 'What's the point?' and that things would 'never change'.

The men also decided to toughen up the 'operational response' that had been implemented in the wake of the December 2013 incident. The diary states there was discussion about having no female cover at Bute House after 8 p.m., a step further than just making sure no women were alone in the residence at night, and that a more senior civil servant in the Scottish government should be informed about what was going on. McElhinney's diary suggests the email from Woman G regarding the Eurostar incident on 28 April was the final straw. All three men testified in court that staffing changes were then implemented in the wake of the complaints. Birt said new rotas were drawn up in April to ensure that no female employee was left alone with Salmond in Bute House, with the plan being for a second male official to work alongside women colleagues at night. The previous rota changes had allowed two female staff members to work the evening shift together, but this new system would mean another man was always present. Asked about this under oath, Salmond insisted he knew nothing about the arrangement. Nicola Sturgeon would later tell Holyrood she was also 'not aware' of any such policy.

In court, Advocate Depute Alex Prentice QC asked Birt if people had learned to live with Salmond's behaviour. The civil servant said the impact on staff had been significant and 'brought up levels of stress that led to mental ill health' and claimed there was 'almost a kind of gallows humour and camaraderie in [Salmond's] private office'. Asked if people were 'frightened' of the First Minister, he replied: 'Yes.'

'The culture built up over a number of years,' he added.

> None of the women felt like they wanted to complain. We felt in a very difficult position where it was difficult for us to do anything further because the civil service had allowed this to build up over time. Frankly, I can't speak for the women, but I can speak for myself. I would not have trusted the civil service procedures at that time to be able to handle such sensitive issues.

Asked if the situation had improved in the intervening years, he replied: 'I'm not sure we have got much better.'

Griffin told the court that after the April incident he alerted David Wilson, director of communities and ministerial support for the Scottish government, to the situation. It is unclear what action, if any, was taken by the senior civil servant.

McElhinney's diary entry for 28 April 2014, which deals with the Eurostar email from Woman G, also suggests Griffin was poised to raise her case with the First Minister in the same way he had done with Woman F the previous December. It reads: '28 April (am) – email from [Woman G] 11.33. FM asking her to have sex on Eurostar. Shared with JG/CB. Met & agreed JG will speak FM on 30 April. (1) this must stop. (2) Changes to late cover at Bute House.'

It is also unclear whether Griffin, who was appointed the Scottish government's director for safer communities in March 2020, followed through with the meeting.

The political sensitivities of the time also played an important role in the wall of silence thrown around the issue. A recurring theme with all the women who raised informal concerns with McElhinney and his team during late 2013 and the first half of 2014 was that they feared formalising their complaints not only because of the power and profile of the First Minister but because of the political context of the time. There was a fevered atmosphere throughout this period as voters prepared to settle whether Scotland's constitutional future lay as a part of the United Kingdom or an independent country. As the figurehead of the Yes campaign, Salmond was under fierce media scrutiny, and it was inevitable that any questions over his personal character would be seized on by the pro-Union side for their own political advantage.

Pressed in court by Jackson on why she did not immediately report the alleged assault if she thought it a criminal act, Woman F said:

This is to misunderstand the context … Going to someone outside was completely unthinkable. This was the run-up to a referendum on independence. Everything we did which was outward-facing had potential ramifications which went well beyond personal experience … If that had got into the public domain then that could potentially have been used against the government, it could potentially have informed public opinion in the run-up to the referendum.

Following the April incident, there were no more allegations of inappropriate behaviour from the First Minister reported to McElhinney, Birt or Griffin until after the independence referendum, when they would receive one final complaint during Salmond's very final days in office.

It was not until he was charged by police years later that they discovered that two other women claimed to have been sexually assaulted by the First Minister in Bute House between May and September 2014 and that this included an alleged attempted rape.

CHAPTER 4

THE DREAM SHALL NEVER DIE

19 SEPTEMBER 2014, 4.08 P.M.

Standing in front of a mirror in the main reception room of Bute House, Alex Salmond turned heartbreak into an opportunity.

'I believe that in this new exciting situation, redolent with possibility, [the] party, Parliament and country would benefit from new leadership. Therefore I have told the national secretary of the SNP that I will not accept the nomination to be a candidate for leader at the annual conference in Perth.'

Ten hours after it became arithmetically impossible for the Yes campaign to win the Scottish independence referendum, the 59-year-old Salmond was resigning as First Minister of Scotland.

Geoff Aberdein, his long-standing chief of staff, was visibly upset at the back of the room where he stood amongst the Scottish government's senior advisers, who had all gathered to watch the speech. A female civil servant, a member of the press team, was also crying. Salmond's subsequent – and dubious – claim that Brian Taylor also had 'a tear or two in his eye' rankled with the scrupulously impartial former BBC Scotland political editor, but there was no doubt emotions were running high.

In classic Salmond style, the whole event was perfectly pitched to the public but laced with political menace behind closed doors.

Resigning quickly with a finely crafted statement urging unity while giving hope to despondent Yes voters was a graceful move, but the decisions about who would be allowed in the packed room to witness this final flourish betrayed bitter score-settling. Journalists deemed hostile were banned from the event, including many who had covered the Holyrood beat for years and attended daily press conferences with Salmond on the campaign trail. A senior press officer doubled as a bouncer outside Bute House, blocking the way of reporters making the case for the free press, including a camera crew from the *Daily Telegraph* who had arrived to film the newspaper's reporter being barred.

The bulk of the speech had been written shortly after 1.31 a.m., when Clackmannanshire's declaration of a No vote pointed to the direction of the referendum result, in the owner's office at Eat on the Green, the fine dining restaurant in Ellon, Aberdeenshire, where Salmond's entourage had been based that evening. The most famous line, which would define the Scottish National Party's attitude towards the constitution in the coming years, was a last-minute impromptu addition: 'For me as leader my time is nearly over. But for Scotland the campaign continues and the dream shall never die.'

Salmond's resignation speech also left hanging the question of his replacement. To the surprise of some journalists in the room, he would not officially endorse his deputy, Nicola Sturgeon. Under questioning, he even suggested a leadership contest might be a healthy development for the party he had led for twenty of the past twenty-four years.

For her part, Sturgeon, who was not present at the press conference, was effusive towards Salmond in an article published shortly afterwards. She said their partnership 'has been unusual in politics – we like and respect each other', adding: 'Alex Salmond is one in a million and although his tenure as First Minister is coming to an end, I have no doubt that he will continue to make a big impact on Scotland for many years to come.'

Just a few hours earlier she had unsuccessfully tried to talk him out of standing down. Salmond and Moira, his wife of forty years, had flown from Aberdeenshire to Edinburgh and arrived at Dynamic Earth, the visitor attraction behind the Scottish Parliament where the Yes campaign was set up on referendum night, to find an exhausted and emotional team of politicians and activists. After making a short concession speech outside for the television cameras, Salmond gathered in one of the venue's green rooms for a tearful encounter with Sturgeon, Aberdein and John Swinney, then Finance Secretary, who would go on to become Sturgeon's Deputy First Minister. 'There was just the four of us there and we gave each other a big hug for a couple of minutes and had a good Scottish greet [cry]. We just had a big greet. We all realised we'd lost,' Aberdein told the *Scottish Sun*.

The quartet were the most senior figures in Salmond's government and had never been closer than that moment as their shared dream of independence was shattered. They would all be key to the subsequent fallout that would split the SNP, with Swinney appointed to handle the response of Sturgeon's administration to the allegations that Salmond had sexually harassed two civil servants, and evidence from Aberdein key to fuelling the claims that she lied to the Scottish Parliament.

Salmond was sure of his resignation by 10 a.m. after some words of wisdom from his wife. 'You do what your instinct tells you. Your instinct is always right,' Moira had told him.

Sturgeon and Swinney made the short trip from Dynamic Earth to the Scottish government headquarters at St Andrew's House, where extra civil servants had been on standby ready to get to work in the event of a Yes vote and the immediate commencement of independence negotiations. After thanking them for their efforts and sending them home, Sturgeon joined Salmond at Bute House, where over bacon rolls she unsuccessfully tried to dissuade him from his decision. She urged him to wait and let the raw emotions of the day settle before making a final call but quickly relented when it became clear he wanted to choose the timing of both his resignation and his departure.

'We hadn't talked about what would happen if we lost the referendum,' Sturgeon told the *Sunday Times* the week after the defeat.

> I met up with him in Edinburgh in the early hours of Friday morning and he told me his decision. I tried to talk him out of it but even as I was doing so I knew he had made up his mind. He wanted to make the decision on his terms and on his timescale. I think he deserves that.

After making his speech and taking questions from those who were allowed inside, Salmond left the room with a weight lifted from his shoulders. One aide told the author David Torrance that Salmond appeared 'demob happy' before he made his evening journey back to the north-east. He and Moira were driven to Preston-field House, the five-star hotel and golf course, where a helicopter was waiting to fly them and his closest constituency staff back to Aberdeenshire. Before boarding, Salmond spotted a photographer trying to snatch some candid shots. He beckoned her over to take a picture of the couple in the helicopter with beaming smiles and their headsets on. Salmond had been angered by an image taken in the early hours of that morning of him looking despondent in the back of his chauffeur-driven car examining the referendum results, which showed 55.3 per cent of Scottish voters had rejected his vision for independence. Ever the pro, he was going to make sure a similar image did not dominate the front pages again.

After landing in Aberdeen, the Salmonds went straight to the Marcliffe Hotel for food. While there, they received a message from their gardener warning them that a media scrum had congregated outside their house in Strichen, so they decided to spend the night in another favourite local hotel, Meldrum House.

Salmond would later note how appropriate it was that he signed off with Moira by his side. 'Being a political spouse is probably the worst job in the world. I think being First Minister is the best job in the world, but being the spouse you get none of the glory and all of the intrusion,' he told *The Courier*. 'Moira has done it all with grace and forbearance, which I'm very grateful for.'

As a couple they are notoriously publicity shy, with Moira only ever having given one interview, to the *Sunday Post* in 1990. 'I'm no Glenys Kinnock,' she said. 'I married Alex, not politics. That's his life and I am happy to be in the background.' The interview also shed light on the couple's domestic situation. The paper noted: 'He can't cook, is reluctant to do housework and still hasn't put up the new pole for her curtains even though she's had it for six months!'

Back in Edinburgh, Salmond's aides, many of whom were operating on snatched moments of sleep over the previous twenty-four hours, staggered blinking past the open champagne bottle that sat on the steps outside Bute House and into the sunlight of Charlotte Square. They decided that the only thing to do was go to the pub.

After one drink at the nearby Cambridge Bar, they moved on to the Star Bar, a local dive with a vociferous independence-supporting owner in Edinburgh's upmarket New Town. Such was Salmond's allure to Yes supporters at the time that Irvine Welsh, the *Trainspotting* author, bought the group a round of drinks after discovering who they worked for. The evening ended at around 2 a.m. with a rendition of 'Freedom Come-All-Ye', the Scots-language socialist and anti-imperialist song written by Hamish Henderson, led by Campbell Gunn, who in addition to his jobs as a journalist and spin doctor had also been a member of the band Runrig. As well as Gunn and Aberdein, Liz Lloyd, who would become Sturgeon's chief of staff, Stuart Nicolson, who served as both politicians' official spokesman, and Delancy Johansson, a policy adviser to Salmond, were all present. Their close relationships would fracture over the coming years even as the chances of independence seemed to increase.

The days that followed showed a change in attitude from Salmond as he refused to attend a special church service organised the Sunday after the vote aimed at healing divisions created by the referendum campaign. With Sturgeon putting the finishing touches to her leadership bid, the Scottish government was left with only Swinney to represent them at the so-called 'service of reconciliation' at St Giles' Cathedral in Edinburgh. Only two other nationalist MSPs – John Mason (Glasgow Shettleston) and Roderick Campbell (North East Fife) – turned up. In contrast, unionist politicians were well represented, including Better Together leader and former Labour Chancellor Alistair Darling, the Liberal Democrat Chief Secretary to the Treasury Danny Alexander and the leaders of Labour, the Conservatives and the Lib Dems at the Scottish Parliament.

In television interviews given on the day of the service, Salmond said voters had been 'misled', blamed older Scots for blocking 'progress for the next generation' and hinted at supporting a unilateral declaration of independence. Although he rolled back from the latter suggestion in subsequent interviews, Sturgeon was frustrated at having to distance herself from the prospect, particularly as it threatened to overshadow her own big announcement.

Five days after Salmond's resignation, Sturgeon used a speech at the Glasgow Royal Concert Hall to declare she would be running to be leader of the SNP and Scotland's first female First Minister. She ran unopposed and with no campaign to fight struggled at times to compete for the limelight with the man who was standing aside.

Salmond's behaviour and mindset in the days and weeks following the referendum became a growing cause for concern amongst his colleagues. This was the First Minister unleashed, with his aides left unconsulted and often in the dark about his activities during the handover period. His quick political understanding and insight in the hours immediately after the referendum defeat had positioned the SNP perfectly for the following May's general election. But his subsequent struggle to deal with the loss of prestige, disappointment at the crushing of his lifelong dream and the recurrence of a tendency to obsess over settling old scores began to cause trouble.

*　　*　　*

The radio plays in the background throughout the day in the special advisers' room in St Andrew's House, the Scottish government's headquarters in the shadow of Calton Hill, Edinburgh. Close attention is paid to the BBC's *Good Morning Scotland* as the news agenda for the day is determined, and then the volume is turned down for the *Morning Call* programme that follows. On 3 October 2014, there was a reason to keep listening.

'You'll never believe who's phoned in. No, seriously, you will never guess who has phoned in. We have Alex from Peterhead. Good morning, Alex,' said host Kaye Adams.

'Eh, not from Peterhead, Kaye, from Strichen,' came the response in the familiar tones of a First Minister prepared to pick a fight over almost any topic, including which part of Aberdeenshire he was calling from.

The volume on the radio in the heart of the government was quickly turned up. One person present recalls: 'We heard the voice and someone said, "Is that Alex?" The next question was, "What the hell is he doing?"'

The answer was having an on-air argument with a Conservative councillor about local authorities pursuing old poll tax debts. A few weeks later, while opening a Lidl supermarket, he would attack Asda for their pre-referendum warning about food price rises in the event of independence. He even found time to write to *The Herald* and complain bitterly about an uncomplimentary article by its former columnist David Torrance, who authored Salmond's unofficial biography.

Internal tensions were also beginning to show. In early October, following a meeting of the SNP's National Executive Committee (NEC) at the Macdonald Holyrood Hotel, which sits behind the Scottish Parliament, Salmond pulled Peter Murrell, the party's chief executive, who is married to Sturgeon, to one side.

The gathering had been one of positivity despite the soul-crushing defeat, but the mood was about to change. Standing in a corridor of the hotel, Salmond told Murrell that 'if all goes according to plan, you should plan an exit because it won't work'. The plan was Sturgeon's unopposed election and what wouldn't work was a husband and wife occupying the two most senior positions in the party. Witnesses described Murrell as looking 'absolutely ashen'.

Allies of Salmond say the conversation was not aggressive and he was pointing out the obvious rather than trying to exert authority in the dying days of his leadership. In a move to 'let him down gently', he said a viable pathway was for Murrell to steer the party through the 2015 general election behind the scenes before departing. 'In some sense it would be fine if it was a family business,' says a source close to Salmond. 'But it's not. It's not Walker's shortbread. It's a public organisation, a membership subscription organisation. It won't do.'

A similar conversation was held in the following days with

Sturgeon, who remained calm and composed, not giving away her thoughts on the suggestion. She would go on to ignore it, in an early sign that she was not going to take her former mentor's advice.

In a public show of defiance, Sturgeon and Murrell gave a joint interview to the *Sunday Herald* the following weekend, complete with a photograph of them together on the sofa in their Glasgow home. The First Minister in waiting denied that becoming Scotland's ultimate power couple would be detrimental to the party. 'I'm comfortable there are no issues that arise,' she said. The overwhelming strength and dominance of the Sturgeon–Murrell household within the SNP would certainly breed resentment over the years that followed and also lead to claims that the governance of the party had suffered. But even the fiercest critic of the arrangement could not have predicted that within six years Salmond would accuse Murrell of being a key player in a 'malicious' plot to have him imprisoned on false charges and remove him from public life.

There was certainly no sign of the future conflict when many of the advisers who had worked for Salmond in government gathered for a farewell drinks reception at Waverley Gate, the prestigious office complex in Edinburgh's former General Post Office. The event 'to mark the departure of the Rt Hon Alex Salmond MSP as First Minister' took place three days after he handed over the SNP leadership to Sturgeon in November. It saw Jennifer Erickson, Salmond's former economic adviser who was by then working for Barack Obama in Washington, fly in from the United States to bid him farewell.

There were also moments of high jinks and joviality that showed staff still loyal to him and enjoying his company. One of these involved a video made by some of his closest aides of a 'final interview' between him and Jackie Bird, the BBC presenter. Alexander

Anderson, a long-standing special adviser, plays Salmond in the video while Aberdein plays Bird, with press officers Aileen Easton and Tim Christie mimicking their own sometimes exasperated responses. 'If you can forgive Geoff's legs and make-up then it does indicate a degree of mutual affection as well as the highest regard,' Salmond wrote in his referendum diaries.

Salmond may have appeared like a man desperate to hog the attention during the transition period, but Sturgeon was far from camera-shy as the handover of power approached. She embarked on a rock star-style journey around venues in Scotland – dubbed #SNPtour by senior nationalist politicians on social media – where warm-up acts got the crowd ready for the First Minister in waiting before Sturgeon delivered a speech then took questions from the audience. Edinburgh's Corn Exchange, Dumfries's Easterbrook Hall, Dundee's Caird Hall and the Eden Court Theatre in Inverness were to build up to an appearance at the 12,000-capacity Hydro in Glasgow, which would take place after her coronation as leader of both party and government.

The SNP sought to capitalise on Sturgeon's burgeoning popularity by promoting a cult of personality more than ever before. Stalls of merchandise were set up at each event which included T-shirts emblazoned with 'Nicola Sturgeon: The Tour' and tops that mimicked the look of classic Scotland football shirts with 'Sturgeon 15' on the back in a nod to the upcoming general election. Critics were quick to note the blurring of lines between party and country that is often associated with the SNP.

Sturgeon used the rallies, which were supplemented with Facebook question-and-answer sessions for those who missed out on tickets, to pledge to be the 'most accessible First Minister ever'. Part of that promise included plans to hold monthly press conferences. These were quickly dropped from her schedule.

Concern over online disinformation as a political campaigning tool had not penetrated the public consciousness in 2014 in the way that it would dominate debate in later years, particularly following the election of Donald Trump as US President in 2016. Nevertheless, fake news was alive and well in Scotland following the independence referendum, with internet claims that the vote was 'rigged'. Examples often focused on the count in Dundee, where repeated fire alarms meant the venue was evacuated. One snippet of video which was widely circulated on Twitter on the night appeared to show a counting officer at the polling station lifting votes from a Yes pile and placing them under No. A separate clip highlighted a Yes vote, bundled with others, sitting on the No pile. At 12.50 a.m. on 19 September, while votes were being counted, the official Yes Dundee campaign tweeted to try to allay fears, saying: 'To clarify, ballot papers have not yet been sorted into Yes/No and are just resting on [the] table where No will go once sorted. No need to worry.' This did not stop Jim Sillars, the former deputy leader of the SNP, amplifying the claims by insisting they should be investigated. A pro-Kremlin vote-monitoring agency, which sent observers to the referendum, denounced the result and claimed it was manufactured to avoid comparisons with a vote in Crimea to secede from Ukraine.

The idea of a rigged referendum continued in the months that followed. During her tour stop in Dundee, Sturgeon was asked by a member of the audience if she was concerned about vote tampering. The First Minister in waiting rejected all suggestions of foul play out of hand and pointed out that if there was any doubt about the integrity of the result then she would be the first person knocking down doors to have it reviewed.

Scottish politics' online ecosystem, and its vulnerability to exploitation from foreign powers, would become a key issue in the tribal feud that erupted between Sturgeon and Salmond in the years that followed. Salmond's decision to host a show on the

Kremlin-backed TV station RT was instrumental in the disintegration of the pair's relationship, and online bloggers with a history
of amplifying Vladimir Putin's propaganda regularly promoted
Salmond's false claims that he had been the victim of a conspiracy
in his criminal case.

*   *   *

One of the final major public displays of unity between Sturgeon
and Salmond was the official handover of power at the SNP's conference. Adoring party members enthusiastically cheered both their
outgoing and incoming leaders on the opening day of the sold-out
event at Perth's Concert Hall. Having received a lengthy standing
ovation before he spoke, Salmond said Scotland had 'changed and
changed utterly' in an echo of Yeats's poem 'Easter, 1916'. It was
a less than subtle suggestion that Scotland would follow Ireland
towards independence as he hailed Sturgeon as a 'woman of extraordinary talent' who would 'make history' as First Minister. For
her part, Sturgeon, who received an equally rapturous reception,
hailed Salmond as 'a hero of our movement and a champion of our
nation'.

In a sign of the rhetorical direction her government would take,
the major policy announcement of Sturgeon's speech was something that would benefit children across the country. 'By the end
of the next parliament, my commitment is that all three- and four-
year-olds and all eligible two-year-olds will receive not sixteen
hours but thirty hours of free childcare each week,' she said. That
very first commitment was not fulfilled, with the extension pushed
back during the Covid-19 pandemic until after the 2021 Holyrood
election.

The conference was a huge success for Sturgeon and demonstrated both the sharp upward trajectory of the party and her desire

to have allies in key positions. There was an atmosphere of celebration despite the referendum loss, in large part down to the tens of thousands of new members who had joined the SNP in the wake of the independence campaign.

As well as Sturgeon's unopposed election, Stewart Hosie, the then husband of Shona Robison, who is one of Sturgeon's closest political friends and ran her leadership campaign, was voted in as deputy leader.

On the plaza outside the concert hall, Salmond lapped up the adulation. Hundreds of people on the streets serenaded their political hero with 'For He's a Jolly Good Fellow' and he could not help but indulge his fans. The man who had worn his arm in a sling for weeks after the referendum because he had shaken too many hands during the campaign disappeared into the group to grip more arms and take selfies. Panicked aides and his protection officer watched aghast, unable to keep up with Salmond as he disappeared from sight. Gunn, who was with Salmond, says: 'If somebody wanted to do him any harm there was just no way we could do anything about it because of all these people cheering and shouting and wanting to shake hands with him. He just disappeared into a mass of people outside the concert hall.' Salmond himself remembered the event with considerably less trepidation. In his referendum diaries, he wrote:

I was in one of the dressing rooms at the back of the Perth Concert Hall, trying to adjust to my first moments of not being SNP leader, a position I'd held for twenty of the last twenty-four years. Political conferences tend to be exhausting and I was just expecting an evening with friends and family. But I agreed to go outside for a few moments because I was told some people had turned up wanting to have their picture taken with me.

There wasn't a handful of folk waiting – there were thousands.

A flash crowd had gathered in response to a single Facebook message. I spent a considerable time walking through the people and talking to as many as I could, before making a speech of thanks to them, just as they had gathered to thank me.

On 18 November 2014, Alex Salmond officially stood down as First Minister of Scotland. He had spent large parts of his final two weeks in office individually responding to letters from home and abroad. He also attracted praise for auctioning personal effects and donating his first ministerial pension to charity.

His final day in office began with Salmond unveiling a tribute to himself. By a duck pond on the campus of Edinburgh's Heriot-Watt University, a sandstone monument was erected bearing the motto: 'The rocks will melt with the sun before I allow tuition fees to be imposed on Scotland's students.' The sentence, adapted from the Robert Burns song 'A Red, Red Rose', is a quote from Salmond in 2011. It was a reference to the SNP's decision in government to remove any charges for Scottish university students. European Union laws meant this had to extend to anyone travelling to study from a country in the bloc, although a loophole meant people from England, Wales and Northern Ireland had to pay up to £9,250 a year. It subsequently emerged that a number of universities – including Salmond's alma mater St Andrews – had turned down an offer to host the stone before Heriot-Watt agreed. The memorial was removed from the campus in 2020 after complaints from fee-paying students.

His Cabinet colleagues clubbed together to present Salmond with an apt leaving present – a personalised golf bag in blue and white with a small saltire. If the gift betrayed a hope that he would depart the stage to concentrate on his putting and leave politics behind, they were to be sorely disappointed.

The most generous – but not uncommon – view of Salmond's leadership style came later that day from Stewart Stevenson, the former MSP who as Salmond's oldest political friend was the only non-party leader allowed a contribution during forty-nine minutes of speeches in the Scottish Parliament to mark his resignation. 'He is the toughest boss I have ever worked for, or with, and the fairest, and he is a team builder. But, however tough he might have been on me or on the rest of us, he has always been tougher on himself,' Stevenson said.

Salmond was teased during the debate by Scottish Labour's Jackie Baillie about his brief period out of the SNP as part of the infamous '79 Group who rebelled against party policy as she accused him of leading a delegation of rebels to walk out of a meeting. 'She should go and look at it again, because I did not walk out – I was flung out. I offer her this in case she is ever in such a position: never go willingly – wait to be expelled, Jackie,' Salmond, who would later quit the party over allegations of sexual harassment, replied.

The following day saw Sturgeon confirmed into high office. Ruth Davidson, then Scottish Conservative leader, made a token challenge for the position but lost by sixty-six votes to fifteen.

In her maiden speech as First Minister, Sturgeon spent more time reflecting on her feminism than she did on her nationalism. She looked up to the Holyrood chamber's VIP gallery, where her niece Harriet Owens was watching proceedings, and reflected on the fact the eight-year-old had not yet learned about the sexism prevalent in Scottish society. She added:

My fervent hope is that she never will – that by the time she is a young woman, she will have no need to know about any of these issues because they will have been consigned to history. If during my tenure as First Minister I can play a part in making that so, for my niece and for every other little girl in this country, I will be very happy indeed.

While Sturgeon was promising to use her platform as Scotland's first female First Minister to secure greater opportunities for women, officials in the office she had just inherited were wrestling with what to do about the legacy of her predecessor.

A young female civil servant had returned from one of Salmond's last public engagements and complained that he had groped her towards the end of the evening.

The glitzy event had been held at Stirling Castle and, as was now standard practice, many of the guests in attendance were desperate to get a selfie with the man of the moment. Years later, the young woman would recall in court how Salmond had been 'very insistent' that she also have her photograph taken with him on the ramparts of the castle. She said as they were posing for the picture, he put his arm around her and then 'reached down and grabbed hold of my backside'. Under cross-examination, she insisted there could be no doubt as to Salmond's intention, as he had done it 'quite forcefully with his full hand' and it had felt 'very deliberate'. The woman said she had been left in 'shock and disbelief' but had tried to 'just keep smiling'. She added: 'I just want to do my job and feel proud of myself doing my job and it felt like I was being demeaned. It was unprofessional but there was nothing I could do about it.'

During his trial, Salmond denied the incident took place and his close friend and business partner, the former SNP MP Tasmina Ahmed-Sheikh, testified she had also been at the event and had seen nothing untoward. He was found not guilty of sexually assaulting the civil servant.

When she returned to work in Edinburgh following the Stirling Castle event, the woman became the third female government employee in the space of a year to inform her line manager that she believed she had been on the receiving end of inappropriate behaviour from Salmond. She would later become Ms B in the Scottish government investigation into Salmond and tell investigators:

> Afterwards I told my line manager about this incident, but didn't feel that I wanted to take a complaint further. Part of the reason for never wanting to complain was the awareness that, even post-referendum, we were at a very sensitive time politically and historically. Additionally, I think anyone that works in private office will agree that you have failed at your job if you somehow become the news story.

It wasn't the last time the woman raised concerns about the culture at the heart of the Scottish government, nor the last time she was ignored. It would take the passage of another three years and the eruption of the Harvey Weinstein scandal before her repeated concerns finally forced an investigation into the former First Minister's conduct.

CHAPTER 5

A NEW HOPE

7 MAY 2015, 10 P.M.

Big Ben struck ten and an earthquake rumbled through British politics.

Sitting in her Glasgow home, Nicola Sturgeon watched as graphics on television news channels morphed into projections of the shape of the House of Commons based on the exit poll for the 2015 general election. It predicted that the Conservatives would comfortably be the largest party, in stark contrast to opinion polls that had shown David Cameron's party neck and neck with Ed Miliband's Labour all the way up to voting day.

There would be questions asked about how public opinion was so badly misread – especially given the Tories did indeed eventually return a majority – but there was one part of the UK where pollsters had been consistently correct.

Standing in front of a virtual Commons chamber, complete with graphic animations of senior politicians that wobbled in an unnerving manner on the computerised front benches, Jeremy Vine told BBC viewers:

We bring on the SNP and you can see them there. A quite sensational result for them. Remember, fifty-nine seats in total in

Scotland. They have won all but one of them under our forecast and at the last election they only had six seats in total. So they have gone from six seats to fifty-eight under Nicola Sturgeon. It is the stand-out result of the night.

During the month running up to 7 May, multiple polling companies had predicted that the SNP would return around 50 per cent of the vote. On the night, they claimed almost exactly half of the number of people who turned out, up from just 20 per cent in the 2010 election. The exit poll sent jaws to the floor across Scottish politics.

During the campaign, a buoyant Sturgeon had deployed humour with her team as a way of expressing her delight at the direction of travel. 'The week before the actual election, there was a poll came out that said the SNP were going to win fifty-eight out of fifty-nine seats,' says Campbell Gunn, who was a serving special adviser (spad) at the time.

And Nicola came out of her office to the spads and said, 'For fuck sake, lads, we're losing one.' Those were her words. It's the only time I've heard her swear, but she was doing it jokingly. I mean, neither she nor any of us expected us to even get fifty-six, as we did.

In the wake of the exit poll, Sturgeon moved to manage expectations. At 10.07 p.m., she tweeted: 'I'd treat the exit poll with HUGE caution. I'm hoping for a good night but I think 58 seats is unlikely! #GE15'.

As it turned out, that startling prediction was only two more MPs than the SNP ended up returning. Nationalists took to using the phrase 'The 56' as a way of identifying themselves, just as

'The 45' became shorthand for independence voters after the 2014 referendum.

Salmond maintains that the result was no surprise to him. In their election day ritual, Moira asked him to predict the outcome, to which he responded by writing '51' on a piece of paper, folding it and handing it to his wife. He was also on hand to calm the nerves of his successor. 'On the way to Strichen, Nicola phones,' he writes in his diaries.

> She had been at a polling station in Govan and was concerned that someone had not met her eye. It is not unusual for this normally ice cool lady to have a campaign wobble. Indeed the only campaign I can remember her not having one was the referendum, which we then lost. Mind you with the Yes results in Glasgow there was probably no reason for her to worry.
>
> I tell her we have an exit poll. 'What does it show?' she asks. 'Prepare for a landslide,' I reply.

Sturgeon was separate from most of her team, who were based at the SNP's offices on the third floor of Gordon Lamb House, just a few minutes' walk away from the Scottish Parliament. Instead, Sturgeon was in Glasgow, surrounded by only her closest allies: Liz Lloyd, her chief of staff; and Noel Dolan, her longest-serving aide as well as a member of her private office and an SNP staffer. After a relentless campaign, she had enjoyed a more relaxed forty-eight hours before the results began to trickle through.

In Edinburgh, party staffers crowded around a long, white rectangular table with a television screen at its end, watching with increasing jubilation as the results rolled in. Amongst them were Sue Ruddick, the party's chief operating officer, who would later claim Salmond had physically assaulted her during campaigning in

2008, and Kirk Torrance, the party's head of digital, who was subsequently key to setting up Salmond's breakaway party, Alba. They were joined by Scottish government special advisers for the night as they followed proceedings fuelled by Irn-Bru, bottled water and tubs of Pringles.

The scale of the SNP's victory was vividly illustrated when the BBC's swingometer was twice unable to properly visualise the shift towards the party: firstly in Glasgow North East, but perhaps most symbolically in Kirkcaldy and Cowdenbeath, where Roger Mullin claimed the seat being vacated by Gordon Brown, the former Labour Prime Minister whose intervention in the independence referendum was seen by many nationalists, including Salmond, as vital to saving the Union. But those results were not the two that caused the greatest cheers amongst the SNP. The group erupted 'like a football crowd' according to one attendee, both when Jim Murphy, then leader of Scottish Labour, lost his seat in East Renfrewshire and when Douglas Alexander, the former Cabinet minister, was ousted from Paisley and Renfrewshire South by twenty-year-old Mhairi Black.

It was decided overnight that a team should be sent to London with Kevin Pringle, who was the brains behind the SNP's slick press operation as it came to power, and Erik Geddes, another senior press officer, being dispatched from Edinburgh on no sleep. They spent the following day on College Green pushing Deputy First Minister John Swinney and Humza Yousaf, then the Europe Minister, in front of any microphone that would broadcast the party's message.

Sturgeon was due to travel to London no matter the election result to attend the 70th anniversary of VE Day and commemorations at the Cenotaph. Officials noted her naturally shy personality asserted itself even in the midst of her triumph as she had to be persuaded to make small talk with David Cameron, Nick

Clegg and Ed Miliband ahead of the ceremony despite the fact her party had just won a handsome victory. She would later claim that Boris Johnson, who was also in attendance in his role as Mayor of London, asked if giving Holyrood enough powers to render it independent in all but name would 'kind of buy you guys off' as they left the ceremony.

The election result was a disaster for the three pro-Union parties. Labour, the once dominant force in Scottish politics, lost forty seats and retained only Edinburgh South's Ian Murray as its sole MP north of the border. Murray saw off Neil Hay, the SNP candidate, who only weeks earlier had been discovered using the social media pseudonym 'Paco McSheepie' to retweet a link referring to supporters of the Union as 'quislings', also claiming that some elderly voters could 'barely remember their own names'. Sturgeon distanced herself from Hay's comments but urged his constituents to vote SNP in a radio interview in the run-up to polling day.

Meanwhile, the Liberal Democrats lost ten MPs, with only Alistair Carmichael, the then Scottish Secretary, retaining his seat by just 817 votes. The Lib Dem losses included Charles Kennedy, after a bitter campaign that saw the former party leader subjected to abuse including anonymous, aggressive notes being left on his car and put through his letterbox. Supporters of Ian Blackford, the SNP candidate who would later become the party's leader at Westminster, launched a #WheresCharlie? campaign on social media, criticising Kennedy's voting rate. Kennedy died of a major haemorrhage linked to his alcoholism less than a month after the election.

Almost immediately after Kennedy's death, Salmond questioned his commitment to the Union, telling the BBC: 'I don't think his heart was in the Better Together campaign.' The comments did not go down well with Sturgeon, who was genuinely upset when she heard of the news during a trip to Brussels. She told reporters that she fondly remembered a trip to Australia in the mid-1990s where the pair had 'skived off' to watch *Trainspotting* together in a Melbourne cinema, the only two Scots in the audience.

There was little change for the Scottish Conservatives, with David Mundell clinging onto their sole seat, though his majority was slashed to 798 votes.

*　　*　　*

Such a dramatic shift in fortunes and power will always come as a shock on the night, but the signs had been there for anyone paying attention in the preceding months. By the time of the 2014 Scottish independence referendum, the SNP had around 25,000 members. Just weeks after voters rejected breaking up Britain, computers in the party's headquarters had crashed when that number doubled to more than 50,000 to make the party the third largest in the UK, a position it was soon to occupy electorally. The total passed 100,000 by March 2015 and it sat at 115,000 shortly after the election, meaning that around one in fifty of Scotland's adult population was a member of the SNP at the time. It was a phenomenal and spontaneous expansion of the party with very little coordinated effort put in to secure the additional membership. The influx would also create its own difficulties in time.

In contrast to the organic growth of the SNP, Sturgeon's start to life as First Minister was carefully stage-managed. The day after taking post she summoned ministers one by one to Bute House and appointed her new, gender-balanced, Cabinet. After being given their new roles, those with a place at the top table had to wait in the building until all the announcements had been made so they could pose together for a photograph on the steps outside the First Minister's official residence.

The desire to have an equal number of men and women in

government led to the sacking of senior figures from the Salmond administration. Mike Russell, the Education Secretary, and Kenny MacAskill, the Justice Secretary, were summoned to Bute House the night before the reshuffle and told their services were no longer required. Swinney was promoted to Deputy First Minister while Shona Robison, a close friend of Sturgeon, became Health Secretary, replacing Alex Neil, a stalwart of the left of the SNP who had previously run for its leadership. Neil was demoted to Social Justice Secretary but retained his place in government after Sturgeon decided his popularity in the party made him a more valuable asset than Russell. He did not enjoy serving under Sturgeon and contrasted how she ran her ministerial team unfavourably with Salmond's approach. 'What Alex did was he conducted the orchestra,' Neil says.

He decided what tune the orchestra was playing, he decided in which way it was going to be played, he decided how many folk were in the orchestra and who was in the orchestra. And if any member of the orchestra wasn't playing the tune properly, he very quickly sorted it out. Sometimes by giving them another instrument to play, as it were – i.e. reshuffling, or sometimes by shuffling them out altogether – but he basically let you get on with the job. Nicola, on the other hand, tries to be the conductor of the orchestra and tries to play everybody's instrument at the same time. And I think that's why a lot of mistakes have been made and why delivery under Nicola of key policies is much less successful than what it had been under Alex.

Dolan, who was one of those advising Sturgeon on the reshuffle, concedes that the ambition for a gender-balanced Cabinet adversely affected the quality of government: 'She had to remove certain people in order to get her gender balance, and certain people were

promoted who helped achieve that gender balance, shall we say.'
However, he argues that Sturgeon attempted to give her Cabinet
greater autonomy than the picture painted by Neil and in fact tried
to model her approach more closely on Salmond's.

> She tried to be supportive even when people were making ques-
> tionable decisions. Her attitude was 'I've got to let them do it'.
> She might not have agreed with what they were doing all the
> time, but she felt she had to let the Cabinet minister do that.
> And some people were very experienced, obviously, but there
> were some new ones and she just let them get on. Some of those
> ones that she let get on, she let get off the Cabinet as well.

Angela Constance, who was made Education Secretary in Sturgeon's first reshuffle, was demoted to Neil's job eighteen months
later as he departed government. She was sacked from the Cabinet altogether in 2018. Constance had admitted that the SNP had
failed to close the gulf between the best and worst state schools
during her time in charge of education and officials around Sturgeon were known not to have been impressed with her performance as a minister. She would, however, be brought back to the
front bench in December 2020 to tackle Scotland's drugs death
crisis after asking awkward questions of the government while
serving as a member of the Holyrood inquiry into the handling of
the Salmond complaints.

The push for gender equality went beyond Sturgeon's ministerial team. Within nine months of her becoming First Minister,
the number of women working for the Scottish government had
increased to overtake the number of men, and in May 2015 it was
announced that Leslie Evans would become the first woman to
hold the post of Permanent Secretary to the Scottish government.

The business of governing played second fiddle to the campaign trail, however, and Sturgeon was undoubtedly the breakout star of the show not just in Scotland but across the UK. In some ways that campaign had started as soon as she officially became First Minister. Her pre-coronation tour culminated on 22 November 2014, the day after her reshuffle, with a headline performance in front of 12,000 screaming fans at Glasgow's cavernous Hydro arena. With a Madonna-style radio microphone strapped to the side of her face, Sturgeon followed in the footsteps of Kylie Minogue, Beyoncé and Lady Gaga by appearing at the venue that had been opened fourteen months previously with a Rod Stewart concert. Standing in the bowl of the amphitheatre as the rapturous crowd gave her a prolonged standing ovation of the type she had become used to over the preceding weeks, she pronounced: 'Democracy rocks.' Her support acts included Eddi Reader, the Scottish singer-songwriter and former frontwoman of Fairground Attraction, the Celtic rock band the Red Hot Chilli Pipers and Salmond, who called her 'the most brilliant young woman in Scottish politics'.

Sturgeonmania and selfies would become central to the campaign as the new leader's ability to reach out across the political divide was almost universally lauded. She sharpened her image during the campaign, donning designer suits and losing a stone in weight through a mixture of healthier eating and regular use of her exercise bike. When she was confirmed as First Minister, the SNP sent out only one press release, which let it be known that her striking red dress was made by Totty Rocks, an independent Edinburgh womenswear fashion label who had worked with the model Kate Moss. Holly Mitchell and Lynsey Blackburn, the designers, were invited to Sturgeon's office for final adjustments before the big occasion and the firm was soon regularly providing outfits for – and being name-checked by – the First Minister and her press operation.

Another clear moment for softening Sturgeon's image came during a kitchen table interview with STV when she was filmed giving Murrell a playful slap on the cheek after he burnt a slice of toast. During the same interview, she also addressed not having any children. 'The idea that you would ever make a conscious decision about these things – some women possibly do and there's nothing wrong with that – but I certainly, we certainly, didn't,' she said. 'So there are areas in your life that I understand there's a curiosity but I also think most members of the public would also understand that everybody's entitled to some privacy.' Seventeen months later Sturgeon would reveal in a book by the journalist Mandy Rhodes that she had suffered a miscarriage in 2010, when she was forty.

During the campaign Sturgeon was surviving on three hours of sleep a night but was seen as fresh and energetic by election watchers north and south of the border. The main leaders' debate on 2 April was a breakthrough moment. A snap YouGov poll for *The Times* found the British public had deemed her the winner. Other polls offered a more mixed assessment, but there was no doubt that Sturgeon, a Scottish nationalist, had found widespread general approval with an audience across the UK. The iconic picture moment came at the end of the debate when Sturgeon, Natalie Bennett of the Greens and Plaid Cymru's Leanne Wood walked across the stage and embraced one another.

A private jet owned by Chris and Colin Weir, SNP supporters who had won a £161 million lottery prize, was used to fly Sturgeon and her team between Edinburgh and Manchester to save on travelling time. That same week, Salmond had been mocked for quaffing pink champagne in a tribute to his beloved Heart of Midlothian FC, who had just secured promotion back into the Scottish Premiership, during separate interviews with the *Spectator* and *New Statesman* magazines. As Sturgeon and her team boarded the private jet for the flight home, they were all offered a drink to toast her success. The First Minister and her aides erupted with laughter as a bottle of pink champagne was produced.

Effusive in his praise the following day, Salmond said that his successor was 'wiping the floor with the old boys' network'. The turn of phrase would be used with venom by Sturgeon against her former mentor in the years to come.

The coverage was not universally positive. The *Daily Mail* memorably branded Sturgeon 'the most dangerous woman in Britain' with a front page that served to gee up Conservative voters in England who feared that Ed Miliband would enter Labour into a coalition with the SNP to ensure he became Prime Minister. Such speculation was almost certainly fuelled by a conversation between Alastair Campbell, who was helping Labour's 2015 campaign, and Geoff Aberdein, Salmond's former chief of staff, in which Tony Blair's former spin doctor was sounded out about the former First Minister becoming Deputy Prime Minister during a trip to Scotland. At a dinner on 4 February with Sir Martin Gilbert, the founder and former chief executive of Aberdeen Asset Management, Aberdein, who was now employed by the investment management company, told Campbell that Sturgeon would have 'mixed feelings' about Salmond's return to Westminster. 'But as the evening wore on – and he mentioned a couple of times that he had been speaking to Alex today – he raised directly the idea of Salmond as DPM in a Labour coalition government,' Campbell wrote in his diaries.

> After the Q&A with Martin, during which I said I felt Labour could win – and said why – Geoff said you don't believe that, you know he can't win a majority, but he might do it with Alex in there as No. 2. I said I would try to sus it out.

Allies of Sturgeon say they were unaware of any such plan but that the conversation was part of an off-books Salmond operation that he thought would boost the SNP's fortunes. Amid the speculation of a deal between two or more parties in the event of a hung parliament, the hope was that Aberdein's suggestion would filter back through Ed Miliband's team and leak into the public domain, setting up a narrative that the SNP would be major players after the votes had been counted. 'In a Westminster election that's vital because unless you're actually challenging for something like that, then you'll get ignored by the London broadcasters,' a party strategist says.

The plan appeared to work, with speculation increasing that Salmond would be the person to demand a senior Cabinet role – Deputy Prime Minister was the one most often referenced – in exchange for propping up Labour. It inspired Conservative posters of Miliband popping his head out of Salmond's jacket pocket, and that narrative shaped much of the campaign across the UK.

Although not sanctioned, Salmond's plan dovetailed with Sturgeon's message, which had been carefully crafted and was aimed at catching the ears of more than just a Scottish audience. At the party's manifesto launch she promised to act 'in the interests of people not just in Scotland but across the UK' if the SNP was to have influence in any hung parliament. 'For as long as Scotland remains part of the Westminster system, we have a shared interest with you in making that system work better for all of us – for the many, not the few,' she said. That final catchline would become synonymous with Jeremy Corbyn's period as Labour leader, but it also echoed language used during Tony Blair's time in charge. Sturgeon's adoption of the rhetoric was representative of a finely tuned campaign to hoover up traditional Labour voters, many of whom had backed Yes in the referendum. This strategy signposted a shift away from the base that Salmond had built in the north-east and rural parts of Scotland. The derisory 'Tartan Tories' nickname had been bestowed on the SNP because it had won in traditional Conservative seats. Although the party's appeal had been broadened by Salmond, and the independence campaign won support from the left, Sturgeon's Ayrshire and Glasgow roots meant the focus was about to shift increasingly towards the central belt, larger towns and cities.

The contrast was highlighted in how Salmond chose to set the agenda in the months running up to the election. A bidding war to hire him as a columnist was won by DC Thomson, with the decision to write jointly for the Aberdeen-based *Press and Journal* and the Dundee-based *Courier* raising some eyebrows. However, on top of the not inconsiderable annual fee of £108,000, the move made sense politically as it allowed him to target voters in his backyard through the *P&J*, a trusted local newspaper – and he wasn't planning a re-election campaign for his seat in the Scottish Parliament.

Salmond realised that staying at Holyrood could see him accused of backseat driving. Instead, he looked to return to an old haunt. 'He has always liked Westminster and I don't think there was any great hesitation going back there or any great soul-searching,' says Dolan.

> It was just something he was going to do and it was the best thing from his point of view. From her point of view having him sitting on the back benches [at Holyrood] was not ideal. In the period from November 2014, when he was still there, he just kept out of the way and let her get on with it. That was what she wanted and was great for her.

However, Sturgeon's team was keen to move on to a new era, with Salmond having far less involvement in the party direction so the new leader could take the spotlight. Other senior figures did not agree with his return to frontline politics, particularly with the SNP seen as lacking a substantial 'elder statesman' to add gravitas to their public profile with well-timed interventions. There is now an acknowledgement that neither Salmond nor Sturgeon, nor anyone in the tight group around them, had put enough thought into what his place in the party should have been after he left office.

Another former official says a return to being an MP meant he lost some of the standing of a former First Minister. 'But to be fair, nobody had ever really worked out what he would do as a "former First Minister" so there was a vacuum there and him defaulting to becoming – or continuing to be – a parliamentarian filled that vacuum,' they say. 'I don't think anybody thought anything like enough about what that role could or should have been.'

Salmond's impending return to Westminster began dominating headlines as soon as it was confirmed that he would be standing in the Liberal Democrat-held Gordon constituency. Part of Sturgeon's election plan saw him deployed across the country to boost the profiles of other candidates, particularly after the publication of his referendum diaries. The old joke about finding a 'rare unsigned copy' seemed to apply to *The Dream Shall Never Die* as Salmond became a one-man whirlwind of publicity. Signing events attracted large crowds as supporters clamoured for personalised copies and selfies, which was seen as a way of exposing the public to would-be MPs.

Sales were high, but the critical reviews were rather mixed. Paddy Ashdown, the former Liberal Democrat leader, described the book as 'the longest exercise in literary masturbation since politics began' as he tried to divert press attention away from his own party's struggling spring conference.

As well as promoting the book and the party, Salmond used the trips around the country to sound out candidates who would be senior figures about the prospect of him running for the party leadership in the House of Commons. That would have seen him replace Angus Robertson, who is close to Sturgeon but has an uneasy relationship with Salmond. 'He was seriously weighing up the notion of going into the leadership at Westminster,' says a source close to Salmond.

There were definitely people who felt much more loyal to Alex. Even some of the older guard felt much more loyal to Alex than to Angus. He had been eyeing up what would be fun if we had held the balance of power. It would have been great to be leader of the group, or Chief Whip, so he could be the one running around cutting deals. That would have been pretty fun in that context. But I think as soon as we were in a position where there was a Tory majority the appeal disappeared a bit.

The move was not discussed with Sturgeon or any of her immediate team, who were frantically trying to find out if the rumours of his canvassing support were correct. 'I think he just decided to keep people guessing,' the source adds. 'He would have beaten Angus if there had been a run.'

While he was considering becoming the boss at Westminster, Salmond's interventions repeatedly opened the door for questions about whether he or Sturgeon was really in charge of the SNP as a whole. In an interview to announce his joining the paper as a columnist, he told *The Courier* in January 2015 that 'home rule' – where all domestic affairs and taxation would be controlled by Holyrood, with defence and foreign affairs reserved to Westminster – would be the SNP's price to prop up a minority Labour government. Sturgeon's spokesman refused to be drawn on the price of any coalition but conceded that the First Minister 'supports what the former First Minister said'.

In fact, the policy itself had long been a back-up plan to independence for the Salmond–Sturgeon government. Salmond had tried to have a third option of 'full devolution' put on the 2014 ballot paper, but it was the only request that saw David Cameron – who famously declared himself 'not too fussy' about the timing of the referendum, to the dismay of his Scottish colleagues – put his foot down during the negotiations between the First Minister and

Prime Minister. Reheating those plans would eventually be a key part of Sturgeon's election campaign.

Salmond's comments to *The Courier* found their way to the Scottish Parliament thanks to opposition leaders using them to attack Sturgeon at First Minister's Questions. Kezia Dugdale, then Scottish Labour's deputy leader, quipped during one session: 'It strikes me that if you want a straight answer from the Scottish National Party, you need to take Alex Salmond out for lunch.'

Such freelancing left Sturgeon unimpressed – and a rare public glimpse of it cut through in an interview with *The Times* in which she said of Salmond's 'joke' that he would be writing the Labour budget: 'I am not going to say whether I thought it was good, bad or funny.'

His appearance at the SNP's spring conference in March would also increase tensions. The party's expanded membership meant it held the event in Glasgow's cavernous SECC, but despite the increased audience, a pre-conference story in *The Herald* about a proposed North American book tour to promote Salmond's diaries dampened the mood in Sturgeon's camp. HarperCollins, his publisher, announced planned signing events in New York and Toronto during the annual Scotland Week festivities in April, which would have seen Salmond miss part of the election campaign.

There was little time between press enquiries landing with the SNP and confirmation of the tour being cancelled. Salmond, who was at a local hustings in the town of Huntly when he was called and told of the queries, was said to be 'particularly livid' about the fact that the information had been made public and pulled the plug.

There was no chance of him missing a lunchtime fringe event to promote the book on the final day of the party conference. The size of the crowd meant that what was supposed to be a low-key intermission soon overshadowed the rest of the day. Salmond did not need much encouragement from the 2,000-strong crowd to move from a wooden secondary podium in the corner of the venue to the one from which his successor had given her keynote address less than twenty-four hours earlier. The symbolism was not lost on the watching press pack, who had repeatedly asked Sturgeon, much to her irritation: 'Who really leads the SNP?'

During the question-and-answer session, Salmond accused the BBC of being biased in the run-up to the independence referendum and waded into a debate about an Angus school's decision to withdraw the award-winning Gregory Burke play *Black Watch* from its drama curriculum over its bad language and sexual dialogue, telling his audience that the head teacher should hang her head in shame. Aides to Sturgeon were visibly frustrated by the attention-grabbing behaviour as the limelight switched from their boss.

Away from the glare of the cameras, new party rules were being approved in an effort to shut down dissent against the Sturgeon leadership. During a private session on the same day that Salmond made his appearance, a set of standing orders were passed by delegates. The changes, which were proposed in Angus Robertson's name, dictated that all party members must 'accept that no member shall, within or outwith the Parliament, publicly criticise a group decision, policy or another member of the group'. This effectively meant that it would be a disciplinary offence for any backbenchers at Holyrood, MPs or ordinary party members to speak out against the decisions of the leadership. It would not prove a deterrent in later years as the SNP's once iron-clad discipline broke down in parallel with the Sturgeon–Salmond relationship.

In the years that followed, Salmond would repeatedly accuse Sturgeon of not pushing hard enough on the constitutional question. Just thirty-six hours after the election, the contrast was already visible between the new and old leaders. Standing under the Forth

Rail Bridge with the other fifty-five victorious candidates and the First Minister, Salmond was asked if Scotland was now closer to independence after the landslide victory. He replied: 'Yes, because the SNP now has an overwhelming mandate from the Scottish people to carry forward Scotland's interests. Now, obviously the timing of any future referendum is a matter for the Scottish people first and foremost and a matter of tactics is certainly a question for Nicola Sturgeon.' The same question was duly put to Sturgeon, who said: 'The election wasn't about independence. I made that clear. The result of the election was not going to influence the independence debate one way or the other.'

Aides to both politicians say the lack of communication between the pair only grew worse once Salmond's base was primarily at Westminster. Once installed in the Commons, he requested the foreign affairs portfolio and immediately set about installing a team of his choice. The day after the new SNP group arrived in London, Salmond approached Stephen Gethins, then the MP for North East Fife, in one of the many corridors of the Palace of Westminster with a simple question. 'Do you want to do Europe?' he asked his former special adviser. The answer was affirmative. He also recruited Tasmina Ahmed-Sheikh, whom he would work closely with and who would join him in co-hosting his television show, to cover international trade, and Patrick Grady, who would later become embroiled in a harassment scandal of his own, as international development spokesman. Tellingly, Salmond made the approaches and appointments rather than Robertson and started 'freewheeling a little bit', to the annoyance of the SNP's leadership at Holyrood.

After his appointment was confirmed, he tweeted: 'We'll provide a strong, consistent #SNP voice which is: – pro-Europe – pro-developing world – against military adventurism.' Sturgeon's closest advisers angrily asked a Salmond ally: 'Is Alex unilaterally setting the SNP's foreign policy?' The questions underlined a fear that their former boss was going to undermine Sturgeon's burgeoning leadership and make it increasingly difficult for her to escape from his shadow despite the switch of parliament. A source close to Salmond says: 'They were a bit like "What's his game here?" Actually, I think he was just enjoying himself. He was back in the fray at Westminster, he had plenty left to say, it was an exciting time.'

During this period, however, Salmond became frustrated at Sturgeon's lack of contact with the Westminster group as a whole and with him personally. 'Nicola is terrible at maintaining those personal connections and making people continue to feel important, as you need to in politics, whereas Alex was actually quite good at that,' says a senior party figure.

> And Alex – he wasn't vying for Nicola's time or demanding to be listened to on this, that or the next thing – but the fact that she wasn't calling him probably made him feel slightly sidelined. He gets the job. He knows that the First Minister cannot be on the phone all the time. But I think he probably expected a wee bit more of a two-way street whereas Nicola was determined to plough her own furrow.

Salmond was by far the biggest political beast in the Westminster group, eclipsing not only Robertson but also Stewart Hosie, the deputy leader of the party, and was frustrated at what he saw as the SNP's inability to take full advantage of its vast increase in MPs and resulting enhanced position in the Westminster pecking order. 'I think he struggled with being out of the limelight,' says Gethins.

> Not being leader any more is hard and he was also carving out a role for himself down there. It's a weird sort of situation because remember Nicola was a wildly popular First Minister and

leader, given the big upsurge in membership. Angus was seen as doing a really good job as leader [in the Commons], and in PMQs, because remember Angus was being compared to Jeremy Corbyn at the time. Like everybody else, Alex was trying to carve out his own niche at that time and that's never something that's easy.

Sturgeon was also pursuing her own approach to party discipline which showed a ruthless streak towards anyone she thought risked damaging her or the SNP's brand. 'Nicola could never be accused of ever knowingly defending a friend or colleague,' a source close to Salmond says. 'A characteristic of Nicola if anyone is in trouble is not to stick her neck out, not to even stick her little finger out.' Others in the party believed that the way individuals were treated depended on whether Sturgeon favours them personally. 'There is a general feeling in the party that the disciplinary regime is not a particularly fair one and what happens to you is based on whether your face fits with the leader,' says Alex Neil.

Perhaps the highest-profile early example was Michelle Thomson. In September 2015, the newly elected Edinburgh West MP found herself at the centre of a storm over allegations around buy-to-let homes being bought for below-market prices and the conduct of a solicitor who had acted for her property firm. Thomson said that she was given no opportunity by Sturgeon to explain her side of the story before being forced to resign the party whip. The move to cut Thomson loose so quickly was generally received positively by the media, but it raised eyebrows amongst some SNP parliamentarians and activists. Police Scotland launched an investigation into Thomson, but the Crown Office eventually ruled that an 'absence of sufficient credible and reliable evidence' meant there was no case to answer. By that time the SNP had refused to endorse Thomson to run again as a candidate in the snap 2017 general election and she had lost her seat as a result. Salmond, who was later critical of a 'difficult' situation that was 'handled badly', lobbied Sturgeon on Thomson's behalf and was said to have been 'very supportive' of the under-fire MP in SNP group meetings. Sturgeon would later describe the Thomson situation as 'not easy' for her party. Then, as winter approached, she cut another of her MPs loose over alleged financial irregularities.

Natalie McGarry is from SNP stock. Her mother is Alice McGarry, a nationalist councillor on Fife Council since 1986, and her aunt, Tricia Marwick, was one of the original intake of Members of the Scottish Parliament in 1999 and served as Holyrood's Presiding Officer, the equivalent of the Speaker in the House of Commons, from 2011 to 2016. McGarry had been heavily involved in the Women for Independence campaign group, formed in 2012. However, concerns were raised with police about the alleged disappearance of more than £25,000 from the group's funds in November 2015 and two days after the missing money was first reported in the *Daily Record*, McGarry became the second SNP MP to resign the whip. Criminal proceedings were launched against McGarry and at the time of writing the case remains unresolved.

If Sturgeon's heavy-handed approach to internal discipline risked alienating some of the new MPs, Salmond remained a hero to many of them. Parliamentarians who had only become involved in party politics as a result of his influence admitted to being 'starstruck' in his presence in the early days of 'The 56' and Salmond knew how to cultivate those relationships. He would host regular boozy curry nights in London, which could sprawl on into the early hours of the morning. As well as these team-building exercises, he was generous with his time and knowledge of parliamentary procedure to those who would listen, giving tips to new MPs about how to ask effective questions in the chamber and how to use parliamentary procedure to their advantage.

Not everyone was overawed. Mhairi Black, aged just twenty and still a student at the University of Glasgow, had become the youngest MP since the eighteenth century. Not long after her election she was called up to see the former First Minister in the plush office he secured in the sought-after 1 Parliament Street building. 'I was just sitting chatting away to him and the whole time I'm thinking, "What's the point of this meant to be – is this a date, do I need to come out to Alex Salmond?",' she told *Holyrood* magazine.

> It was fine, really, he was just giving me tips here and there and then he says, 'I'm sure Taz [Ahmed-Sheikh] will take you out to go shopping or something at some point and you'll find your own style.' He then said that the last time he'd had this conversation it was with a young woman called Nicola Sturgeon. I thought, 'Oh, very good' and I just left the awkward silence hanging when he asked me if I wanted him to arrange it with Taz. I'm like, 'I am never going to be told how to dress, especially by a man.'

If that was a puncturing moment, it appeared to be in the minority. As he gave the journalist Jamie Ross a tour of the Palace of Westminster shortly after his victory, he told how several Labour and Conservative MPs had approached him for advice. Salmond also reiterated his disdain for the mainstream media, with whom he was regularly agreeing to interviews, and voiced some concerns over unregulated online outlets. Ross wrote: 'As for noted pro-independence blog Wings Over Scotland, Salmond believes it sometimes "takes conspiracy theories to the end degree" and is uncomfortable at the decision of Stuart Campbell, the site's owner, to adopt the persona of a reverend: "I'm innately suspicious of someone who calls himself a reverend who isn't."' Years later, his relationship with Campbell would flourish as the controversial website, which was influential with some Scottish nationalists, pushed the idea of a conspiracy against Salmond more than any other outlet.

He may have been influential over part of the new intake of MPs, but Salmond's actions in Westminster were also causing headaches for his successor. A month after the election, Sturgeon was forced to defend him against allegations of sexism after he clashed with Anna Soubry. The then Conservative minister interrupted Salmond and asked him to 'move on' during a Commons debate. In a response that Soubry said betrayed an 'attitude [that] belongs firmly in the nineteenth century', Salmond told her she should 'behave better' before adding: 'Behave yourself, woman.'

The comments were put to Sturgeon during a trip to New York. Her response gave no indication that she was aware of the concerns that had been raised about the culture in Salmond's government. She told HuffPost: 'I understand it was language that not everybody thinks should be used but it was in a boisterous House of Commons debate. The fundamental question, "does that language indicate that Alex Salmond is sexist?" Absolutely not, there's no man I know who is less sexist.'

The trip to the US had been a successful publicity push for Sturgeon, whose appearance on the popular satirical news programme *The Daily Show* had garnered particular praise. It also presented an opportunity for her team to snipe at Salmond. When a travelling journalist being quizzed by border control said he was covering the engagements of Scotland's First Minister, the American immigration officer replied: 'Nicola Sturgeon?' An aide to Sturgeon briefed the *Mail on Sunday*'s diary column: 'It is a level of public recognition her predecessor could only dream of.'

For his part, Salmond insisted his comments to Soubry were 'not in the slightest' chauvinistic, telling *Newsnight*: 'That's a Scottish idiom. I've said, "Behave yourself, man" many times in the

Scottish Parliament. I think it was merited on the occasion. There was certainly nothing sexist in it, whatever else you might think.' There is no evidence of Salmond ever using the phrase in the Scottish Parliament's Official Record, the equivalent of Hansard at Westminster.

The former First Minister was also sparking controversy by making regular appearances on RT, the Kremlin-backed television channel formerly called Russia Today. During one of his 2015 appearances, Salmond attacked the BBC, with whom he had an uneasy relationship following the independence referendum, as a 'mouthpiece of Tory propaganda'. Despite Sturgeon being opposed to her politicians appearing on the network, SNP MPs say Salmond was 'encouraging others to do so' and inviting RT representatives to drinks functions on the parliamentary estate.

It is worth noting that unlike Conservative and Labour MPs who received up to £1,000 an hour to appear on the channel, which regularly pushes Kremlin propaganda, there is no record or suggestion of Salmond accepting any fees for his appearances while he was an MP.

However, after he lost his seat in 2017 he signed up for a weekly chat show on the channel. The decision was the final straw in the breakdown of his relationship with Sturgeon.

CHAPTER 6

FROM RUSSIA WITH LOVE

9 NOVEMBER 2017, 8.01 P.M.

On the twenty-eighth floor of London's iconic Millbank Tower, Andrew Nicoll stared into a familiar pair of brown eyes. The veteran *Scottish Sun* political editor had been invited to a secretive event to launch the next phase of Alex Salmond's career and was bemused to find a photograph of the former First Minister proudly adorning the wall. 'Neither of us knew what was about to happen,' says Nicoll, who attended the bash with his editor, Alan Muir.

> We were amongst the first to arrive and we sat down on face-to-face leather sofas and looked out at the lights of London. There was nothing to do. Nothing to drink. Nothing to nibble. So I wandered over to gaze in stunned silence at a photo portrait of Salmond framed on the wall. There was another, in exactly the same style, hanging alongside. The name meant nothing to me, so I asked Alan to google the bloke. He turned out to be an RT presenter. That was our first hint.

The Alex Salmond Show – produced by his close friend and former SNP MP Tasmina Ahmed-Sheikh – had been given a trial run at that summer's Edinburgh Festival before being shopped around various broadcasters. It was assumed the show would be picked up by Rupert Murdoch's Sky, as the media tycoon was known to be personally friendly with Salmond and another of his companies, HarperCollins, had published *The Dream Shall Never Die*.

It became obvious that was not the case as the room filled up with Russian nationals and other broadcasters associated with the controversial Kremlin-backed station, including the former Glasgow MP George Galloway. Final confirmation that Salmond had signed up with a channel widely described as a propaganda outlet for Vladimir Putin's regime came when a press pack adorned with the RT logo was distributed to the guests. Nicoll took a picture and tweeted it, alerting the Scottish political world to the news.

Nicola Sturgeon was in the departure lounge of London City Airport with Scottish Brexit Minister Michael Russell preparing to fly to Jersey for a British–Irish Council summit when an official accompanying her spotted the tweet. The First Minister was absolutely furious not to have been given warning of Salmond's plans. Russell, who had been one of the guests on the Edinburgh Festival version of the show, was also livid. 'There was a stunned silence when the news filtered through to them,' says one source in attendance. 'Nicola was completely aghast. They simply couldn't believe that he would do such a thing.' The First Minister almost immediately sent a WhatsApp message to her predecessor simply saying: 'No wonder you didn't want to tell me.'

In the Scottish Parliament's bar, which is always busy on a Thursday night after First Minister's Questions, politicians and journalists digested the shocking news over pints of lager and glasses of wine. Alyn Smith, at that time an SNP MEP, was holding court with a group of newspaper reporters in a snug corner of the drinking den affectionately known as Margo's in tribute to the late nationalist MSP Margo MacDonald. On seeing Nicoll's tweet, Smith's reaction was immediate and visceral. 'What the fuck is he thinking?' he said, before adding: 'And that's on the record.' Several of the journalists immediately raced back to their offices in another part of the building to file copy on the unfolding drama.

Back in London, Salmond had finally arrived at the event, seemingly oblivious to the controversy his latest career move was already causing. He had been given a conspicuous makeover and was wearing a new three-piece tweed suit and open-neck shirt which, according to Nicoll, made him look 'like Mr Toad having a weekend off'.

Other launch attendees were more favourably disposed to Salmond's new job. A question-and-answer session with the invited audience brushed over RT's dubious output until Nicoll, who had followed every twist and turn of Salmond's career for thirty years, commandeered the microphone and asked bluntly: 'Is there nobody you won't work for?'

'It was a bit of a "guy on the piano stops playing" moment,' recalls Nicoll. 'And then Salmond did his wee mocking chuckle thing: "Ahuhhuhhuh, well, people used to say that when I was writing for the *Scottish Sun*, but I said, if it's good enough for Andy Nicoll, it's good enough for me."'

The gruff journalist, who had a second career as an award-winning literary novelist, was disgusted by Salmond's response. 'Say what you like about Rupert Murdoch, he's never launched a germ warfare attack on a UK city or left a trail of radioactive isotopes leading to a murder site. He employs journalists; he doesn't murder them,' he says now.

Nicoll immediately left the venue and returned to his hotel room to write up the story for the next day's paper. He also spoke briefly to Muir, who had helped Salmond edit his referendum diaries, and advised him to leave too. 'He decided I was right, but as he was leaving, he met Moira Salmond,' says Nicoll. 'She asked him: "How do you think this will play?"'

"'I don't know. These people shoot reporters," he said. But she just patted his arm and laughed and said, "Oh, Alan! Oh, Alan.'"

Moira's curiosity about how the move would be received suggests the Salmonds did harbour concerns about RT – but not to a sufficient degree to turn down the station's money. It is also telling that Salmond failed to consult any of his long-standing allies or advisers prior to the announcement. Former SNP MP Stephen Gethins, who carried out peace-building work in the western Balkans and south Caucasus before becoming a special adviser to Salmond, says his old boss had a 'real blind spot' when it came to Russia.

I spent time in Moscow with Russian human rights activists, and in St Petersburg. He'd clearly never spent time with the human rights activists who still show the scars of having been beaten up. LGBT activists with black eyes, lawyers who had lost their jobs because they tried to maintain the rule of law, the mothers of Russia who campaign for their kids who have been killed in Putin's various wars, who are roughed up by the police on a regular basis. This is an unpleasant authoritarian regime, which no one should have anything to do with. And I think that was the point when Alex really broke with the party.

Gethins says he was 'astonished' Salmond took the show on RT given his background.

When I wrote my book, I was rereading some of his foreign policy speeches pre-2015. They were fantastic, they laid the groundwork and I included some of them in the book because they're so good. And to have gone from that position and that handle on international affairs to be presenting RT along with George Galloway… I'm not sure why he did it and I think he's unnecessarily tarnished his reputation by doing so. It was a big severing moment for him and Nicola as well. It was for all of us who had been close to him.

Sturgeon's official response to Salmond's show was not as critical as her private assessment but still made clear the politicians were increasingly estranged. 'His choice of channel would not have been my choice,' she said in a statement. 'Of course, Alex is not currently an elected politician and is free to do as he wishes – but had I been asked, I would have advised against RT and suggested he seek a different channel to air what I am sure will be an entertaining show.'

Her embarrassment was made all the more acute when Ireland's Taoiseach, Leo Varadkar, took her aside after a joint press conference in Jersey at which the issue had been raised and incredulously asked if it was true Salmond had signed up with the station. 'I'm afraid so,' she replied.

*　　*　　*

Throwing in his lot with RT may have caused a definitive break with mainstream SNP opinion, but Salmond had been slowly drifting further away from his party colleagues for months. He had started the previous year by landing a broadcast job on a more respectable station when he signed up to present a weekly radio show on LBC, receiving a total of £15,000 for his six months of work. While a regular high-profile platform for him to air his views was a nagging concern for those around Sturgeon, Salmond was keen to stress in interviews that he was no longer calling the shots.

That did not stop him dreaming, telling the *Scottish Sun* in April 2016 that he missed being in charge of the Scottish government and was still adjusting to his new role. 'You wake up in the morning and think you're still First Minister, particularly when there is some emergency,' he said.

I will hear an item on the radio and think, 'Right, I need to summon the resilience committee.' Then I go, 'No, no, that's not me any more. Nicola can go and summon the resilience committee.' I miss things like that, as I loved all that sort of stuff. But it was the right time to stand down.

Salmond took a back seat during the 2016 Holyrood election campaign and jetted to the US a month before the vote to give a talk at the Hudson Union Society in New York City and promote his referendum diaries, having declined such a trip a year previously.

He was departing the Scottish Parliament but was unhappy with the SNP's selection of Gillian Martin as his replacement for the Aberdeenshire East seat, having unsuccessfully tried to introduce a last-minute rival into the race. In an old blog that emerged as she was selected, Martin had made a series of controversial remarks and called Salmond a 'smug git'.

But irritations about candidate selection aside, Salmond was still on reasonably good terms with the majority of his former colleagues during this period. 'He was one of the people put out in the media on the day of the manifesto launch, so he was still trusted enough to be given access to the manifesto in advance and to defend it and push it in the media,' says one SNP source active in the 2016 campaign.

So the relationship was still pretty good at that stage although there was increasingly a sense that he had to be handled, and the best way to do that with Alex Salmond is to ensure he is getting the attention that he feels he deserves.

Of course he did have views on what was going on politically and the decisions made by the government. I think anyone who used to run the show would feel that way, but I don't think he was attempting to do all that much backseat driving.

Despite the impending Brexit referendum, Sturgeon's focus was on the Holyrood election campaign, her first time asking the public to elect her as the leader of the Scottish government. To hammer home that point, she adopted a tactic Salmond had deployed in the 2007 and 2011 elections and had the slogan 'Nicola Sturgeon for First Minister' appear on ballot papers.

The campaign itself was built almost entirely around Sturgeon's personal popularity. While the 2011 push had been based on the slogan 'Team, Record, Vision' and stressed the party's strength and depth, this was a one-woman show. The front cover of the SNP's manifesto simply featured a full-page photograph of Sturgeon with the word 'Re-elect' written in bold typeface above her head. The messaging was strikingly similar to Salmond's 2011 pledge book, but while its cover had contained other pictures – including one of his ministers – the effort five years later was all about the new leader. In scenes reminiscent of the poster for the film *Being John Malkovich*, Sturgeon and her ministerial team held copies of the booklet above their heads on the stage during the manifesto launch while other politicians and supporters in the audience did the same. The result was a picture featuring hundreds of Sturgeons staring down the barrel of the camera over the shoulders of the real-life First Minister.

It was one of the more memorable moments of a low-key campaign in which Sturgeon promised to put her 'neck on the line' over the Scottish government's attempts to close the poverty-related attainment gap in education. 'I want to be judged on it, and I'm going to be making sure that the information's there to enable people to do that,' she said. In fact, Scotland withdrew from two international benchmarks used to compare education standards between nations, and spending watchdog Audit Scotland concluded before the 2021 election: 'Progress on closing the [attainment] gap has been limited and falls short of the Scottish Government's aims.'

The manifesto itself attempted to fudge the independence question by setting two tests that appeared likely to kick the issue into the long grass:

> We believe that the Scottish Parliament should have the right to hold another referendum if there is clear and sustained evidence that independence has become the preferred option of a majority of the Scottish people – or if there is a significant and material change in the circumstances that prevailed in 2014, such as Scotland being taken out of the EU against our will.

On election night, the SNP's vote share in constituencies increased slightly, but a combination of a fall in the Holyrood regional list ballot and the proportional nature of the system meant that Sturgeon returned six fewer MSPs than Salmond had in 2011, losing her majority in the process. This would prove crucial in the years that followed, allowing opponents to overturn legislation and dangle votes of no confidence over ministers at key moments.

The election also saw a significant change to Sturgeon's tight inner circle, with Noel Dolan, who had been her closest aide for twelve years, retiring as a special adviser. His departure meant that Liz Lloyd, Sturgeon's chief of staff, would have even greater influence. It was amid this change that Sturgeon faced the first major crisis of her time as First Minister and it was one of both a personal and political nature.

On 17 May, the *Daily Mail* splashed with a sensationalist front-page headline: TWO SNP MPS IN COMMONS LOVE TRIANGLE. The nationalists were embroiled in an old-fashioned sex scandal. Stewart Hosie, the SNP's deputy leader, and Angus MacNeil, the Western Isles MP, had both been involved in separate affairs with Westminster journalist Serena Cowdy. The *Mail* chronicled the relationships in salacious detail, including Cowdy reportedly painting the SNP as romantic revolutionaries and describing them as 'the Mujahideen of British politicians'. The headlines were problematic enough, but the fact that Hosie was married to Shona Robison, the Health Secretary and one of Sturgeon's oldest and closest friends, meant the First Minister had an emotional investment in the situation.

MacNeil had months earlier announced his separation from his wife – eight years after it was revealed that he had had a drunken encounter with two teenage girls in a hotel room while she was pregnant and in hospital – and was largely left alone by the party hierarchy. But Sturgeon made it clear to Hosie that he had to resign as her number two – a demand that was officially beyond her remit given he had been elected to his position by party members. Nevertheless, he announced that he would stand down at the SNP's conference in October. In a resignation letter released by the party the day before Sturgeon travelled to London to address the MP group, including Hosie, he apologised for 'any hurt and upset' he had caused his friends, family and colleagues.

The almost unanimous view within the SNP was that Sturgeon's relationship with Robison was behind Hosie's downfall and that things would have been different under Salmond. 'The First Minister has very high standards when it comes to these things, but I think there's very little doubt that the Shona element there was the deciding factor,' says one source. 'You know Alex wouldn't have cared. I mean, he would have shrugged his shoulders, told Stewart to be more discreet in future and there would have been no more consequences from it than that.'

Hosie may have lost his job because of the scandal, but there was little chance of Robison, who had been under severe political pressure for failings as Health Secretary, being moved from her brief in the ministerial reshuffle that took place in the middle of the drama. Sturgeon would not do anything that would be seen to diminish her friend. Significantly, she moved Deputy First Minister John Swinney from finance to education in an effort to show it was her main priority and promoted Derek Mackay, who was seen as a potential successor as First Minister, to Swinney's old brief.

The changes also saw Alex Neil depart government in a move that, while widely anticipated, still led to bad blood with the SNP veteran. As Social Justice Secretary he had put forward a policy paper earlier that year proposing using Holyrood's new powers over welfare to create a payment for the families of underprivileged children. He said this would have cost £500 million per annum after five years and was projected to reduce child poverty by one third. Neil says he was aware of opposition to his work from within the government but sent the paper to Sturgeon anyway.

'Within an hour she sent me a reply saying she doesn't read unaffordable proposals,' he recalls.

To which I replied, how do you know it's unaffordable if you haven't read it? It was her over-caution, her conservatism – small c – and there was no discussion. With Alex [Salmond] he would have said come in and we'll discuss it, and we would have talked it through and probably reached a compromise and it would then have gone to the Cabinet. With Nicola there's none of that, especially if she's in one of her moods. It's her way or the highway. And on this issue it was the highway and I knew then this wasn't a government that was going to deliver in the way that the Salmond government had delivered.

Neil says he came close to resigning in anger at the refusal to consider his plans but was dissuaded from doing so by his special adviser and others in the SNP because they 'didn't want me rocking the boat' ahead of the Holyrood election. Instead, he was called into Sturgeon's office in the Scottish Parliament on 18 May and told he would be going to the back benches. 'I wanted to go and she wanted rid of me,' he says. 'I'm sorry I didn't do it earlier when she wouldn't even discuss what was a forward-looking radical policy on child poverty.'

Sturgeon would later introduce a £10 a week payment to the parents of children on benefits. Another legacy of the sacking was that Neil would become one of the first senior SNP figures to publicly criticise her leadership, including defying party policy to back Brexit.

*   *   *

The decision on Britain's membership of the European Union seemed relatively low budget to much of Scotland, with little of the passion shown two years previously during the independence referendum. It was literally low budget for the SNP, who spent just £90,830 on their campaign.

Salmond was the SNP's international affairs spokesman at Westminster but had little involvement with the party's strategy. Shortly after arriving in the Commons, he had helped Gethins lay ultimately unsuccessful amendments to try to delay the referendum, but the SNP's push for a Remain vote ended up being run by Humza Yousaf, the Europe Minister at Holyrood, a position which has no powers over foreign affairs. Senior figures who were devising the strategy say Salmond was no longer being briefed and that he 'moaned about our campaign an awful lot' as more distance grew between him and the centre of a party that had been almost entirely focused on the Holyrood election.

Salmond did appear on two high-profile debates, telling an audience of young voters assembled by the BBC that a Leave result would mean another independence referendum being held within two years. He also squared off against Boris Johnson in an online event the week before polling day. Sandwiched between those two broadcasts, Sturgeon took on Johnson as part of an ITV debate in which she deflected attacks by Leave representatives by saying the prospect of a second independence referendum was merely 'speculation'. She was widely seen as being impressive against the future Prime Minister, as was Salmond in the online head-to-head, although the most memorable line of the evening went to Amber Rudd, the then UK Energy Secretary, who said of Johnson: 'He is the life and soul of the party, but he is not the man you want driving you home at the end of the evening.'

In the aftermath of the referendum the SNP would face criticism from some pro-EU voices for not campaigning hard enough, but the result in Scotland was still overwhelming, with Remain winning by 62 per cent to 38 per cent. Votes in other parts of the UK pushed Leave to an overall victory. The shocking result left British politics punch-drunk for years, but Sturgeon appeared to have possessed foresight ahead of the ballots being counted. Fergus Mutch, then the SNP's head of communications, recalls:

> I was with her on the morning of the referendum when she went to vote and do the photocall for that. As we were walking down from her house to the polling station, which was only five minutes away, I asked her how she thought it was going and she said, 'I think it will be Remain in Scotland and the rest of the UK will be Leave – and it will be narrow.' 'OK,' I joked with her, 'that's not necessarily unhelpful, is it?' and she just gave me a smile.

When the result was confirmed, Sturgeon wasted no time in making sure the ensuing chaos would reignite Scotland's constitutional question. Within hours she was standing in exactly the same spot in Bute House where Salmond had announced his resignation, revealing that Scottish government officials had started laying the groundwork for a second independence referendum. With the flag of Europe hanging behind her right shoulder and a saltire to her left, the First Minister repeated her predecessor's pre-vote prediction that another contest would have to be held within two years so that people north of the border could choose whether to stay within the UK before it left the EU. She said it was 'highly likely' there would be another independence referendum, adding: 'There are many people who voted against independence in 2014 who are today reassessing their decision. Indeed, a very large number of them have contacted me already.'

Sturgeon was publicly supported by Salmond, who said Scotland was a 'united country' in its support of EU membership as he cited the SNP's manifesto pledge that Brexit would mean a second independence referendum.

Meanwhile, chaos was engulfing Westminster. David Cameron resigned as Prime Minister and was succeeded by Theresa May just two and a half weeks later. Upon entering Downing Street, May quickly started strategising alongside Scottish Conservative leader Ruth Davidson and Scottish Secretary David Mundell about what to do when Sturgeon eventually made her official request for the powers to hold another referendum. They correctly anticipated that Sturgeon would argue that a contest should take place between the autumn of 2018 and the spring of 2019. They also devised a rebuttal that would prove effective when Sturgeon finally laid her cards on the table.

She did so at 11.40 a.m. on 13 March 2017, announcing that, having seen 'efforts at compromise' through a softer Brexit be 'met with a brick wall of intransigence', it was time to press the emergency exit button. 'I know there are some who want me to rule out a referendum completely or delay the decision until much further down the line,' she said from a podium in Bute House.

I understand why some take that view. And of course these views weigh heavily on me. But so does this – and this, for me, is a key consideration: if I ruled out a referendum, I would be deciding – completely unilaterally – that Scotland will follow the UK to a hard Brexit come what may, no matter how damaging to our economy and our society it turns out to be.

That should not be the decision of just one politician – not even the First Minister. By taking the steps I have set out today, I am ensuring that Scotland's future will be decided not just by me or the Scottish government. It will be decided by the people of Scotland. It will be Scotland's choice. And I trust the people to make that choice.

The decision to push for another vote, which would come to be seen as one of the most significant of her career, had been made after consultation with a small group of advisers ahead of being put to the Cabinet a few days before the speech. 'The First Minister came in with a foregone conclusion of where she wanted to go with things and went round the table and all of the Cabinet spoke in favour of her approach apart from maybe two people in the meeting,' says one attendee. 'One of them was [Rural Economy Secretary] Fergus Ewing. Fergus's point was, "What's the rush? Will people be sympathetic on going all guns blazing on a second referendum just three years after the first one?"'

Salmond was one of the voices encouraging Sturgeon to set aside her innate caution and move faster, having repeatedly suggested autumn 2018 as a potential date for a new referendum. He was supportive after the announcement, denying that his successor had been 'backed into a corner' and predicting a 'resounding vote in favour of independence'.

But May's reply to the demand was simple and effective. 'My message is clear – now is not the time,' the Prime Minister said. 'I think it would not be fair to the people of Scotland because they'd be being asked to take a crucial decision without the necessary information, without knowing what the future partnership will be or what the alternative of an independent Scotland would look like.' This response had been tried and tested through focus groups that made ministers confident the rebuttal would resonate. Public opinion polls also showed declining or static support for independence in the wake of Sturgeon's announcement, following an initial surge in the immediate aftermath of the Brexit vote.

The need to reconcile the drive for another referendum with a public who were uncertain about creating more upheaval was brought into sharp focus when, the month after Sturgeon set out her battleplan, May announced a snap general election to be held on 8 June. The timing couldn't have been worse for the SNP, who had been banking on building up public support for a second independence vote over the coming months. Instead, they were faced with fighting an election on the issue within a matter of weeks. One senior SNP strategist says:

> It was an extremely tough sell. I remember spending the most painful couple of days ever focus-grouping what the message would be. The focus groups were telling us that 'Yes to independence' or 'Take independence forwards' or 'Vote SNP for independence' were all just absolutely toxic. By contrast, everyone had already heard the 'Say no to indyref2' coming forth from the Tories and it was simple and easy to understand.

For the first time in living memory, the SNP had a muddled position on the constitution. They were uncertain of what to say about independence and also risked alienating the third of Scottish voters who supported Brexit, many of whom had traditionally backed the nationalists.

Sturgeon attempted to turn the tide by replicating the winning strategy of the 2015 campaign, including flying around the country in a helicopter with her image emblazoned on its side. Frequent visits were made in the 'Nicolopter', as it was dubbed by the media, to the seats deemed most vulnerable to either the Conservatives or a relatively resurgent Labour Party who were gathering momentum under Jeremy Corbyn.

Despite being well ahead in the polls, the SNP leader's frustration at the direction of the campaign and the prospect of losing seats was beginning to show. During the final televised Scottish leaders debate she disclosed a private conversation with Kezia Dugdale and claimed the Scottish Labour leader had said her party needed to embrace a second independence vote after Brexit.

Dugdale had got under Sturgeon's skin during the STV event at the Tron Theatre in Glasgow, but the spur of the moment decision to make the claim went against all the advice she had received before walking up to the stage. During preparations for the debate in a nearby hotel with close aides, she was urged not to make reference to the discussions. The SNP was already sensitive about confidentiality after being accused of launching a 'dirty tricks' campaign the previous year when the news leaked that Dugdale had applied for work experience with Richard Lochhead, a nationalist minister, when she was twenty-one. Riled by Dugdale telling her that voters now referred to her as 'that woman', Sturgeon saw red and blurted out the accusation. She also repeated it under questioning from Davidson a moment later.

As Labour's spin operation immediately began accusing the First Minister of lying – and being 'insulting and demeaning' to high office in the process – Sturgeon realised she had made a major error. Her immediate reaction was panicked and remorseful, but she has never apologised to Dugdale for making the claim.

Salmond was also trying to repeat the successful 2015 playbook by touring potentially vulnerable seats – particularly those of his allies, such as Joanna Cherry and Tasmina Ahmed-Sheikh – as part of efforts to motivate a comparatively lacklustre nationalist base.

But there was trouble brewing for him closer to home. The Conservatives had started to find the north-east of Scotland more fertile ground, making gains in the 2016 Holyrood election. The region's fishermen were particularly sceptical of an independent Scotland rejoining the EU. A combination of a big Tory push and what he saw as an underwhelming SNP campaign meant Salmond was on the back foot on his home turf for the first time in his political career.

At 4.20 a.m. on 9 June 2017, Scottish and UK political observers were left stunned as Conservative Colin Clark earned himself the nickname of the 'Salmond slayer' by removing the former First Minister from his Gordon constituency. Standing on the stage with his hands clasped in front of him, Salmond remained impassive as the returning officer read out the results, which gave Clark a majority of 2,607 following a twenty-point swing towards the Tories. The former First Minister's only hint of emotion was a slight raise of his eyebrows at the vociferous nature of the cheers from Conservative supporters.

Delivering his concession speech, he laughed as those same activists booed after he correctly predicted that May was going to fall short of a majority in the Commons. He also paid tribute to his family, having endured personal tragedy just three days before the election when his father, Robert, died aged ninety-five. In the speech he said he had 'suffered some grievous blows recently which put the whole political world in perspective' but suggested he was not ready to leave the front line. As he prepared to depart the podium, Salmond said: 'I'd like to leave you with a phrase from an old Jacobite song. "So laugh false whigs in the midst o' your glee. Ye've no seen the last o' my bonnets and me."'

The former First Minister may have struck a defiant tone as he exited the public stage, but behind the scenes he was furious with the SNP leadership for campaign failures he believed cost him his seat. The party had lost twenty-one MPs in total, including another high-profile casualty in the form of Westminster leader Angus Robertson, who was ousted from his Moray constituency by future Scottish Tory leader Douglas Ross. Figures close to both Sturgeon and Salmond agree the immediate aftermath of the defeat was of crucial importance in the disintegration of the pair's relationship. Salmond was said to be in a 'vile mood' when a party staffer phoned to relay their commiserations and also declined to take a subsequent call from Sturgeon. At a private lunch with journalists just days after the election, he even directly criticised the First Minister, saying she had run a 'crap campaign'.

The episode had echoes of the aftermath of the independence referendum, when Salmond struggled to acknowledge his role in the defeat and looked for others to blame. 'He blamed the national operation for losing him his seat, but locally he had also run a shit campaign,' says a source who canvassed in Gordon during the election.

> He was doing what he had done in previous elections, scooting about the country, showing up in Edinburgh and Perthshire and trying to help out his colleagues like Jo Cherry and Tasmina. Actually he should have realised he had a massive fight on his hands in Gordon. The Tories had been putting a lot into it because they knew just what a scalp it would be to end Alex Salmond's career.

A week after the election, Salmond rose in St Ninian's Craigmailen Church, Linlithgow, to deliver the eulogy at his father's funeral. He mixed the personal with the political as he touched on Robert's military service, love of football, passion for the SNP and loyalty to friends and family. Senior party figures Derek Mackay, Alex Neil, Fiona Hyslop and Tasmina Ahmed-Sheikh were all at the service, as were former aides Geoff Aberdein and Kevin Pringle, while Fergus Mutch, who had worked for Salmond, played the bagpipes. Sturgeon was noticeable by her absence, instead taking part in First Minister's Questions at Holyrood, and attendees remarked upon the lack of any representation from her top team, including her husband, the SNP chief executive Peter Murrell.

Sturgeon did have a lot on her plate in the post-election period. The loss of Robertson meant the party needed a new Westminster leader. She reached out to Stephen Gethins as her first choice to take over. But in a blow to her plans the North East Fife MP, whose second child was born the week before and who had survived the election with a wafer-thin majority of just two votes, declined the advances. Instead, a contest developed between Ian Blackford (Ross, Skye and Lochaber), Joanna Cherry (Edinburgh South West) and Drew Hendry (Inverness, Nairn, Badenoch and Strathspey). Blackford eventually defeated Cherry by a single vote of SNP MPs.

Sturgeon made little attempt to find a role for her former mentor amid the turmoil, which SNP figures sympathetic to Salmond believe was a mistake. 'They should have thought of something useful for him to do in Scottish public life because he was going to carve out something for himself anyway,' says one source.

Just ignoring him was the worst thing they could have done. They should have kept in touch with him, found out what he was up to, opened doors for him. But that is not Nicola's style. She is a bit brutal about it to be honest and she has never thought of it as her role to babysit Alex Salmond. Why should she? For right or wrong, Alex Salmond sees that as a betrayal. His perception is he made her and she owes him, and one thing about Alex is he values loyalty above and beyond all else.

Andrew Wilson, the former SNP MSP who is an extremely in-fluential figure in the nationalist movement, believes Salmond's craving for attention led him down the path to RT. 'Alex gets more energy from daily or regular attention and adulation than from ir-regular but substantial respect and admiration,' he says. 'What the SNP and the national movement lack is an elder statesperson, like John Major, who can pop up from time to time and speak truth and help. He could have chosen that, but instead he chose to do the fringe and Russia Today.'

It didn't take long for Salmond's residency at the Assembly Rooms in Edinburgh to cause problems for his former colleagues. The very first performance of *Alex Salmond… Unleashed* on 13 August sparked controversy as he unveiled his 'good pal' David Davis, the Conservative MP, as a mystery guest.

As he warmed up the audience ahead of introducing the then Brexit Secretary, he attempted a risqué joke: 'I promised you today we'd either have Theresa May or Nicola Sturgeon or Ruth David-son or Melania Trump, but I couldn't make any of these wonderful women come…' After a drum roll, he added: '…to the show.'

For the second time since he had left office, Sturgeon was forced to defend Salmond over allegations that he had made sexist com-ments towards women. 'I think I would know if he was sexist, and emphatically he is not,' she told the BBC. 'He is not sexist.'

The coming weeks would cause her to re-evaluate everything she thought she knew about Salmond's behaviour towards women.

CHAPTER 7

#METOO

4 NOVEMBER 2017, 7.27 P.M.

Nicola Sturgeon had just sacked a government minister embroiled in a sexual harassment scandal when she first learned of allegations about Alex Salmond.

The First Minister had accepted Mark McDonald's resignation by phone in the departure lounge of Heathrow Airport and was back at home getting ready to attend an SNP function in Glasgow when her husband, Peter Murrell, received a troubling email. Sky News journalist James Matthews had informed them he was poised to broadcast a report alleging that Salmond had been accused of acting inappropriately towards Edinburgh Airport staff a decade earlier but the party had swept it under the carpet.

The email had sparked panic with the on-duty SNP press officer, who contacted Sturgeon's chief of staff Liz Lloyd to ask for help. Lloyd volunteered to call the First Minister about the situation but by the time she did so Sturgeon had already been told by her husband and was pondering what to do. 'I'll phone him,' she told her most senior aide before arranging a conversation that would take place the following morning. Both Sturgeon and Murrell insist it was the first time they had heard of the allegations.

'In early November 2017, the SNP received an enquiry from

Sky News about allegations of sexual misconduct on the part of Alex Salmond,' Sturgeon later recalled to the Holyrood inquiry into her government's mishandling of separate claims against her predecessor.

> I spoke to Mr Salmond about this allegation at the time. He denied it and, as it happened, Sky did not run a story about it at that time. Since the identity of the individuals was not made known to us and they did not approach the SNP directly, there was no further action that it would have been possible to take. However, even though he assured me to the contrary, all of the circumstances surrounding this episode left me with a lingering concern that allegations about Mr Salmond could materialise at some stage.

It may have been news to the SNP's power couple, but rumours about Salmond's conduct at Edinburgh Airport had been circulating in the Scottish political bubble for years.

He used the facility regularly from 2007 to 2010 as he was juggling a dual mandate as MP and MSP. This meant he often had to make quick dashes to vote at the House of Commons before returning shortly afterwards to resume his first ministerial duties. Given these circumstances, the airport had granted him special privileges to speed up the check-in and boarding process on the flight to London. This involved access to a VIP security lane, usually reserved for staff, which included a shortcut through private areas of the building on the journey to the departure gate and eliminated the need to go through the normal metal detectors and search areas.

It was during these trips that members of staff tasked with escorting Salmond through the airport and onto the plane took exception to his behaviour. At least three women expressed concern about the situation to their bosses but stressed they did not want to make official complaints about the most powerful man in the country, especially as they would likely have to deal with him in the course of their future work duties. Instead, a solution was found in which airport management would make an informal approach to Salmond's team and alert them to the fact that the First Minister's behaviour was causing unease. Angus Robertson, who at that time was the SNP's Westminster leader, was called by a senior airport boss and informed of the situation.

Years later, Robertson gave his version of events to the Holyrood committee. In a written statement, he acknowledged that there had been 'one instance where unspecified behaviour was mentioned to me'.

In 2009 I was called by an Edinburgh Airport manager about Alex Salmond's perceived 'inappropriateness' towards female staff at the airport. I was asked if I could informally broach the subject with Mr Salmond to make him aware of this perception. I raised the matter directly with Mr Salmond, who denied he had acted inappropriately in any way. I communicated back to the Edinburgh Airport manager that a conversation had happened. The matter being resolved, and without a formal complaint having been made, it was not reported further.

Sources at the airport say staff had no further issues with Salmond, and the former First Minister has always played down the accusations. Sources close to him have said it relates to a remark he made to a female member of staff after an alarm had gone off during a security scan. In reference to a pair of high heels that were thought to have triggered the device, he is claimed to have said words to the effect of: 'I bet that's not the only thing those heels will set off.'

Salmond later told the Holyrood committee:

It would not have been front-page news in any newspaper if it had ever been publicised at the time, given what I know about it – that was the first indication of anything of that nature in all my years in public life. That was in November 2017. It came from a report from ten years before of a supposed incident, and it was dealt with. It seemed to cause the Permanent Secretary a great deal of consternation.

The Edinburgh Airport story was front-page news for the *Daily Record* when it eventually broke in November 2018, but, as he successfully saw off the Sky News enquiry a year earlier, Salmond asked civil servants directly to provide supportive statements to his lawyers. Permanent Secretary Leslie Evans took issue with the approaches and raised the issue directly with Sturgeon.

'I spoke to him the morning after we got the press query,' the First Minister told Irish barrister James Hamilton when he was carrying out his investigation of her conduct.

He seemed pretty shaken by it at that point and said he had to get to the bottom of what it was. I spoke to him again later that day when he appeared much more bullish. But the following day the Permanent Secretary had indicated to me that he had been, or his lawyers, or a bit of both, I'm not sure, had been contacting people in the Scottish government effectively asking people that he had worked with or that might have been with him going through Edinburgh Airport to back him up and that that has caused a bit of, some disquiet on the part of those people who had been contacted. And she asked me to ask him to stop that, which I did, and he said he already had all the information he needed.

Sturgeon added that Salmond's contact 'had appeared to almost stir something, a hornet's nest had been stirred kind of thing'.

*   *   *

The historical allegations were being revisited as the #MeToo movement swept the world. Tarana Burke, the American activist, started campaigning with the phrase 'me too' in 2006 as a way of highlighting sexual abuse, but it caught fire in October 2017 when the actor Alyssa Milano posted on social media: 'If you've been sexually harassed or assaulted write "me too" as a reply to this tweet.'

Milano was one of dozens of women who accused film producer Harvey Weinstein before he was eventually tried and sentenced to twenty-three years in prison for one count of rape and one count of a criminal sexual act. The shockwaves of the scandal were reverberating from Hollywood to the UK as women felt more empowered to speak up about their experiences and news desks demanded that reporters uncover fresh scandals to emulate the *New York Times* exposé of Weinstein.

The film and music industries were being heavily scrutinised but there was another field where power imbalances were already well known: politics.

UK Defence Secretary Michael Fallon lost his job after a series of allegations of inappropriate behaviour, and it was not long before Holyrood was in the spotlight. Labour MSP Monica Lennon told the *Sunday Mail* she was sexually assaulted by a senior male colleague at a social event in 2013 in front of several witnesses. Although she made an initial complaint to her party, Lennon decided not to take it any further because she felt she would not be believed.

The extent of the problem north of the border was brought into sharp focus when Aamer Anwar, a high-profile lawyer, claimed that women at all levels in the Scottish Parliament had been targeted by men. 'It's a catalogue of sexual harassment, stalking, social media abuse, sexual innuendos, verbal sexual abuse, touching, sexual assaults, requests for sex, cover-up, isolation and bullying,' he told the *Sunday Herald*.

The same weekend, Salmond also found himself answering questions on sexual harassment amid the deluge of media coverage. On an episode of ITV's *After the News* broadcast on 27 October – just a week before the Sky News enquiry reached Nicola Sturgeon – Salmond said sexism was 'rife in the House of Commons but then it's rife across society'. He picked out politics, alongside television, cinema and the media, as an industry more prone to inappropriate behaviour 'because the social and the business are intermixed' and noted that the problems were not new. He joined fellow panellist Julia Hartley-Brewer in criticising then Prime Minister Theresa May for urging women who were victims of 'unwanted sexual behaviour' to go to parliamentary authorities and the police. 'I think it's fatuous,' Salmond said, in comments which are even more striking with the benefit of hindsight. 'I mean, 99 per cent of what we're talking about are not police matters. But that doesn't make it right, incidentally, it's wrong.' He also agreed with Hartley-Brewer when she said that many cases of unwanted attention involved drunk men thinking a woman was interested in them: 'No doubt, I'm sure many men are stupid enough [to misread signals from women].'

Institutions across the country were re-examining their procedures as public opinion demanded change. It would not be long before high-profile figures were accused of problematic behaviour.

Mark McDonald, the Minister for Childcare and Early Years in Sturgeon's government, was the first Scottish politician to be caught up in the new wave of scrutiny. The Aberdeen Donside MSP had been taken aside on 2 November by Lloyd and Deputy First Minister John Swinney and informed that he was the subject of 'chatter' about his behaviour. Two days later, McDonald was presented with a screenshot of a private exchange on Twitter between him and a woman. It read: 'That's twice you've dingyed [ignored] me now. Twice. It's OK tho I understand.' He added: 'My phone wanted to autocorrect dingyed to fingered there. Which I'm so glad I noticed before I sent that message.' McDonald then had the telephone conversation with Sturgeon, who was waiting to fly home from a Brexit summit in London, before emailing to officially confirm his departure. 'In recent days I have been made aware that some of my behaviour, where I thought I was being humorous or friendly, has made some women feel uncomfortable or led them to question my intentions,' he wrote at 5.31 p.m., just two hours before the SNP would receive the Salmond allegation. 'I offer an unreserved apology for that to any woman concerned. Given my role in government I believe it would be inappropriate for me to continue in office at this time and I am writing to tender my resignation.'

McDonald later quit the SNP after it carried out an internal investigation into his conduct, which concluded he had sent inappropriate and unwanted text and social media messages, caused distress through unwanted attention and exploited his position of power. He was subsequently suspended from Holyrood for a month after the Commissioner for Ethical Standards in Public Life ruled the messages, sent in September 2016, breached the code of conduct by creating an 'intimidating, degrading, humiliating or offensive environment'.

McDonald, who separated from his wife in the wake of the scandal, had been a long-term fixture in the nationalist movement. He was present at the Marcliffe Hotel in Aberdeen when Salmond announced his 2004 leadership bid, served as a councillor in the city from 2007, and was appointed parliamentary liaison officer to the then First Minister after becoming an MSP in 2011. The father of two resisted pressure from Sturgeon to quit Holyrood entirely after holding discussions with Salmond, who thought his former aide was being treated unfairly by the party. McDonald, who stood down from Holyrood at the 2021 election after serving as an independent MSP for three and a half years, said he contemplated suicide due to the pressure he came under during his suspension from the SNP.

Alex Neil, the former Health Secretary and a Salmond ally, says:

> When Nicola tried to force Mark McDonald out of the Parliament, Mark, on Alex's advice, stood firm on that. Alex's view was the same as mine: that while Mark had been stupid and maybe merited losing his job as a government minister and getting a one-month suspension from the Parliament, he didn't deserve to be driven out of public office.

Sturgeon's handling of disciplinary matters would become an increasing source of tension within the SNP in the months that followed.

*　　*　　*

It was at the very end of the Scottish government's morning Cabinet meeting on 31 October that Nicola Sturgeon raised the issue of sexual harassment. She had already written to Presiding Officer Ken Macintosh to ask what support was being offered to staff, particularly young women, at Holyrood. The First Minister also told her government colleagues that decisive action was needed. 'It appeared that such behaviour was representative of a culture that had gone unchallenged in many workplaces for a long period of time,' the minutes of the meeting in the government's headquarters of St Andrew's House record.

> If the right actions were taken now to ensure zero tolerance of such unacceptable behaviours and that every workplace had robust procedures in place to address them, then this could be

a watershed moment which would provide the catalyst for the cultural change that was necessary to change these deep-rooted behaviours once and for all.

It was decided that Swinney would make a statement to Parliament stressing the need for men to recognise and alter their behaviour if sexual harassment and abuse was to be stamped out. 'The government wants to make clear that it is the conduct and behaviour of men that needs to change if we are to end the sexual harassment and abuse of women, whether that be in their workplace, their social life or in their home,' he later told a hushed Holyrood chamber.

As the most senior male minister in the Scottish government, I wanted to answer this question and to make clear that it is up to men to make these changes and men must examine their own behaviour. Sexual harassment or abuse in the workplace or anywhere else is completely unacceptable and must stop, just as the underlying attitudes and inequalities that perpetuate it must also stop.

An anonymised survey was sent to everyone working at the Scottish Parliament, including MSPs and their staff, as part of attempts to gauge the scale of the problem. An abuse hotline was also set up for people to report their concerns, and every person who worked in the building was told to take part in anti-harassment training. The scale of reaction had taken even the most seasoned of politicians and political observers by surprise. 'I remember the #MeToo stuff being really quite shocking – not in the sense that we had not known that this kind of stuff happened, but the fact that it was coming out into the open and people were prepared to confront these things was a big moment,' Sturgeon later told the Holyrood inquiry. 'I remember, as I am sure others do, doing interviews at the time and talking about a watershed moment. There was a sense that we had to live up to that and be prepared to meet the moment.'

At the Cabinet meeting, Sturgeon announced that Permanent Secretary Leslie Evans had been tasked with turning the rhetoric into reality by drawing up a new government procedure for dealing with harassment complaints. Responding to the politicians' sense of urgency – and the atmosphere prevalent in wider society – the work proceeded at pace. Senior officials controversially introduced a mechanism by which former government ministers could be investigated over sexual misconduct claims even once they had left office. In the months that followed, the fact that this decision was made just days after McDonald resigned and Salmond contacted civil servants about the Sky News story would be cited as evidence that the ex post facto measure was designed to ensnare them. The former First Minister continues to criticise this retrospective element of the procedure to this day.

The proposal had the explicit support of Sturgeon, who on 22 November wrote to Evans to say the policy should 'address concerns – should any be raised – about the conduct of current Scottish government ministers and also former ministers, including from previous administrations'. However, it sounded alarm bells with the government's colleagues in Whitehall, where Cabinet Office officials warned they were 'very uncomfortable about highlighting a process for complaints about Ministers and former Ministers' and queried whether it went beyond the policy in place for civil servants.

'It would have been very hard to draw a conclusion at that time that historical complaints and the relative difficulty in investigating historical complaints were not a pretty central part of the #MeToo concerns,' Sturgeon told the committee. 'They were. To come to a conclusion that nobody would have thought that that was a legitimate or priority issue is something that I struggle with, as somebody who paid a lot of attention to the debate at the time.'

The dispute over the fairness of the policy investigating historical complaints may have been significant for Salmond, but it was not what would ultimately lead to its failure. Instead, a flaw in how the officials implemented the new procedure would see it struck down in court, humiliate the civil servants involved, cost the taxpayer more than £600,000 in government legal expenses and nearly end Sturgeon's career. The devastating consequences all sprang from a scarcely believable misunderstanding over the meaning of the words 'prior involvement'.

* * *

One government employee carefully following the drafting of the new harassment procedure was the woman who had received an apology from Salmond over his behaviour in the bedroom of Bute House.

Evans had been quick off the mark in promoting the forthcoming changes, sending supportive all-staff emails on the subject and appointing Gillian Russell, the director of safer communities, to act as a 'confidential sounding board for any member of staff who had experienced harassment'. The initial message encouraging staff to share concerns was sent out on 2 November and the civil servant, who would become known as Ms A to protect her identity during the government inquiry, replied the next day to urge officials to listen to people who had previously felt unable to make formal complaints. 'As an organisation we have already failed in our duty of care to staff in this situation, and the review has the potential to be a valuable opportunity to help us learn the lessons we need to take from that on how we can better support people,' she wrote.

If we are serious about creating an environment in which anyone experiencing unacceptable behaviour feels able to speak up and has the confidence that their complaint will be handled appropriately, we need to make sure we're hearing their voices in the first place, and to achieve that we need to give people a confidential and confidence-inspiring channel.

On 7 November, the same day the first draft of the policy was circulated amongst senior civil servants, the woman who had previously complained to her bosses about Salmond's alleged behaviour at Stirling Castle made contact with Barbara Allison, the government's director of communications, ministerial support and facilities. She also wanted to ensure that procedures being put in place would successfully guard against the type of behaviour complained about in 2014. Unlike Ms A, she made reference to her previous experiences during this initial exchange. This was the first time that officials involved in the new procedure had specific confirmation that there had been concerns about Salmond's previous behaviour. Their response to that revelation would set the course for what followed.

The Permanent Secretary was told of the issues raised by the woman, who would be given the pseudonym Ms B during the government's investigation of Salmond.

Ms A then met Sturgeon's principal private secretary, John Somers, in his office on 20 November and told him about how her complaint against Salmond had been dealt with in 2013. She said she wanted to share her experience – not necessarily to make a complaint but to try to improve how the government handled any such issues in the future.

Somers had been told Ms A wanted to see him to discuss a 'personal issue' and struggled to digest the 'overwhelming' information now being put to him. He asked to speak to Allison, who was his line manager, and after a second meeting with Ms A the following day, it was agreed that she too should meet the government director. The prospect was also raised of Ms A discussing her experiences with Sturgeon. Somers told the Holyrood committee:

> At the end of the second meeting, I said that, if she felt that she was not being taken seriously and that no one was listening to her, she should come back to speak to me and that, if she wanted to meet with the First Minister, I would set that up.

He never spoke to Ms A about the situation again.

In email, text and telephone conversations with other officials, Ms A made it clear that she did want to share her experiences with Sturgeon. 'Whilst we are trying to ensure that their concerns are dealt with, we are not necessarily making that an option,' Allison said about Ms A's request in one note to her fellow senior civil servants involved in the process.

Allison and Russell had been joined in leading the initiative by Nicola Richards, who as the director for people was effectively the Scottish government's HR boss, and Judith Mackinnon, who held the title of head of people advice. Mackinnon began working for the government in the summer of 2017 after a spell at the Scottish Police Authority, where she was the head of HR governance. During her time at the SPA, recruitment rules were broken in the hiring process for a new chief financial officer, financial watchdog Audit Scotland criticised a lucrative relocation package for ex-Deputy Chief Constable Rose Fitzpatrick, and former SPA chairman Andrew Flanagan was accused of bullying by an ex-board member. It is unclear what involvement, if any, Mackinnon had in dealing with these controversies.

Mackinnon, who was sent an anonymised note of Ms A's concerns in late November, and Richards had various conversations via email and text messages with Ms A and Ms B at the start of December. In these discussions, both women were told that other potential complainants were 'considering their position'. Ms A was also given a draft copy of the new harassment procedure before it had been signed off.

Meanwhile, a brief consultation was held with trade unions, who argued for a fully independent investigative process rather than complaints being dealt with by the civil service. Eight days later, with that recommendation ignored, the policy was officially rubber stamped by Sturgeon on 20 December. With a new procedure in place, retrospective complaints could now be made against former ministers.

At 10.33 a.m. on 16 January 2018, Mackinnon emailed a Scottish government lawyer with a short message that did not betray the significance of what was about to happen. 'Formal complaint coming in tomorrow – so just clearing schedule for investigation,' she wrote. In fact, Ms A officially asked the government to investigate her claims within two hours.

'Following my meeting with Gillian Russell in November about experiences of inappropriate behaviour while working [redacted], I'd like to make a formal complaint to the Scottish Government,' she wrote in an email to Richards following a conversation between the pair earlier in the day. 'Please find attached the note of that meeting, which summarises the experiences.'

Mackinnon was appointed investigating officer within hours despite her previous dealings with the complainers. Paragraph 10 of the Scottish government's complaints handling procedure said the investigating officer 'will have had no prior involvement with any aspect of the matter being raised'. This conflict is what would ultimately lead to Salmond winning his judicial review against the government.

At least two other senior civil servants were considered as potential investigating officers, but it was decided that Mackinnon should take the lead because almost every other potential candidate had either worked for or had dealings with Salmond while he was First Minister. 'It ultimately fell to Judith because she hadn't been in government at the time so she couldn't have prior involvement so couldn't be prejudiced because of her view of him,' says one senior official.

Exactly a week later, Ms B told Richards she wanted to take things further and the HR manager sent both WhatsApp and text messages to Mackinnon informing her of the news. Once the initial statement had been submitted, Mackinnon texted Richards: 'Got [Ms B] complaint. Pretty grim reading.' Her boss simply replied: 'Oh dear...'

This sparked a process of interviews not only with the complainers but with other witnesses. While giving evidence about their alleged incidents with Salmond, the two women also revealed that another of their colleagues had experienced issues. They were referring to the government official who said Salmond had tried to kiss her in the sitting room of Bute House and made sexually suggestive comments towards her on the Eurostar.

Mackinnon contacted this third official, who would ultimately become Woman G in the criminal trial, to ask if she also wanted to make a complaint. However, at an in-person meeting she became concerned that the government was underestimating the dangers of taking on the former First Minister. She would later explain in court that she declined to take part in the process because she was 'concerned about her position'. 'I was concerned about the implications of preparing an internal Scottish government investigation, but also the fact the Scottish government was handling it,' she said. 'I felt regret at not being in a position to share those experiences. I felt there was too much risk and I was not willing to take part in it.'

With striking foresight, the woman had also asked Mackinnon what plans the officials had in place 'in the event of retaliation from Mr Salmond'. She said: 'What would happen if he [Salmond] were to take it to judicial review? That may happen.' But she said she was told it would not be in his 'interests to do that'. Woman G said she believed those leading the investigation 'really had no idea who they were dealing with'.

If the civil servants had underestimated the forcefulness with which the former First Minister would defend his reputation, they were about to be taught a painful lesson.

* * *

Geoff Aberdein had convened a conference call involving three of the brightest minds in modern Scottish nationalism, but independence was nowhere near the agenda. He wanted the advice of Kevin Pringle, the SNP's former media guru, and Duncan Hamilton, the advocate and ex-MSP, about a personal quandary: whether to tell Alex Salmond he was being investigated for alleged sexual harassment.

On 6 March 2018, Aberdein, who served as Salmond's chief of staff, had met a government official, who cannot be named for legal reasons, for what was meant to be a catch-up between two old colleagues. Rumours were circulating at the time that the former First Minister was plotting a comeback to the Scottish Parliament in the event of Mark McDonald resigning as an MSP and causing a by-election.

Salmond and his allies have always denied the suggestion he was considering another tilt at Holyrood, but the subject was raised with Aberdein by the official, who warned that such a move would be extremely difficult given his decision to launch a talk show on RT. There are contradictory accounts over what exactly happened next.

The official claims they asked Aberdein if he was aware of any issues of concern about Salmond during his time in office. Suspicion was growing within Sturgeon's team that he could be under the microscope. The previous week, the content of a civil service briefing provided for First Minister's Questions on the issue of sexual harassment had changed. It had previously stated that there were no complaints about current or former ministers and that fewer than five cases of sexual harassment had been reported in the civil service. Both statements had been removed.

They were replaced with a note confirming that concerns had been raised and were being considered in line with procedures. It made no mention of former ministers in general or Salmond in particular, but there had been a number of media enquiries about the former First Minister over the previous months – a fact that was also playing on the minds of Sturgeon's team.

According to the official's account, Aberdein referenced two incidents. One was not sexual in nature, but the other involved Ms A. But according to Aberdein, the only discussion of Salmond was about media coverage, specifically his RT programme.

A second, equally disputed, meeting was held on 9 March. Aberdein's 'clear recollection' is that the official not only told him that the Scottish government had received complaints about Salmond but also disclosed Ms A's identity. His accusation would rock the government to its foundations years later, as it cast doubt on Sturgeon's account of when she learned about the investigation into Salmond. It also suggested that one of her senior officials had breached the confidentiality of a sexual harassment complainer by passing her name to someone closely associated with the man at the centre of the allegations.

However, the official insisted Aberdein had misunderstood the conversation and they had no knowledge of any investigations – only suspicions. It should also be noted that Aberdein had been told about the incident back in 2013, had discussed it with the woman involved, and so was already well aware of her identity.

James Hamilton, the former Director of Public Prosecutions in

Ireland, examined this dispute as part of his independent investigation into whether Sturgeon broke the ministerial code. In his written judgment, Hamilton said that despite an 'elaborate explanation' of how there could have been crossed wires, he found Aberdein's account of the conversation and 'the existence of complaints and the identity of a complainer ... credible'. He added: 'It remains the fact that the name which Mr Aberdein said was given to him was in fact the name of one of the complainers against Mr Salmond.'

Shortly after the meeting, Aberdein contacted Lorraine Kay, a former civil servant who worked in Salmond's private office and was by now, like Aberdein, employed at Aberdeen Standard, to relay the contents of the conversation that had shaken him. In a written statement to the Scottish Parliament's inquiry into the handling of the allegations, Kay said:

> I met with Geoff after his meeting with [Redacted], and was shocked to hear that the Scottish Government had received two complaints about Mr Salmond. Geoff also shared with me that [Redacted] had named one of the complainants – I recall this clearly as I knew the individual concerned. I believe I was the first person Geoff spoke to about this issue.

Aberdein quickly set up the conference call with Pringle and Hamilton and asked for their advice about what he should do. It was agreed that Salmond should be informed of the investigation and that Aberdein should be the one to tell him.

His former boss was travelling in a car with other people sitting beside him when he took the call. Far from being shocked as the information was relayed to him, Salmond said nothing. He had been digesting the bombshell news for forty-eight hours after receiving an email from Evans on 7 March.

It told him that an investigation into two formal complaints had been ongoing since 17 January. 'At this stage I am required to consider whether the report of the investigation to date gives cause for concern over your behaviour towards current or former civil servants,' the Permanent Secretary wrote. 'I have taken a view that there is such a cause for concern. I must emphasise that no decision has been taken as to whether these complaints are well-founded.'

Evans told Salmond that Mackinnon was the investigating officer and he should contact her to make a statement and potentially suggest witnesses for interview. In a nod to his actions after the Sky News enquiry about Edinburgh Airport, the Permanent Secretary warned the former First Minister not to directly contact any other civil servants about the case. 'Let me assure you that we are handling this process with the utmost care and commitment to confidentiality,' she added.

> This is an internal process and, in line with our usual practice, we will not make public comment on the investigation. To protect the integrity and confidentiality of this process, and as set out in the procedure, the First Minister has not been made aware of these complaints. The First Minister will only be informed of these complaints and the outcome when the investigation is complete. At that point the First Minister will be made aware of the outcome both in her capacity as First Minister and in her capacity as party leader. The First Minister will be advised if you have declined to cooperate.

Salmond had no intention of cooperating with the investigation and planned to advise the First Minister of that himself. In fact, he would go over Evans's head and ask his former protégée to kill the investigation before it could damage either of their reputations.

CHAPTER 8

THE DECISION REPORT

22 AUGUST 2018, 10.56 A.M.

Leslie Evans's conclusions were as categoric as they were shocking. The Permanent Secretary to the Scottish government, the country's most senior civil servant, had determined that Alex Salmond's behaviour towards two female officials during his time as First Minister had amounted to sexual harassment. Ruling on complaints from Ms A and Ms B, Evans wrote that his conduct on a number of occasions was 'unwanted and of a sexual nature' and had the effect of 'violating' their 'dignity' and 'creating an intimidating, degrading, humiliating and offensive environment'.

Some of the allegations were considered so serious that Evans decided they should be referred to the police – despite both women expressing reservations about becoming involved in a criminal investigation.

The Permanent Secretary's role under the new harassment procedure, drawn up quickly in response to the Harvey Weinstein scandal, was to act as 'decision maker' – in effect to consider the evidence gathered by investigating officer Judith Mackinnon and determine whether each specific complaint about the former First Minister was 'well founded'. Her conclusions followed a 217-day investigation into Salmond's conduct which would eventually lead to a humiliating civil court defeat for the Scottish government, spark a huge police investigation and criminal trial and fracture relationships at the very heart of the SNP.

The decision report, completed on 21 August 2018 and circulated to Salmond and the two complainers the following morning, considered eleven separate allegations – each referred to as a 'cause for concern'. Evans concluded that the former First Minister had behaved inappropriately on a number of occasions and that the pattern of his behaviour amounted to harassment. She upheld five of the individual complaints as 'well founded', dismissed three as 'not well founded' and reserved judgement on three others for procedural reasons.

Explaining how she had approached her deliberations, Evans wrote:

> I have also taken account of the particular context of these complaints, including the working environment of Ms A and Ms B and their professional relationships with the FFM. I consider it relevant that, as First Minister of Scotland, the FFM was in a position of considerable power and trust, including in his dealings with all staff. This power dynamic would inevitably be more pronounced in the case of young and/or junior members of staff. Ms A and Ms B were both young and relatively junior. I consider the significant imbalance in the power relationship with staff to be a relevant factor when considering each cause for concern. I also consider the impact on Ms A and Ms B and corroboration available from witness statements to be relevant factors.

The findings would ultimately be struck down in the Court of Session after the government admitted that procedural flaws in how it had carried out the investigation meant the process was unlawful, unfair and 'tainted by apparent bias'. The conclusions were 'reduced' by the court, a Scottish legal term meaning they were set aside or annulled by the judicial review process, and the report was never issued publicly. However, despite subsequent claims by Salmond that he had been vindicated in two court cases, this did not mean that the complaints had been judged to be unfounded. The Court of Session simply ruled that they had not been properly investigated. At the time of writing, the original complaints are officially still on the books of the Scottish government and could theoretically be re-examined at any point.

A decision on reopening the investigation was initially delayed in order to let the criminal case against Salmond proceed but has not been revisited in the wake of his acquittal and the subsequent parliamentary inquiries.

Now – more than three years after the completion of the original government probe into Salmond's conduct – the details of the complaints he faced, his substantive response and Evans's conclusions can be revealed for the first time.

*　　*　　*

Ms A's four complaints – three of which would be upheld – alleged a rapidly escalating pattern of behaviour by Salmond that ultimately resulted in the December 2013 Bute House encounter that would become a charge of sexual assault with intent to rape. The earliest incident dated back to 2013, when Salmond was alleged to have approached the civil servant from behind in a hotel room, placed his hands over her eyes and spun her around in a seeming attempt to 'make her feel dizzy'. Salmond denied the incident took place and pointed out that he had not visited the location given for the alleged incident during the timeframe cited by Ms A, who admitted she may have got the date wrong.

Evans described Salmond's behaviour on this occasion to be

'inappropriate' and said it was 'the event rather than the exact date that is of most importance'. She added:

> I cannot find any reasonable justification for this action between a minister and [an] official – even as a 'playful' intervention – but particularly given the FFM is said to have approached from behind, and without warning. These circumstances lead me to conclude that the FFM would not have undertaken this action had the official been male. By any reasonable measure, I conclude that this alleged behaviour would be inappropriate and particularly between a minister and a civil servant.

The complaint was upheld as 'well founded', with Evans saying: 'The conduct was unwanted and had the effect of violating Ms A's dignity and occurred because of her sex.'

The complaint which was judged to be not well founded also took place in a hotel room during Scottish government business. The decision report sets out the circumstances:

> The FFM asked Ms A in to his room and requested that she turn off the lights, in order to show her the lights of the city outside the bedroom window. This was not a planned work meeting. The conversation was personal to him, for example, discussing the positives and negatives of being the First Minister and his frustrations with the Scottish government. Ms A felt that in the context of sitting with the lights off this was strange. The conversation continued for two hours.

Salmond denied that the behaviour referred to was harassment and pointed out that Ms A did not allege that anything improper took place. Other witnesses interviewed as part of the inquiry corroborated Salmond's unusual working hours. One witness said: '[I] remember speaking to colleagues who would say FFM had asked them to have a drink at the end of the day – male and female – and they'd laugh with each other at the techniques they used to get out of it.' Another added that he often 'went to Bute House or FFM's hotel late at night to get government business done. Similarly other members of staff – men and women – did so too.'

Evans determined that it had been an 'inappropriate conversation' for Salmond to instigate but that it did not amount to harassment. She added:

> Having reviewed the later allegations and in light of the findings overall, I have concluded that this appears to be the beginning of what can later be seen as a pattern of behaviour and focused attention on Ms A. However, I am not satisfied that in and of itself it amounts to harassment, including harassment related to sex.

The third complaint by Ms A was alleged to have taken place in Bute House in November 2013. The decision report describes it as follows: 'When Ms A was alone in FFM's company late in the evening on official business on FFM's instruction, in a private part of the building, FFM kissed her on the lips as she was leaving the room. This was "more than a peck".' Ms A said she was 'taken aback and shocked mainly because she had no idea how to respond'. Salmond denied the event took place at all, saying he had 'no memory whatsoever' of the incident and that the 'timescale was too vague to identify the circumstances'. Evans said she noted the 'commonalities' with the two earlier complaints and added:

> Having reviewed the later allegations and in light of the findings overall, I have concluded that this is the early stages of what can later be seen as a pattern of inappropriate behaviour and focused attention towards a female official who did not feel in a position

to challenge. I have noted the FFM comments about the vagueness of the timescale and that he has no memory of the incident.
It is relevant, however, that Ms A has a clear memory of it as she
did not know how to respond. I consider Ms A's recollection to
be credible. It follows on from other incidents and suggests an
escalation in the FFM's behaviour towards Ms A.

She found the complaint to be well founded.

The 'escalation' referred to by Evans culminated in the December
2013 incident in Bute House. In her decision report, Evans notes
that Ms A had presented a 'detailed and comprehensive' account of
the circumstances. It read:

> Ms A was working in Bute House late at night. The FFM said
> they would need to move from the sitting room to the bedroom
> as the sitting room was too cold. Ms A accompanied the FFM
> to his bedroom where they had a work conversation, to begin
> with at least. The FFM produced a bottle of Chinese spirits. He
> was drinking and encouraged Ms A to drink with him. Ms A
> described 'FFM pouring drink into her glass but as she didn't
> like drinking with him she just sipped her drink, nevertheless he
> kept topping her glass. It got to the ridiculous stage of almost
> being filled to the brim'.

The account to the government investigation by Ms A was almost
identical to what she would later lay out to the High Court in Edinburgh. The decision report summarises it as follows:

> The FFM requested that Ms A take her boots off. She felt it
> would have been difficult to say no to this. Although she would
> normally take her shoes off in a hotel room, in this particular

context Ms A thought that the FFM's request was 'loaded'. From her statement it appears Ms A formed the view that this was not a meeting as such. She attempted to leave the room. She tried to find a balance between not putting the FFM in a bad mood and being able to make her exit. He did not want her to leave. The bed was by the door. As Ms A was making her way towards the door the FFM told her to get on the bed. Ms A sat on the bed. She felt she had to.

The decision report directly quotes Ms A's harrowing description of what happened when she was on the bed: 'He groped me repeatedly over the bodice of my dress and under the skirt of my dress. He was saying things like "you're ravishing" over and over again. FFM was wandering around kissing different parts of my face.' She told the government investigation that Salmond had been lying on top of her and that although she did not remember him being 'aggressively violent', he did keep her pinned down for a 'few minutes'. The report recounts her version of events: 'The FFM touched her sexually on the breasts and bottom. She resisted this verbally. Ms A felt as if the FFM would not have stopped of his own accord unless she had stopped it.'

The harassment investigation also took witness statements from colleagues of Ms A – including Chris Birt – whom she had told about the incident immediately afterwards. Evans wrote:

The impact on Ms A is evident from the statement of witnesses she spoke to at the time: 'It was clear she was vulnerable and clearly something horrible had happened to her'. I note the conflict and personal compromise expressed by civil servants in coming forward to complain and give evidence. The content of some of the statements points to individuals questioning both their own moral compass and values as professional civil servants … Another witness noted how seriously Ms A had viewed the incident and how shaken and threatened she had been by it.

Salmond disputed Ms A's version of events, saying: 'For the avoidance of any doubt [I] absolutely deny that any instructions were ever given by me at any time or on any such matters, or that I have at any time engaged in a non-consensual way on such issues.'

In response, Ms A said: 'I would emphatically say that it was not consensual – which is central to the fact that I made a complaint at the time.' Evans noted that Ms A's claim was 'supported by her timeous action after the event and the witness statements'.

The Permanent Secretary pointed out that neither party denied an incident occurred but there was a 'difference of opinion' over the exact circumstances and whether the contact had been consensual. She added:

> The witness statements set out that two witnesses decided that at the very least they had to speak to the FFM and ask him what he thought he was doing and to explain to him he could not do this and that they wouldn't be able to staff the FFM's office and provide a service if he carried on with this kind of behaviour.

Salmond objected to the government investigating this complaint at all, as he insisted it had already been dealt with at the time and resolved by way of the apology. The former First Minister's lawyers, Levy & McRae, raised this with Evans on several occasions during the course of the investigation. On 26 April 2018, they wrote: 'Now you are purporting to raise the whole matter again applying a procedure which was not in existence then and which did not come into existence until over three years after our client ceased to be a Minister. This is both unfair and incompetent.' Salmond elaborated on this point in his own submission to the government: 'In short, I had every reasonable expectation that this complaint had been dealt with properly and resolved according to the rules then in existence five years ago.'

However, Evans concluded that the issue had not been suitably dealt with at the time. 'This "informal" resolution was unsatisfactory for a range of reasons,' she wrote. 'No formal record was kept of the incident and no HR involvement was sought, both of which would have been appropriate for an incident of this nature under the Fairness at Work procedure.'

The Permanent Secretary also suggested that the fact Salmond had continued his alleged inappropriate conduct to other female staff members after the December 2013 incident undermined his apology to Ms A.

She said:

Ms A made it clear that she accepted his apology, and agrees with the account of how the incident was handled at the time. However a few months later she became aware that another female member of staff (who did not wish action to be taken at the time and who has not made a complaint under this procedure) had allegedly experienced inappropriate behaviour. I am satisfied that Ms A accepted the apology as the best outcome in the circumstances at the time but that any sense of resolution felt by her was eroded when hearing of other alleged experiences of sexual harassment subsequent to the apology.

Evans concluded the complaint could be considered by the new process and determined that it was 'well founded'.

* * *

Two of the allegations considered by Evans did not relate directly to Ms A or Ms B but focused on Salmond's general behaviour. These included claims that he:

- conducted official business with civil servants, including female staff, in his hotel room while dressed only in his underwear;
- asked female civil servants, including two very junior staff, to 'twirl' to show him their clothing and appearance;
- hid a female official's shoes and made her search for them;
- touched the hair of female officials;
- insisted that female officials travelled in the back of government cars with him and not in the front;
- insisted that both male and female junior officials remain with him in his hotel room on official business late into the evening even when they had no genuine business to attend to;
- expected female officials to attend to his personal care, in particular to: brush his hair, tie his tie and tie his shoelaces.

The complaint also alleged that he:

- shouted and swore at civil service officials;
- threw things at male civil servants;
- expected officials to drink alcohol with him late into the evening while on official business;
- subjected officials to personal insults and verbal abuse such that some were reduced to tears.

In her decision report, Evans did not come to a conclusion on these complaints after Salmond's legal team complained about their vagueness.

* * *

Ms B first began to worry about Alex Salmond's conduct during a government trip to England in the run-up to the independence referendum. In her statement of complaint to the Scottish government, she recalled how the way one of her colleagues prepared herself for interactions with Salmond sounded alarm bells. 'In the lift before we got to his room, I noticed she buttoned up an extra two buttons on her blouse,' she told Mackinnon. 'She said something to the effect of "I've learned not to tempt him".'

This was Ms B's first insight into what appears to have been an ingrained feature of the civil service's approach to working with Salmond – a series of informal measures, procedures and protocols to protect female staff. However, she says she did not learn the full scale of what was going on behind the scenes until some weeks later when a chance conversation in the office led to her being told about the rota changes that had been put in place at Bute House. 'One day I was sitting in the office next to my colleague when she mentioned in a jokey way FM loving to touch a former [staff member's] hair,' she recounted to the government investigation years later. 'When I responded incredulously, her face dropped – she said something to the effect of, "haven't you been told?"'

According to her account, Ms B was then taken into a meeting room with Ms A and the civil servant who had complained about Salmond's behaviour on the Eurostar.

> [They] explained that following complaints they had both made about FM's inappropriate behaviour to them and others, it had been agreed that if my post had been filled by a young woman that they would be warned on accepting the job. This had not happened.
>
> They also explained that there was an agreement when doing the rota for work, that no young women were to be left alone at

Bute House at night. As we often had to stay there until the small hours of the morning (until FM dismissed us as he was going to sleep) there was always also a male colleague rota'd on. Although in practice, especially after returning late at night after events, this was not always the case.

Ms B said she then spoke to Chris Birt and Joe Griffin, who were angry and apologetic about the fact that she had not been made aware of the situation regarding young female staff members and the First Minister. It is notable that, as is the case with other officials who complained about Salmond's conduct, her statement is not critical of how her immediate superiors handled the situation but instead blames a toxic culture that had been allowed to build up by the leadership of the civil service over a long number of years. 'We were a very close-knit team and considered our colleagues to be good friends,' she said. 'We agreed that anytime something happened that I was uncomfortable with, that I would let my line manager know and that if I wanted to escalate it they would support me in doing so.'

In the months that followed, the most serious complaint Ms B would make was the November 2014 incident at Stirling Castle, which she reported to Birt at the time and which would subsequently see Salmond acquitted of a charge of sexual assault in the criminal case. But the 2018 government harassment inquiry also catalogued a number of other incidents of alleged harassment at the lower end of the scale. In her evidence to the government, Ms B painted a picture of Salmond as a politician who regularly mistreated staff. 'More than anything, working for the FM was like being in an abusive relationship,' she said.

When he was being cruel, he made you feel like you deserved

it. But at times he was very caring and great fun to be around, and it was these times that you began to live for – even just for him to be polite or civil one day to you felt like it made up for everything else.

Ms B's very first encounter with Salmond had set the tone for her future experiences. She said she was driving with the then First Minister in a government car when the nature of his conversation struck her as being inappropriate. 'In the car journey back, I sat in the front and my colleague in the back,' she recalled years later.

> He started engaging in 'banter' where he was comparing himself now to an old photo of himself where he was much heavier. He kept repeatedly saying how much 'sexier' he was now that he'd lost weight and 'don't you think I'm so sexy'. At the time I just laughed nervously and thought this must just be what he was like.

When the government put this allegation to Salmond in 2018, he denied that it occurred and suggested the misunderstanding could perhaps be traced to a comment he had made about a viral social media account that gained notoriety in the run-up to the independence referendum. At the time, more than 30,000 people followed the spoof @AngrySalmond Twitter account, which used a picture of the politician wearing a pink beret and sunglasses taken from a photoshoot to promote a breast cancer campaign. It purported to be a stream-of-consciousness rendering of the First Minister's response to contemporary events.

Salmond's submission to the government inquiry insisted:

> The only matter which could explain this bizarre suggestion is

that a parody site had recently been launched exactly at that time called 'Angry Salmond' under the hashtag 'sexy socialism'. I found it amusing and often asked people what they thought of the site and who they thought might be responsible. I can only speculate that some of the comment had been misunderstood.

It is certainly true that the politician took a keen interest in the Angry Salmond account. He told the *Scottish Sun* in September 2014:

I actually get sore from laughing at it. I was getting my hair cut in Aberdeen and I was reading out the Angry Salmond tweets – heavily censored of course because there's a lot of swearies. But I love the slogan sexy socialism. I'm thinking of adopting it. Sexy social democracy has a certain ring to it.

The account's output was edgy, profane, pro-independence but gently mocking of Salmond's ego. A fairly typical tweet took the following swipe at then Deputy Prime Minister Nick Clegg on 28 March 2014: 'Nick Clegg invited me out for a beer once. I laughed for about five minutes before telling him to fuck off. #VoteYes'.

There was fevered speculation in the political bubble about who was behind the account, with many in government believing some of the satire was so on point that those responsible must have personally known Salmond. The politician was equally interested in the identity of the authors and even made a public plea to be let into the secret. The account's success saw the creator given a regular column in the pro-independence newspaper *The National* in the aftermath of the referendum before he was eventually unmasked as former cinema usher Chris McPhail.

In a 2021 podcast, he claimed the experience of meeting Salmond had made him realise the First Minister had not quite understood he was the butt of the joke. 'The thing at the time we clocked was he didn't recognise it as being a parody account,' said McPhail.

> He thought it was a fan account. I don't actually know how much of this account he actually saw, but the joke squarely landed on him to the point where when I first met him I was almost apologising for this. The thing that always stuck with me was him saying to me, 'How did you get inside my head?' That was the penny drop moment of, oh wait a minute here, the character we created was a character, it was a joke, but he was admitting, 'That's me, that's what I am like.'

Regardless of how the Angry Salmond account had inspired the First Minister's comments to Ms B in the car that day, Evans concluded that his behaviour on this occasion did not meet the threshold for harassment. In her decision report, the Permanent Secretary said:

> I find Ms B's account credible and accept that the incident occurred. It was an inappropriate comment for the FFM to make and it made Ms B feel uncomfortable. However, I am not satisfied that taken alone this amounts to harassment. Taking the above into account, I do not consider that this cause for concern is well founded.

Another episode that would become a focus of the government inquiry related to Salmond's repeated comments about staff members' appearance and outfits. Ms B related one incident in which she was made to feel uncomfortable after she went to Bute House to prepare him for an outdoor ceremony. 'When I arrived in his study, he said how pretty my dress was and asked me to "stand there" and "give him a twirl",' she said.

In response, Salmond said there had been nothing untoward or sexual in the comment and he made similar remarks to male members of staff. 'There had been discussion about appropriate wear for me and the staff ... particularly since heavy rain was expected and the Events Team had produced saltire plastic macs,' he said in his submission to the government inquiry.

> When Ms B arrived suitably dressed I suggested that she twirl as I have suggested to other [staff] and they had on occasion asked me to do so. No offence was meant nor apparently taken at the time to this light hearted conversation and this does not even approach what could reasonably be thought of as harassment.

Salmond also directed the investigation to a male witness who recalled the former First Minister asking him to twirl on an occasion when he had been wearing special trousers for the Ryder Cup golf tournament. A female witness cited by Salmond also said: 'On occasion he asked me to twirl but despite it not being very "PC" I think it was intended to be complimentary and not in a harassing or demeaning manner.'

Ms B disputed Salmond's interpretation of these events, saying:

> The fact that we then had a conversation afterwards does not mean that I did not take offence at the time. FFM clearly does not understand what could be considered harassment. Asking any member of staff, female or otherwise, to twirl is grossly inappropriate, regardless of his intention. And likewise, me continuing to do my job does not mean that I was not uncomfortable or not offended.

In her decision report, Evans concluded this incident also did not amount to harassment on its own.

> I conclude this behaviour was inappropriate, whether directed towards a man or woman, and in this specific instance it appears to form part of a course of conduct which Ms B found harassing and demeaning. I view the considerable imbalance in the power dynamic to be relevant. Ms B did not feel empowered to say 'no' and the sense of humiliation she felt is clear from her statement.
>
> I find Ms B's account credible and accept that the incident occurred. It was an inappropriate comment for the FFM to have made. However, I am not satisfied that at this stage it amounts to harassment.
>
> Taking the above into account, I do not consider that this cause for concern is well founded in itself. However, when taken with other incidents it may demonstrate a course of conduct which would appear to a reasonable person to amount to harassment.

One of the other incidents referred to by Evans had allegedly taken place the same day at an evening reception Ms B attended with Salmond. 'During this time, he got quite drunk and as I was speaking to another attendee at a table of about ten, he reached over and put his hand on my face and under my chin to speak to me,' she recalled.

> He later pulled on my ponytail as I was speaking to people. I was utterly mortified and it made me feel like he was treating me as his property to show off to other men, and diminished me professionally. His actions made me feel horrible. I felt it was worse because there were people there and this had been a display of power.

Ms B noted that she had told her line manager about both these incidents at the time, and he was subsequently interviewed as part of the harassment inquiry. The decision report notes: 'The [manager] recognised this was inappropriate behaviour and asked Ms B if there was anything she wanted him (the witness) to do. The witness just said that Ms B just wanted to let him know about this incident but she did not ask him to do anything about it.'

Salmond denied that the behaviour complained about took place but did not offer a substantial rebuttal as Ms B had initially got the date of the event wrong and placed it on an evening when the former First Minister was having dinner with the Queen at Balmoral.

Evans accepted there had been some confusion about the exact date but determined that the complaint was well founded, saying:

> I find Ms B's account credible and accept the incident occurred. I view the considerable power imbalance to be relevant. Ms B described feeling humiliated and treated like property. Taking the above into account I believe this cause for concern is well founded. The conduct was unwanted and had the effect of violating Ms B's dignity and occurred because of her sex.

Ms B also complained of an incident of alleged harassment that did not have a sexual aspect but centred on the bullying behaviour that several of Salmond's supporters would later acknowledge he could exhibit. This particular example was said to have taken place when travelling to an event in the run-up to the independence referendum when Ms B said there was a breakdown in communication with a government driver over the exact destination.

'When FM heard this, he made the driver pull over and stop the car,' she said.

He then proceeded to yell and point his finger directly in my face saying that I was a disgrace and that I had let my colleague (the driver) down. He went on and on telling me that he could go to 'any primary school in the area and find a five-year-old that could do your job better'.

Throughout the day, we had a number of car journeys. Each time we got into the car he would start shouting at me including for things that were entirely party matters (e.g. Why were people not out canvassing the area the night before). I put this down to concerns about the referendum and chalked it up to experience. I felt that if I could handle this level of abuse I could handle anything.

Salmond denied the incident and objected to the fact that Mackinnon had not traced the driver to corroborate Ms B's account during the investigation. In response, Evans decided not to make a finding in relation to this complaint, although she noted that she found Ms B's account 'credible'.

It was the alleged incident at Stirling Castle that formed the most substantial element of Ms B's statement to the government harassment inquiry, described in the decision report as the 'main issue of complaint'. The civil servant's version of events presented to the government was the same as she would outline in court two years later. 'A professional photographer was hired to take photographs and the FM was having parting shots taken out on the ramparts,' she told the inquiry.

I had no intention of having my photo taken; however, he insisted I join the photo. While the photo was being taken, he reached his arm behind my back and grabbed my backside. I was really shocked but didn't know what to do, especially as we were having our picture taken and I didn't want to create a scene.

Salmond's submission to the government investigation echoed

the defence that would ultimately be accepted by the jury in the criminal trial. 'This simply did not happen and furthermore can be shown not to have happened,' he said.

> Numerous witnesses can testify that no one was 'instructed' to have their photo taken. Numerous witnesses can testify that there was a queue to have these photos taken with just about every- one attending the dinner including staff members keen to have an individual photo to remember the evening. The photos were taken outside with a lion rampant in the background. Numerous witnesses will testify that nothing inappropriate occurred.

Two witnesses cited by Salmond at the criminal case would later testify that they had seen nothing untoward. However, in her response to Salmond's statement Ms B said no witnesses had a proper vantage point for the incident: 'Since no one was standing behind us (as FFM rightly points out the photos were taken with the lion rampant in the background) no one would be able to see where his hand was.'

Ms B's manager told the harassment inquiry that he had been informed about the incident, adding that he had offered to speak to Salmond about it but she had declined as the First Minister was just days away from leaving office. The manager added: 'This was on the lower end of the spectrum, with FFM just being a dirty old man and we knew he was going at that stage. Ms B was just keen to let me know this had happened and the protections needed to be there.'

In her decision report, Evans said she suspected a 'certain level of inevitability and resignation seems to have set in given others' responses to this event'. She found that Salmond's behaviour in Stirling Castle had again amounted to harassment, adding:

The conduct was unwanted and of a sexual nature. It had the purpose or effect of violating Ms B's dignity and creating an intimidating, degrading, humiliating and offensive environment. In addition, this conduct, when taken with other incidents ... forms parts of a course of conduct which would appear to a reasonable person to amount to harassment.

Ms B had made repeated attempts to get the Scottish government to take the sexual harassment of civil servants more seriously. Her statement to the harassment inquiry revealed that in addition to the various reports to her line manager in 2014 she also raised the issue with a senior civil servant in the months after Salmond's departure.

Equalities expert Robin Iffla was drafted in by the Scottish government to do training in the wake of a 2016 staff survey that found that one in ten civil servants said they had been bullied or harassed at work. Of those subjected to such behaviour, only 43 per cent reported it and just 16 per cent felt the problem had been resolved. Part of Iffla's work included a discussion on what to do if you witnessed inappropriate behaviour in the workplace. Given her previous experiences, Ms B was left 'incredibly hurt and upset' by the suggestion that staff should report instances of misconduct if it was to be properly tackled. She asked to speak to Lisa Bird, the principal private secretary of the new First Minister, Nicola Sturgeon. 'I told her that bullying and sexual harassment had taken place under FFM (which may have explained some of the employee survey results),' she said.

I explained that I wanted procedures put in place to ensure that staff (and particularly young staff) were not ever placed in the same situation again. I explained that being alone, in hotel rooms, cars etc., often after ministers had been drinking, was unavoidable but that it was the responsibility of the organisation to make sure this happened as safely as possible.

She asked for definitive action to help in the event of similar situations arising for staff in those types of jobs. It is unclear what action, if any, Bird took after this meeting.

'What troubled me was the feeling this had been allowed to happen incrementally over many years by a lack of process within SG [Scottish government],' added Ms B.

> I don't believe there was any single person that can take responsibility for this other than FM. But at the same time, I believe, both organisationally and personally, that he engaged in unchallenged escalating behaviour that allowed him to feel impunity to act as he did. Everyone was afraid of him and no one wanted to put themselves in the line of fire (understandably) to stand up to him.

Ms B said that 'in the grand scheme of things' the alleged behaviour she experienced was 'at the low end of the scale'. She added:

> But they were part of a pattern of behaviour FM employed towards many of us – pushing to see what he could get away with. But I also know that if someone else was telling me about this I'd be horrified.
>
> I feel that it's important to speak truth to power and I had failed in doing so. I felt complicit and morally compromised. I felt ashamed and angry that I hadn't done more or said anything, especially as I knew that my colleagues, my friends, had … suffered more than me and I hadn't spoken up. I felt ashamed that I didn't speak up for myself when I felt boundaries had been

crossed. I felt angry that more senior people in the SG and SNP clearly knew but felt powerless to do anything.

Ms A and Ms B had spent years attempting to get senior officials in the Scottish government to take harassment issues seriously. They were finally about to rocket to the very top of the political agenda.

CHAPTER 9

ACCUSED

Nicola Sturgeon's stomach churned as she stood, shaken, in the bathroom of her Glasgow home. In the kitchen sat Alex Salmond, her predecessor as First Minister. He had just told her he was being investigated by the Scottish government over allegations of sexual harassment.

From a letter sent to Salmond by Permanent Secretary Leslie Evans outlining the claims against her former mentor, Sturgeon – who later said she was 'shocked and upset by the reality of what I read' – digested the detailed claims of the incident with Ms A in the bedroom at Bute House in December 2013.

'Reading that letter is a moment in my life that I will never forget,' she told the Holyrood inquiry into the government's unlawful handling of the claims.

> Although he denied the allegations, he gave me his account of one of the incidents that was complained of, which he said he had apologised for at the time. What he described constituted, in my view, deeply inappropriate behaviour on his part – which is perhaps another reason why that moment is embedded so strongly in my mind.

As well as the seriousness of the allegation itself – Ms A's claim would become a charge of sexual assault with intent to rape in the criminal trial – Sturgeon felt an acute sense of personal betrayal as its significance sank in. When she had questioned Salmond about the Edinburgh Airport allegations the previous November, he had insisted there were no skeletons in his closet.

'He said something to me about, you know, you can't have stories like this running because you get one and the floodgates will open kind of thing, which he immediately qualified and said, "Oh no, that's not to say that I think there is anything there,"' Sturgeon later told James Hamilton as part of the standards investigation into her handling of the incident.

Now it had emerged by Salmond's own admission that he had apologised for inappropriate behaviour towards a female civil servant during his time leading the country. This was the moment that Sturgeon decided she could no longer trust the man she has called 'the most influential and important person in my adult life' outside of her parents and husband. 'Somebody that I loved, on a level,' she would later tell the *New Yorker*.

Recalling the April meeting to the magazine, she said: 'I remember leaving the room at one point. I think I said that I was going to make a cup of tea, and going to the bathroom and feeling physically sick.'

Ahead of the gathering, Sturgeon's chief of staff Liz Lloyd had travelled through from Edinburgh to the First Minister's modern detached house on an estate in the east of Glasgow. Peter Murrell, Sturgeon's husband and the SNP chief executive, was not at home. He would later say he had gone in the opposite direction to work at the party's headquarters in Scotland's capital on Easter Monday.

Salmond was making his way from his home in Strichen with his suitcase in tow. After the meeting with Sturgeon, he would fly to the US to record a series of programmes for RT from New York and Washington DC. First he took the train from Aberdeenshire to Glasgow's Queen Street Station and met his former chief of staff Geoff Aberdein and the lawyer and former SNP MSP Duncan Hamilton at the neighbouring Copthorne Hotel. They discussed the meeting before taking a taxi to Sturgeon's house. After formalities, the two senior politicians moved to the kitchen at Salmond's request, leaving the aides in the front room. It was there that he laid out the details of the allegations facing him over the course of an hour-long conversation. He asked Sturgeon to intervene on his behalf and was satisfied upon leaving that his former deputy was going to come to his aid. In the other room, Aberdein and Hamilton were going over much of the same material and issues with Lloyd. Murrell arrived home but rather than join either meeting went upstairs to take a shower.

Sturgeon and Salmond rejoined their aides and a discussion ensued involving the entire group, again leaving the former First Minister under the impression his successor would help him resolve the situation informally. 'We discussed mediation,' his lawyer Duncan Hamilton said in written evidence to the Holyrood committee.

> My clear recollection is that her words were 'If it comes to it, I will intervene.' From a legal perspective, that was the most important aspect of the meeting. I therefore remember it clearly. I discussed the commitment to intervene with Mr Salmond and Mr Aberdein after we left the meeting specifically because it seemed very likely that mediation would be achieved. From Mr Salmond's perspective, that was the desired outcome. The First Minister did later change her mind. She was entitled to do so. That change was, however, a matter of surprise.

Sturgeon had always denied offering to intervene but admitted to the committee that she was equivocal during the meeting. 'I was perhaps trying to – how will I best put this? – let a long-standing friend and colleague down gently,' she said. 'Perhaps I did that too gently and he left with an impression that I did not intend to give him. I think that I was clear, and I certainly intended to be clear.'

The meeting had been arranged four days earlier in the First Minister's office. Aberdein had made contact after his exchanges with the government official and subsequent telephone conversations with Salmond. The ten-minute meeting on 29 March would raise questions about the honesty of Sturgeon's version of events.

When Aberdein arrived at Holyrood, he found birthday celebrations under way for a civil servant he had worked closely with and so joined the party before asking the First Minister, who was also present, if they could talk privately.

The main thrust of the discussion was Aberdein trying to persuade Sturgeon to meet Salmond over allegations of inappropriate behaviour. Aberdein would later tell James Hamilton that he provided a broad summary of the complaints being made against Salmond but that he was not aware of the detail of the allegations to relay them to the First Minister. Sturgeon has maintained she did not know that the claims were being investigated by her government until Salmond told her on 2 April. 'To the best of my recollection, no, he [Aberdein] did not give me details, it was very much he wanted to get me to agree to see Alex,' she told Hamilton.

Alex and I were very close, but we hadn't been speaking as much as normal. You know, I was First Minister, he was off doing other things, he had lost his seat. He wanted me to see Alex and agree to a meeting. He was telling me that he was very worried about Alex, a lot of the discussion was about Alex's state of mind. You know, he seemed to be indicating that he had never heard Alex be quite so upset about anything previously, that he was very distressed, that he thought he might be about to resign his SNP membership because of the nature of the issue he was upset about.

Appearing before the Holyrood inquiry, she conceded that Aberdein did 'indicate that a harassment-type issue had arisen, but my recollection is that he did so in general terms'.

Salmond vociferously denied ever considering quitting the SNP over the investigation. Asked directly at the Holyrood committee, he said: 'I did not threaten resignation. There was nothing to threaten resignation about. I am not sure that "threatening resignation" is the right term, anyway. The answer is no.'

The content of the meetings – specifically whether Sturgeon knew about the Scottish government investigation before 2 April – came under intense scrutiny because of statements the First Minister made to Holyrood in the aftermath of Salmond's judicial review victory. She told MSPs that as well as the 2 April gathering, the pair had met on 7 June ahead of an SNP conference in Aberdeen and again at her home on 14 July. Telephone calls took place on 23 April and 18 July, the latter marking the last time Sturgeon and Salmond spoke to each other. She did not mention the 29 March meeting and it only became public knowledge during Aberdein's evidence to the criminal trial. This left Sturgeon open to a charge of misleading Parliament through an effective lie of omission. It also damaged her defence to another aspect of wrongdoing she was accused of. The Scottish ministerial code states: 'A private secretary or official should be present for all discussions relating to government business.' The 'basic facts' of those meetings should then be recorded, with all meetings published three months later. If a minister ends up 'discussing official business without an official present – for example at a party conference, social occasion or on holiday – any significant content ... should be passed back to their

Private Offices as soon as possible after the event, who should arrange for the basic facts of such meetings to be recorded,' the code adds.

Sturgeon would argue that her 2 April meeting with Salmond was a 'party matter' so did not need to be recorded. The suggestion that she knew it would be centred on the Scottish government's harassment policy – plus the fact that she was accompanied by Lloyd, who is on the public payroll, rather than SNP chief executive Murrell – cast serious doubt over the claim and left her open to accusations of having broken the code.

Sturgeon subsequently insisted that she did not tell Evans about the meetings or the fact that she was aware of the investigation because she did not want, even inadvertently, to be seen as putting pressure on the Permanent Secretary. Despite that, she continued to discuss the case with Salmond.

She received a WhatsApp message from her predecessor at 8.31 p.m. on 22 April asking to speak to her in a voice call using the encrypted service the following morning. A first attempt failed because of poor signal as Sturgeon was travelling up Scotland's A9 towards Inverness, but when they eventually spoke for around fifteen minutes, Salmond said his legal team would formally ask for mediation with the women that day. Sturgeon, with Lloyd beside her in the room, refused to try to persuade Evans to accept the offer.

Their relationship was straining to near breaking point. Between 31 May and 1 June, the pair exchanged eleven messages as Salmond tried to convince her to agree to another in-person meeting. He insisted a further telephone call was 'not appropriate' as there was 'material you need to see and assess privately'. The mood darkened yet again when Sturgeon said she wanted a 'quick chat first to understand the purpose of giving me material' and stated: 'We've already spoken about why I think me intervening is not [the] right

thing to do.' After a two-day delay, an unimpressed Salmond finally replied to his successor. His message was the first time the
First Minister realised with horror that her mentor was seriously
considering taking her administration to court. 'My recollection of
our Monday 2 April meeting was rather different,' he said.

> You wanted to assist but then decided against an intervention
> to help resolve the position amicably. Now is different. I was in-
> tending to give you sight of the petition for JR [judicial review]
> drafted by senior counsel. You are a lawyer and can judge for
> yourself the prospects of success which I am advised are excel-
> lent. This will follow ANY adverse finding against me by the PS
> [Permanent Secretary] in a process which is unlawful.

He repeated his view that Sturgeon was 'perfectly entitled' to intervene and suggested she was obligated to do so if there was a
risk that her government was acting unlawfully. Salmond warned,
correctly, that a legal battle would be more bruising for the government than it would be for him, particularly given the shambolic
nature of the investigation, as he suggested the fallout risked causing political damage to the First Minister.

Salmond added:

> The JR will be rough for me since the hearing will almost cer-
> tainly be made public but at least I will have the opportunity
> to clear my name and good prospects of doing so – but for
> the Government? One further thing to consider. Thus far we
> have been able to confine evidence offered to the general (and
> mostly ridiculous) matters. This has had the benefit of keeping
> everything well clear of [the] current administration. When we
> go to Court we will have to produce evidence to demonstrate
> prior process (which incidentally the PS has admitted!). If you

want to discuss privately then I can come to you in the north east on Monday.

Sturgeon – who would later tell Hamilton that the 'intimidatory' tone of the message 'changed her view of the matter' – was in Aberdeen for the SNP conference that weekend and agreed to meet Salmond in the private Platinum reception of the Hilton Double-Tree hotel on the city's Beach Boulevard on 7 June.

An increasingly trenchant First Minister refused to take a copy of the legal opinion offered to her by Salmond, reiterated that she would not intervene in the process and urged him to consider addressing the substance of the allegations. She later said the threat of impending legal action and a fear of being 'cornered' by her predecessor at the conference meant she wanted to hold the meeting on her terms.

By this point Sturgeon had spoken to Evans and revealed that she had been in discussion with Salmond about the ongoing government investigation. These facts were finally put in writing to the Permanent Secretary the day before the meeting in Aberdeen.

Salmond – who would write to Evans six days later stating that it would be a breach of confidentiality to share details of the investigation with Sturgeon, in a letter that stressed his right to privacy and argued the government had no jurisdiction to examine him under the new procedure – did not attend the conference but at the meeting again told the First Minister he intended to take legal action against the government if the situation was not resolved to his satisfaction.

In retrospect, there were signs that the stress of the encounters was taking its toll on Sturgeon. The day after meeting Salmond, she struggled in an interview with *Channel 4 News* and was unable to remember the set-up costs proposed for an independent Scotland in the SNP's recent Growth Commission report. She also struggled to recall the price tag for creating Scotland's new social security agency. Observers were surprised at the inability of the normally commanding First Minister to recall the detail as she said: 'I don't have all of those figures right at the tip of my fingers right now.'

If the full extent of the issues being posed by Salmond behind the scenes was not known, there were still public signs of discord between the two. On 13 June, SNP Westminster leader Ian Blackford led a televised mass walkout from the House of Commons during Prime Minister's Questions. After calling for an emergency debate about how the EU Withdrawal Bill would affect devolution, he ignored eight demands from Speaker John Bercow to sit down before marching his thirty-four MPs out of the chamber amid jeers and waves from Conservative MPs.

Blackford was banned from Parliament for the rest of the day, but by the weekend Salmond had taken credit for the move, telling the *Sunday Herald* he had suggested the stunt in a phone call the night before. 'One of the iron laws of parliamentary politics is that if you always play the Westminster game then you will always lose,' he said.

> And the way to turn that round successfully is to target interventions at those occasions which mean so much to the Westminster establishment – PMQs, Budgets, State Openings, etc. – and then use their own procedures against them. Certainly, that was my advice to Ian Blackford when he phoned me last Tuesday night and I was delighted to see him carry it through.

The disruptive behaviour mirrored one of the iconic moments in Salmond's career, when he was thrown out of the Commons in 1988 after interrupting then Chancellor Nigel Lawson during the Budget to protest against the poll tax.

However, senior SNP figures dispute Salmond's account and say Blackford had phoned him as a 'reaching-out exercise' to ask his thoughts on the planned walkout. 'And then of course Alex leaked, saying, "Oh, I told them to do it,"' says a source close to the SNP leadership. 'It was total bollocks and of course that meant it became very difficult to talk to him about anything.'

Whatever the facts of the conversation, Salmond's decision to make public his involvement just days after his meeting with Sturgeon could be regarded as an attempt to undermine his successor by talking up his influence over one of the SNP's more memorable moments at Westminster.

Meanwhile, his hopes of securing mediation from the Scottish government had hit a brick wall. His first attempt, on 23 April, had been rejected by Evans without consultation with the women who had made the allegations. When he made a second approach three days later, she put the offer to the complainers, who also turned it down. One of the women later told a private session of the Holyrood committee:

> I felt absolutely unable to take part in any mediation at that point – because I did not want to enter into that conversation, because I was quite anxious about that potential encounter, but also because it was very clear that he was, at that point, not accepting any responsibility for any of his behaviours or actions. Therefore, I did not see what could possibly be achieved through mediation at that point.

With his hopes for an informal resolution now dashed, the former First Minister's focus switched to arbitration, in which an independent panel or retired judge would rule in private on the legal issues he had raised about the government's policy.

Salmond's new strategy was not concentrated on the substance of the complaints but the technicalities of the process. Giving evidence to the Holyrood committee, Sturgeon said: 'It is not immediately obvious to me that arbitration would have been the right thing or would necessarily have been a quicker, cheaper or more effective way of dealing with those things' as she defended the Permanent Secretary's decision not to engage. All through the discussions, Evans insisted the government's investigation procedure was 'fair and legally sound' and as a result would not benefit from the arbitration process. She also argued that bringing in an independent arbiter would be inappropriate and unfair to the complainers and further delay the investigation.

Salmond was concentrating on convincing the civil service to once again bend to his will and did not contact Sturgeon for almost a month. When he finally did get in touch, there were two issues he wanted to discuss. The first was a freedom of information request submitted on 18 June specifically asking if there had been any complaints about his conduct. The other was arbitration.

On the latter point, he told the First Minister in a WhatsApp message that Evans's argument 'entirely misses the point'. He added:

> The SG may well believe it is lawful. My Senior Counsel believes it is unlawful. That's the whole point of the arbitration. The legality will have to be resolved either in private (in a confidential and binding arbitration) or in public at the Court of Session. The SG, and you, have everything to gain from arbitration. If my legal advice is wrong, I will accept that and the current process proceeds. If the SG legal advice is wrong, you discover that without losing in a public court.

He added that the process also guaranteed anonymity for the complainers. Of course, it gave him the same protection, which was key to his argument about the FOI request. He urged Sturgeon to ensure that the government used an exemption covering personal data as a means of stopping the information becoming public, adding: 'It is critical that this happens.'

Sturgeon did not respond to the message, but it was she who instigated the next, and final, meeting between the formerly close political allies. She had one of her officials send Salmond a WhatsApp message telling him the First Minister wanted another face-to-face encounter. This took place on 14 July, with the venue once again Sturgeon's Glasgow home, but on this occasion it was just the two senior nationalists present. Salmond's initial unhappiness at his perception that Sturgeon was personally blocking his arbitration plan was eased, while the First Minister suggested he engage with the substance of the complaints themselves rather than focus on a legal battle. In a message sent at 10.42 p.m. the following day, Salmond told Sturgeon he was 'grateful that you will correct the impression being given that you are against arbitration or that it is somehow against your interests'. He once again said he could not see a downside for anyone involved in pursuing that route and suggested he had taken on board her guidance. 'I am also giving much thought to your advice and thinking deeply about how arbitration on process might open up the space and opportunity to address and resolve the underlying matters, as far as is possible, to everyone's satisfaction,' he added.

Sturgeon, who had subsequently told Evans she had no view on arbitration and did not want to influence the process, did not respond to the message. Instead, she telephoned Salmond at 1.05 p.m. on 18 July to say arbitration had been rejected on the advice of the government's law officers and once again urged him to submit a defence against the complaints.

In her evidence to Hamilton, Sturgeon said she made the call as part of a last-ditch attempt to stop their relationship breaking down entirely and to draw a line under their contact about the investigation ahead of her taking a two-day summer break. A paranoid Salmond would later attribute more malign motivation to his successor.

In his written evidence to Hamilton, he claimed Sturgeon had downplayed the seriousness of the allegations he was facing and encouraged him to engage in the process by putting forward a written defence.

He added:

My view is now that it was believed that my submission of a rebuttal would weaken the case for Judicial Review (my involvement in rebutting the substance of the complaints being seen to cure the procedural unfairness) and that the First Minister's phone call of 18th July 2018 and the Permanent Secretary's letter of the same date suggesting that it was in my 'interests' to submit a substantive response was designed to achieve that.

At 8.50 p.m. that night, Salmond WhatsApped Sturgeon a copy of a letter from Evans also encouraging him to submit a response. She ignored both that and a subsequent message sent at 10.37 p.m. on 20 July in which Salmond said: 'A full rebuttal of all complaints went in by the deadline today. Let us see how it is judged.'

The pair have had no contact since.

*   *   *

Viewers of *The Alex Salmond Show* on 23 August 2018 would have seen the former First Minister looking relaxed and in his element in a blue and green striped shirt under a dark suit jacket as he interviewed a poet and a talk radio show host about the constitutional future of Catalonia. By the time the programme aired, he was back in Edinburgh Airport and was locked in discussion with his legal team. It was now 169 days since Salmond had first been told he was being investigated and the Scottish government was on the verge of making its findings public.

Despite a last-ditch attempt by his lawyers to have the outcome 'considered with the strictest confidence', officials had told Salmond at 2.07 p.m. that they intended to release a statement just three hours later. Its key sentence was the most shocking ever drafted by a Holyrood administration: 'At this time I can confirm that the Scottish Government has received two complaints in relation to Alex Salmond under that procedure.'

Salmond was incensed and immediately launched a legal bid to block the government's revelations. He decamped from the airport to the Edinburgh home of Ronnie Clancy, the QC who prosecuted the Lockerbie bomber Abdelbaset al-Megrahi, to begin drafting a court order, or interim interdict, banning publication. He also began the process of contesting the legality of the government's complaints procedure in a judicial review.

Thirteen minutes after Salmond was told of the government's plans, Nicola Richards sent an email to Ms B titled: 'update – for real'. The HR boss wrote: 'Deep breath, we now have an agreed position on the statement and we are intending to issue a public statement at 5pm. We have just informed the FFM of this timeline but as you're aware any statement may still be blocked if we get an interdict mean time.'

What was unknown to most of those involved at this point was that the *Daily Record* had already received its anonymous note and was closing in on the story. That changed around 4 p.m. when, shortly after receiving an initial enquiry from the paper, a government lawyer contacted Salmond's legal team and told them that the *Record* 'seems to know the story'. Salmond and Clancy were joined by Callum Anderson, a partner in the law firm Levy & McRae, while his colleague David McKie tried to find a judge in Glasgow who could rule on the interdict. If they were to be contacted by a news organisation, the aim was to obtain the Scottish version of an injunction to block publication.

The newspaper's enquiry also caused panic in the Scottish government as hastily arranged conference calls took place about how, or if, ministers could respond. Senior officials cancelled plans to attend events at the Edinburgh Festival as, according to one, 'the shit very much hit the fan'. Attempts were being made to deal with both the prospect of a media report and the concurrent exchanges with Salmond's lawyers that were stymying the ability to make any information public.

Salmond's threat of legal action seemed to be successful, with the government backtracking on the plan to issue a statement. At 7.35 p.m., having appeared to keep a lid on the scandal but unaware of how close the *Record* was to substantiating the story, McKie wrote twenty-two words as part of an email to the government that left open a window of opportunity for journalists. 'We and our client have had no approaches from any media organisation and so no interim interdict applications are being sought tonight,' he said.

Less than forty minutes later, everything changed. Salmond's phone lit up with David Clegg's number. The former First Minister looked to Clancy, who was sitting beside him. The QC told him to take the call but give nothing away.

Salmond's battle for privacy had been in vain. Everything was about to spill out into the open in the messiest manner imaginable.

CHAPTER 10

TAINTED BY APPARENT BIAS

29 AUGUST 2018, 8.30 P.M.

I did not come into politics to facilitate opposition attacks on the SNP and, with Parliament returning next week, I have tendered my resignation to remove this line of opposition attack. Most of all I am conscious that if the party felt forced into suspending me it would cause substantial internal division.

Alex Salmond quit the SNP six days after the *Daily Record* revealed he was being investigated by the police over alleged sexual assault. He used his resignation to launch an online crowdfunding appeal to finance a judicial review of the Scottish government's separate harassment inquiry. He was taking his case to the highest civil court in the land in order to have Permanent Secretary Leslie Evans's decision report rendered null and void. The appeal raised £100,007 – more than double its original target – in less than three days, with 4,146 people making donations before the former First Minister closed the fund. In the event of his victory, he said, 'every penny of surplus funds, which will be substantial in the event of a successful judicial review, will be distributed to good causes in Scotland and beyond'. SNP MSP Colin Beattie, the party's treasurer, gave £20 and left the comment: 'Fairness and transparency.' In an obvious show of defiance, Sturgeon and some of her senior aides simultaneously shared online fundraising appeals by the charities Scottish Women's Aid and Rape Crisis.

It was left to Ian Blackford, a Sturgeon loyalist who had been involved in a bitter fallout with Salmond over party finances in the year 2000 and was now the SNP Westminster leader, to boldly try to pretend everything was fine. 'This is a party, this a movement, that is pretty united,' he told a Scottish Parliamentary Journalists' Association event.

On 31 August, the First Minister addressed her MSPs and MPs face to face for the first time since the crisis had erupted. Witnesses say she struggled to maintain her composure during the annual awayday at Napier University in Edinburgh. One politician present says they had 'never seen her so distressed – never' as Sturgeon's composure left her during the presentation. 'All of a sudden she's among pals,' they say.

> She felt secure that nobody in that room was going to talk and she started talking about it and it just all came out in a torrent. She was just so distressed. She basically started out very Nicola, 'You'll have read what's in the papers.' She was being very controlled. And then there was just a break in her voice, and she was like, 'I'm just finding this so hard to deal with, please excuse me.' Somebody brought her a drink of water.

While the personal cost of the saga was bearing heavily on Sturgeon, the government was still feeling positive about winning the judicial review. It hired two of the country's most senior lawyers in Roddy Dunlop and Christine O'Neill. In their first appraisal of the case, delivered in September, the QCs had been cautiously optimistic, saying that most of the claims brought by Salmond about the retrospective nature of the policy and how it was applied were 'weak', although they warned of a 'real risk' the court would rule the investigation of the former First Minister was procedurally unfair.

However, on Halloween night Dunlop wrote an email that sent waves of horror through the corridors of power. He was furious after discovering what turned out to be the fatal flaw in the government's investigation into the harassment complaints against Salmond. As part of routine disclosure of evidence, the government had revealed that Judith Mackinnon had spoken to Ms B on 7 December 2017, before she had formally submitted her complaint to the government.

The admission was the first time the lawyers had told of Mackinnon's prior contact with the female complainers and, unlike the officials involved in the investigation, they immediately realised the grave implications. Dunlop warned in no uncertain terms that it could be deemed a breach of the 'no prior involvement' clause of the Scottish government's harassment procedure. 'It would be wrong for me to suggest that this revelation is anything other than an extremely concerning one,' he warned, adding that the government had to decide whether or not to disclose the failing and, if so, consider conceding the court battle. 'I can well understand the angst that even suggesting [this] will provoke, but if the proceedings are vitiated [damaged] then it makes little sense to continue to defend the indefensible,' Dunlop wrote.

Despite this stark advice it would take months for Sturgeon and her most senior civil servants to accept the reality of their situation.

Dunlop said one benefit of collapsing the case at this stage would be that the original investigation would simply be set aside, meaning the complaints could be re-examined in a manner less likely to be struck down by the courts.

He had spoken to Lord Advocate James Wolffe before sending his sobering note at 10.50 p.m. on 31 October. He said Scotland's most senior law officer, who sits in Sturgeon's Cabinet, shared 'both my firm advice that this issue will have to be disclosed, and my concern as to the potential repercussions for the wider case'.

Two days later, at a meeting with the government's in-house legal team and Sturgeon's chief of staff Liz Lloyd, Dunlop warned that Salmond would demand that internal emails and notes be released as part of an 'attempt to impugn the integrity of the process' of the investigation. The QC was then summoned to Bute House on 13 November for a meeting with the First Minister, Lloyd and Evans, but his advice to consider collapsing the case again went ignored.

The government argued that because Mackinnon was not aware of the incidents at the time they happened – because she had not yet joined the Scottish government – it did not matter that she had subsequently discussed the prospect of making complaints with the women.

Sources say the attitude from the top of the government became 'quite derogatory' towards Dunlop after the initial warnings about the case's viability, with suggestions being made that 'counsel was not getting it and was not on side'.

Dunlop was privately considering his own position. He told friends he had warned Wolffe that the only reason he was staying on the case was 'because it is you'. The pair are not believed to be personally close, but Dunlop's professional respect for the Lord Advocate meant he was reluctant to quit representing the government unless the situation became untenable. This is exactly what was about to unfold – in an even more dramatic fashion than either Dunlop or O'Neill had predicted.

The prior contact between Ms B and Mackinnon was disclosed to Salmond's team on 15 November, prompting him to widen his legal challenge of the procedure. This led to further information being obtained from the government which showed that Mackinnon's contact with both Ms A and Ms B before they made their complaints had been even more extensive than the lawyers originally realised.

In legal advice given to the government on 6 December, they said Salmond's court challenge was now 'more likely than not to succeed'. They warned:

> Ultimately, our own view is that the 'least worst' option would be to concede the Petition. We understand how unpalatable that advice will be, and we do not tender it lightly. But we cannot let the respondents sail forth into January's hearing without the now very real risks of doing so being crystal clear to all involved.

Dunlop and O'Neill added that carrying on would lead to 'far higher' expenses and 'the real prospect of damaging criticism' from the judge in the case, Lord Pentland.

Sturgeon, Evans and Wolffe all saw the damning analysis on the day it was sent but, in keeping with their previous attitude, appeared to shrug it off. In an email sent at 00.53 on 7 December, Paul Cackette, the Scottish government's former legal director, said both the First Minister and Permanent Secretary were 'unclear – in effect – about what has changed since the last notes and FM meeting that leads you to write as you do'. Dunlop said the worries he conveyed directly to Sturgeon during the Bute House gathering 'have deepened in light of the documents now disclosed'.

On 10 December, a crunch meeting lasting an hour and forty-five minutes was held between Dunlop and the government's in-house lawyers at which the QC's recommendation was once again ignored. Wolffe – who had made clear there was 'no question of conceding' – argued 'that even if prospects are not certain it is important that our case is heard'.

The wheels of the government's case were wobbling dangerously at this point, but they would come perilously close to falling off entirely over the following seven days, prompting Dunlop and O'Neill to threaten to walk away.

The cause of their anger began when O'Neill discovered on 12 December that information had been withheld from the court without her say-so. During the investigation of Salmond, an email between government officials about how to handle complaints against ministers and former ministers specifically discussing 'the circumstances in which complaints of harassment should be reported to the police' had been copied to a Police Scotland staff member. Civil servants said the message was sent to the police worker in error with the recipient's address included instead of Nicola Richards's because of a mistake using the email's predictive function. Two emails were sent to the wrong person.

O'Neill told civil servants to disclose all of the information but, without her knowledge, this instruction was ignored by officials, who decided that GDPR concerns for the police staff member outweighed the need to provide everything to the court. They did not tell O'Neill of their decision and she learned about it only when Salmond's team questioned why the email address had been redacted. This had two consequences. One was that, as the lawyers correctly predicted, the officials' disdainful attitude towards pro-ceedings would 'add fuel to the fire of the petitioner's [Salmond's] "conspiracy theory"'.

The second was that a furious O'Neill came to the view that 'we could not properly advise the court that the Scottish government had discharged its duty of candour'.

In effect, the government's own lawyers were making the stag-gering admission that it had not been entirely honest with the court. Salmond's lawyers agreed with the sentiment, and they suc-cessfully pushed for a Commission and Diligence, a process under Scots law to obtain evidence that is used when witnesses have failed to produce documents.

The move was opposed by the Scottish government, which said no other relevant documents existed. 'Remarkably, the Scottish government had even signed a certificate confirming to the court that no documents existed,' Salmond would later tell the Holyrood committee. Even at this point, the government's in-house lawyers were still telling officials there was nothing to be concerned about. One civil servant was wrongly told that no witnesses would have to appear, while another senior figure was reassured that the hearings would be a formality. It subsequently emerged that the Scottish government's legal department was 'a dysfunctional mess', in the words of one official closely involved in the judicial review. Two of its senior figures had recently died, leaving them understaffed, and those who remained were ignoring the advice of junior lawyers with experience of commissions. The episode led to the department losing the confidence of ministers and it was shut out of dealings with the criminal trial and Holyrood committee.

The decision to hold the commission delighted Salmond's legal team. At a lunch at Glasgow's Marriott Hotel for the Journalists' Charity Scotland on 14 December, the day the court agreed to the hearings, allies of Salmond bragged there had been a breakthrough in the case.

Senior UK government minister Michael Gove had given the keynote speech, but it was David McKie, one of Salmond's lawyers, who had to fend off the most media attention. He remained tight-lipped as reporters flocked to his table at the event as news filtered through from the court but was upbeat as he declined to dampen speculation that the decision was good for his client.

The commission hearings were estimated to cost £50,000 per day, but it quickly became clear that the price paid by the government would be far higher both financially and reputationally.

* * *

'Given the potential for harm we simply wish all concerned – and we include the First Minister in this – to be absolutely certain that they wish us to plough on regardless notwithstanding the concerns which we have outlined.'

By 17 December, an increasingly frustrated Dunlop and O'Neill were at the end of their tether and warned they were on the verge of quitting in an extraordinary memo to ministers. It accurately predicted the legal, political and financial outcomes of continuing to take on Salmond – who they said had adopted a 'scorched earth' approach to defending his name – despite ministers having a fatal flaw in their case. 'It is clear that there is no concern on his part as to who might be criticised, or harmed, as a result of these proceedings,' they wrote of Salmond.

> We understand that this is well understood by those 'in the crosshairs' – most obviously the Permanent Secretary and the First Minister. If instructions are to proceed notwithstanding then so be it – we are not in a position where we are professionally unable to mount a defence (because, for example, there is no statable defence). We are, however, perilously close to such a situation.

The lawyers bluntly reiterated their view that Salmond would win and that they were 'entirely unconvinced' about the benefits of continuing to fight the case. 'Leaving aside the large expenses bill that would inevitably arise, the personal and political fallout of an adverse decision – especially if, as may be the case, it is attended by judicial criticism – seems to us to be something which eclipses by some way the possibility of helpful judicial comments.'

They said the appointment of Mackinnon as the investigating officer despite her having previously discussed the case with both complainers was 'on reflection indefensible'. They added that the government might be able to 'stem the substantial expenses bill that we have no doubt is presently being incurred' and protect itself from some criticism by conceding the case.

'We are acutely aware that much of this has already been said, and discounted,' they wrote. 'The decision to proceed has been taken by very experienced legal and political minds, who are entitled to proceed as they wish. However, we are – independently but also mutually – unable to see that the benefits in proceeding come close to meeting the potential detriments in so doing.'

Nicola Sturgeon was on the roof of the Scottish government's offices in Glasgow for an interview with *Channel 4 News* when one of her private secretaries handed the devastating note to the special adviser accompanying her. The official read its contents with increasing levels of horror before presenting the document to the First Minister.

The blood drained from Sturgeon's face as she realised just how bad the situation was. There was no outburst from a politician who almost always remains calm and quiet in moments of crisis, but she had come to the same conclusion as her aide. 'The game's a bogey, this is done.'

Even worse was to follow when searches for the Commission and Diligence uncovered new evidence, which led to a 9.15 p.m. crisis meeting on 18 December, the day before the first hearing at the Court of Session, involving counsel and the government's internal law officers.

It had emerged that Mackinnon had still not disclosed all of her meetings with the women before they made their complaints. This had led to the lawyers giving false statements to the court about the number of meetings. 'We have averred that there was no further meeting with Ms A before she made her complaint. That is, it would now appear, plainly and demonstrably untrue,' they said.

Mackinnon had given counsel two draft affidavits, written

statements made under oath, which had incorrectly sworn the number of meetings she had held with Ms A. If either of the drafts had been formalised, signed and lodged, it would have potentially opened Salmond's investigating officer to a perjury charge. The failure to disclose the whole truth in the document was 'frankly, alarming', the lawyers said.

It was also disclosed to the legal team that Mackinnon had made arrangements to meet Ms B before she had made her complaint. The lawyers said this was done before Mackinnon 'could have had any legitimate interest in speaking to Ms B'.

In a withering note explaining the situation on 19 December, the legal team said their 'dismay at this case deepens yet further' and that they had 'each experienced extreme professional embarrassment as a result of assurances which we have given ... turning out to be false as a result of the revelation of further documents, highly relevant yet undisclosed'.

When she gave evidence under oath to the Holyrood inquiry into the government's mishandling of the allegations, Sturgeon said that note was 'catastrophic and it was what led to the ultimate concession'. The government actually continued the case into the New Year, although senior figures insist moves were being made to collapse proceedings as quickly as possible.

*　*　*

It was not long before reality crashed home elsewhere in the government. Further forensic searches of computer records, emails and other documents were about to begin in St Andrew's House, this time on the instruction of the Lord Advocate. Pale faces avoided each other's eyes in a crisis summit called to demand the information be provided following another devastating day in court on 21 December.

Evans was in the room alongside the most senior officials with any involvement in the investigation of Salmond. A decision had already been taken not to use email to inform anyone of what was being discussed because of the sensitivity of the topic.

Dunlop had suffered hours of embarrassment during the second behind-closed-doors commission hearing and almost immediately expressed his fury to Wolffe. It had transpired in the most embarrassing way possible that even more material had not been provided to the court. Giving evidence under oath during the private session, Donald Cameron, Evans's principal private secretary, swore there were no more documents to be turned over. At that point he was informed by Salmond's legal team that while he was on the stand, the Scottish government had in fact emailed more evidence. This prompted Dunlop to set out his feelings in no uncertain terms. The Lord Advocate responded by ordering the searches to be carried out.

Civil servants, some of whom had only had a passing involvement in the case against Salmond, were told they had an extremely tight timescale to produce all the relevant documents. 'That was one of the most heart-stopping meetings I've ever been in,' says one person present left horrified by the government's shambolic response. 'We were really shocked and angry because there was nothing warming us up to this.'

Around the time of that second hearing, Wolffe asked Dunlop 'to provide a list of work that would require to be undertaken if the case was to be progressed'. But as documents flooded into the court following the session and subsequent crisis meeting, O'Neill highlighted 'new information over the last twenty-four hours' that caused further damage to the case. This included Mackinnon being privy to more information about Ms B's complaints than had previously been disclosed and having met Ms A 'immediately' before she lodged her complaint. In what Dunlop described in an email sent on the evening of 21 December as a 'watershed moment where the case moved from very difficult to unstateable', Mackinnon told the commission that she could not remember the meeting. This left her 'unable to rebut the rather obvious inferences that will otherwise be drawn from the fact that it occurred', the lawyer told the government.

The hearings had been excruciating for Dunlop. After informing the court that not all the documents had arrived, he gave a mea culpa on behalf of ministers, saying: 'It is entirely regrettable and I can only apologise to the commissioner and ultimately to the court for the piecemeal nature of what is happening and, frankly, I am personally horrified of [sic] the way this is unfolding but I can only make available what is available.'

As he revealed the Scottish government had set a deadline of 7 January – the day before the judicial review hearings were due to formally begin – for providing all the documents, Dunlop admitted eight times that his client's behaviour was either regrettable or unacceptable.

Ronnie Clancy, who was acting as Salmond's QC, was personally kind towards Dunlop but professionally merciless. 'As of last Friday, when the matter was before Lord Pentland, the respondents were willing to certify that the procedure had been exhausted and that all documents had been found and we now know that in all sorts of ways that was simply not accurate,' he told the court.

It was during these hearings that Dunlop revealed the Lord Advocate's instruction that the Permanent Secretary's offices and emails be searched.

Dunlop signed off his withering email to the Scottish government on 21 December with an ironic note: 'I wish you all a merry festive season.'

Many of the tight group of government staff involved in the process worked through the holidays gathering documents. One says it was 'the worst Christmas/New Year ever experienced when the signs started to come through very clearly that any attempt by us to try and win the judicial review was quite frankly deluded'.

Just a few days after Santa's annual visit, a bombshell dropped that gave Salmond the best present he could have hoped for. On 28 December, the date of the third commission hearing, O'Neill wrote to the Scottish government on behalf of herself and Dunlop threatening to quit if the case was not dropped by 3 January.

It was on that deadline day that the government privately told Salmond's lawyers they would be conceding the case. One ally says Salmond was 'the most animated I had heard him' as he absorbed his impending victory, but there was little time for resting.

The Court of Session hearing was set for 10 a.m. on 8 January, a crisp, cold and sunny winter's day in Edinburgh. As he crossed the cobbles outside the court and emptied his pockets to pass through an airport-style security scanner, Salmond was visibly upbeat. In a room in the basement of the court, he, Clancy, McKie and Campbell Gunn, his spokesman, ran through the procedure and the plan for what would happen after the judgment. They then listened as Lord Pentland declared the actions of officials investigating the harassment complaints were 'unlawful in respect that they were procedurally unfair' and had been 'tainted by apparent bias'. A smiling Salmond then shook hands with his lawyers. The ruling effectively meant that the findings against the former First Minister were null and void, although the Scottish government was free to re-examine the complaints.

Salmond moved outside, strolling from within the quadrangle where the entrance of the court is contained out to the front of St Giles' Cathedral. A semi-circle of media had been vaguely arranged, but it quickly enveloped him as a full scrum. He was flanked, to the surprise of some, not only by Kenny MacAskill, the former Justice Secretary, who had increasingly become a critic of the SNP's leadership under Sturgeon, but also Tricia Marwick, Holyrood's first female Presiding Officer, who was not known for a close relationship with Salmond.

After making his statement, Salmond took questions, which quickly turned to the continuing police investigation. He was asked, not for the first or the last time, if he was entirely innocent of sexual misconduct. Salmond replied: 'I'm certainly not guilty of any criminality. I've never said, incidentally, that I'm an angel.'

Warming to another theme he would return to over the coming years, Salmond urged Sturgeon to concentrate on securing independence when he was asked about her involvement in the case.

After the official statement and question-and-answer session had finished, Gunn retreated to a quiet area with a small group of journalists. Two days previously, Salmond had emailed him a list of key themes he wanted hammered home, titled 'Briefing Points for Campbell'. The first point was to 'reflect on the enormity of what has just happened', while there was also a desire to focus on 'huge volumes of material [being] extracted like teeth under oath from Scottish Government officials' and the accurate prediction that there would be a high six-figure cost to the taxpayer. In a sign of the arguments that he would deploy in the years to follow, the note states that documents disclosed in the Commission and Diligence 'showed that complaints had been canvassed'.

He was also keen to point out that the government had conceded the case after Salmond's lawyers had asked that Lloyd and John Somers, the First Minister's principal private secretary, give evidence to the judicial review. This focused more on Somers than Lloyd, with the suspicion from Salmond that the government was not willing to have the senior civil servant questioned under oath about his meetings with Ms A. 'What Alex I think was suggesting was that John Somers doesn't interview people and if he was setting up a meeting it was for Nicola,' Gunn says now. 'So I think he probably thought that John Somers had organised a meeting with Ms A for Nicola, which turned out not to be the case. But at the time Alex was convinced that they collapsed the case because they didn't want John Somers and Liz Lloyd giving evidence.'

When Somers appeared under oath at the Holyrood inquiry, he said he met Ms A on 20 November 2017 because she wanted to raise concerns about her experience. It was agreed the following day that she would meet Barbara Allison, who was the government's director of people at the time. Somers said he never heard from Ms A again and did not share any of the information with anyone else until he disclosed the meetings as part of the judicial review.

Government diaries show that Somers met Lloyd and Cameron for a meeting titled 'catch-up' the next evening, having held a second meeting with Ms A earlier that day. He told the committee that he could 'definitively and categorically say that I made no reference to the meetings with Ms A, at that meeting, or to anyone other than my line manager'.

Salmond's main focus immediately after the civil court victory was Evans. He called for her to resign in his press statement, saying: 'On a day of abject humiliation for the Scottish government that seems to me like a correct and proper response.' A handwritten note at the bottom of the printed-off briefing document shows Gunn recording that Salmond wanted the Permanent Secretary's words 'the procedure I introduced' repeated to the press.

At Holyrood, Sturgeon was unwilling to give any ground and was firm in her backing of Evans. The motivation behind that public show of support – and the decision to not only stick by the Permanent Secretary but later extend her contract after the costs for the failed case spiralled to more than £600,000 in external legal fees alone – has been the subject of much angry speculation within parts of the civil service.

'It was the Scottish government, the Permanent Secretary – yes, at the behest of Nicola Sturgeon, but the Permanent Secretary – who was extremely exposed,' says one figure.

> That's why when Alex Salmond came out, he said he was going after [Evans] right from the get-go. I'm still absolutely gob-smacked, but clearly she dug her heels in and has been either protected because there's a particular rapport between her and Nicola Sturgeon – there's not – or kept in place as fodder, in the event of push coming to shove and someone having to go.

There was a 'big panic' amongst Sturgeon's aides after the outcome of the case. Some officials were concerned that what was seen as a 'major wobble' could have led to the First Minister – who even some of her supporters conceded was 'looking like shit' – quitting.

'Nicola took it pretty bad,' says a close ally.

> I don't think she was ever seriously considering resigning, but I think she thought it all had the potential to lead down that path. The government had screwed it up, she was going to have to be the one to take responsibility for it and knowing Alex, as she did, he would not stop there – so there was definitely a bit of trepidation about what was going to come next.

In an effort to rally the troops, Deputy First Minister John Swinney, an almost universally respected figure in the SNP group at Holyrood, addressed the weekly meeting of MSPs. Behind the glass fronted door just off the Scottish Parliament's 'black and white corridor' that allows access to the debating chamber, Swinney urged those assembled to focus on domestic policy issues rather than the internal party soap opera that was coming to life.

That afternoon, Sturgeon gave a statement to the Parliament

about the outcome of the case, which she said 'has no implications one way or another on the substance of the complaints or on the credibility of the complainants'. She added:

> It is deeply regrettable, perhaps that is an understatement, that because of a failure in the application of one aspect of the procedure, the Scottish government has had to settle this matter today. This morning, the Permanent Secretary apologised to all involved. In echoing that, I want also to express my regret – in particular, about the difficult position in which the complainants have been placed. I know that the Permanent Secretary has spoken directly to both women. I can only imagine how difficult the decision to raise concerns, as well as the publicity around the investigation and the judicial review, must have been for them in recent months. They had every right to expect the process to be robust and beyond reproach in every aspect, and for it to reach a lasting conclusion. I am sorry that, on this occasion, that has not been the case.

Sturgeon also publicly confirmed for the first time that she had met Salmond three times and held two telephone conversations with him about the Scottish government's investigation. In response to a question by Jackson Carlaw, then Scottish Conservative leader, Sturgeon said that she 'was informed of the investigation by Alex Salmond' at the first meeting on 2 April 2018. She argued that no record of the conversations needed to be taken because they took place in her capacity as SNP leader rather than First Minister, despite the fact that they were discussing the investigation of the former First Minister under her government's new policy.

On hearing this, Salmond and his allies bristled, because they were aware of the 29 March meeting involving Geoff Aberdein, Salmond's former chief of staff, in Sturgeon's parliamentary office.

They did not allow it to dampen their spirits. On 10 January, Salmond gathered those closest to the case – Clancy, McKie, Callum Anderson and Gunn – for a celebratory meal at the Inter-Continental Edinburgh the George hotel, still almost universally known by its former name, the George.

Salmond's allies were simultaneously taking action within the SNP. At a meeting of the party's National Executive Committee on 12 January, Joanna Cherry, a QC, MP and at the time the party's justice spokeswoman at Westminster, cited the judicial review and raised concerns 'that complaints processes are not robust enough', according to a minute of the meeting. Kirsten Oswald, the SNP's chair and business convener and a Sturgeon loyalist, shut down the discussion, saying that the 'NEC had no jurisdiction over a Scottish government matter and cautioned members against raising matters that could not possibly be progressed by discussion at the meeting'. The exchanges became increasingly heated as the gathering turned into 'a tears and snotters affair', according to those present. 'Jo raised the issue, Nicola wasn't at that meeting, of course, and there was a complete attempt to shut that down,' says a Salmond ally who was in attendance.

> In hindsight I think it is ironic that Kirsten Oswald has tried to shut it down saying it was not a matter for the party, this is a matter for the Scottish government. Fast forward a year and there is the argument that this isn't a Scottish government matter, this was a party matter. It seemed that those in government weren't allowed to talk about it because it was a matter for the party and those in the party weren't allowed to talk about it because it was a matter for the government.

Sturgeon also came under considerable pressure at Holyrood over what she knew and when, as further details began to emerge about her contact with Salmond. This culminated in her referring herself to the independent adviser on the ministerial code, Ireland's former Director of Public Prosecutions James Hamilton, who can investigate whether senior politicians in government have broken the rules. This would be the first and so far only investigation for Hamilton, who was appointed by Salmond late into his term and reappointed by Sturgeon in 2015.

Despite Salmond's initial joy at the result in the civil case, there was trouble coming down the line and it had almost overtaken the court victory. Sitting before the Holyrood inquiry in February 2021, Salmond set out his view that senior civil servants hoped 'that the police investigation would come to the rescue' once it became clear he was going to win the judicial review. He told MSPs 'that was very, very close to happening' without revealing exactly how fine the margins were.

On Boxing Day 2018, while government officials were watching their case collapse, a senior officer from Police Scotland telephoned McKie to ask that Salmond come in for an interview. The date offered was 8 January 2019.

The unwelcome Christmas present was swiftly rejected as McKie urged the detective to consider how it would look if Salmond was questioned on the day he was due to appear for his civil case against the Scottish government.

Instead, a date was booked for 23 January at Dalkeith Police Station. The scale and severity of the criminal charges facing Salmond would shock all of Scotland.

CHAPTER 11

OPERATION DIEM

24 JANUARY 2019, 3.01 P.M.

Standing shivering outside Edinburgh Sheriff Court, journalists gaped in disbelief at their phones. An email had arrived from the Crown Office, Scotland's prosecution service, containing arguably the most dramatic charge sheet in Scottish legal history.

Case reference – ED19001446.

Full name – Alexander Elliot Anderson Salmond.

DOB – 31/12/1954.

General Address – Aberdeenshire.

Charges:

i) Breach of the Peace

ii) Indecent Assault

iii) Sexual Offences (Scotland) Act 2009 S3 (Sexual Assault)

iv) Indecent Assault

v) Sexual Offences (Scotland) Act 2009 S3 (Sexual Assault)

vi) Sexual Offences (Scotland) Act 2009 S3 (Sexual Assault)

vii) Sexual Offences (Scotland) Act 2009 S3 (Sexual Assault)

viii) Sexual Offences (Scotland) Act 2009 S3 (Sexual Assault)

ix) Sexual Offences (Scotland) Act 2009 S3 (Sexual Assault)

x) Sexual Offences (Scotland) Act 2009 S1 (Attempted Rape)

xi) Sexual Offences (Scotland) Act 2009 S3 (Sexual Assault)

xii) Sexual Offences (Scotland) Act 2009 S1 (Attempted Rape)

xiii) Sexual Offences (Scotland) Act 2009 S3 (Sexual Assault)

xiv) Sexual Offences (Scotland) Act 2009 S3 (Sexual Assault).

Plea – No plea.

Outcome – Continued for further examination and released on bail.

Next appearance – TBC.

By this point, those same reporters had already jostled for position with television cameras and photographers against waist-high metal crash barriers to hear Alex Salmond make a statement denying any criminality. Those trying to question him had not known the number or nature of the charges despite the fact that he had appeared in court almost an hour earlier.

The journalists' shock on reading the charge sheet had been exacerbated by Salmond's defiant public demeanour in the previous days. He had been on a high when hosting the celebration dinner with his victorious legal team from the civil court case. A week later, he had convened his solicitors from Levy & McRae at the firm's Glasgow offices. The agenda was to discuss what could be said legally in comments to the press and how to address any questions that would be put to him in the period before his scheduled police interview. At this point Salmond had no idea of the scope of the criminal investigation, nor whether he was going for a preliminary interview or to be formally charged.

At 7 p.m. on 22 January, Salmond held a meeting with lawyer Callum Anderson and press adviser Campbell Gunn at the George. He was being interviewed by detectives the following day and wanted to go over the case in preparation for the interrogation. Those present said that although Salmond 'always took the issues seriously', he did not seem panicked or 'overly nervous' about the interview during the brief meeting, which was conducted without refreshments.

On 23 January, Anderson drove Salmond eight miles down the A7 from central Edinburgh to Dalkeith Police Station, a brown building that serves as a monument to 1960s brutalist architecture. The situation that emerged during the course of the interview was much more severe than Salmond or his legal team had imagined. Detectives formally arrested and charged him with twenty-one offences, including two counts of attempted rape. In a hammer blow for Salmond, many of the complainers were women he had worked closely with and considered friends and allies.

The seriousness and sheer number of the charges floored the former First Minister and his legal team. One of the attempted rape charges was the 2013 Bute House incident, although it would be downgraded to sexual assault with intent to rape by the time of the trial. The other was made by a former government official who had worked closely with Salmond for years and claimed he had tried to force her to have sex with him, again in Bute House, in June 2014. It was during the police interview that he discovered that this woman – and others who had worked closely with him – had made extremely serious allegations against him.

In the tried and tested tactics of Scottish criminal prosecution, all possible allegations had been put to him in the first instance; only fourteen would survive the night and be led in court the following day.

It can now be revealed that Salmond had originally faced charges related to the Edinburgh Airport incident which first sparked rumours about his conduct, but they were dropped before trial. These included two allegations of breach of the peace involving sexualised communications and a single charge of indecent assault on the airport campus. All were said to have taken place at an 'unknown' point in 2007.

The original charge sheet also included an allegation of 'culpable and reckless conduct' which named a Scottish government driver as the complainant. Salmond had no idea what was being referred to and had to be told it was a story widely shared amongst his team of special advisers. It related to a bottle of sparkling water being handed to the then First Minister by his spokesman Ross Inge-brigtsen in a ministerial car. Upon opening, the bottle promptly exploded, soaking everyone in the vehicle. Another accusation that was later dropped was that of physical assault against the SNP's chief operating officer Sue Ruddick during campaigning for the 2008 Glenrothes by-election.

Police agreed to release Salmond on the condition that he presented himself to the court at 2 p.m. the following day. He returned to the George and arranged a pre-appearance crisis gathering of his advisers. The meeting was scheduled for noon on 24 January, but all hell broke loose at 9.03 a.m. when Colin Mackay, STV's political editor, tweeted: 'Former First Minister @AlexSalmond was arrested by Police Scotland and is expected to appear in court this afternoon.'

The Scottish press pack was well aware of Salmond's favoured hotel and a scrum of photographers duly descended on George Street, making life difficult for those due to attend the emergency meeting. In a scene reminiscent of a spy novel, Gunn was told to wait at noon in a basement cafe on nearby Hanover Street, where he would be met by a member of staff. From there, he was escorted along a small lane which runs to the back of the hotel and into the building via its kitchen, then up to Salmond's room, where he was drinking coffee with Joanna Cherry, the SNP MP and QC.

Cherry left relatively quickly and over sandwiches and coffee Salmond, Gunn and Anderson discussed what would happen during the appearance and how to coordinate the media. This included drawing up a statement which they asked hotel staff to print out multiple copies of so it could be handed out to journalists at the court.

The trio left the hotel through the same convoluted route by which Salmond's guests had arrived. A car was waiting for them outside, but the journey still almost turned to farce. The driver was not familiar with Edinburgh's city centre, which can be confusing to navigate, and began to head in the wrong direction before Gunn stepped in. As well as the throng of journalists, who had been outside the sheriff court for around four hours amid increasing rumours about the seriousness of the charges, they were greeted by well-wishers who cheered Salmond's arrival. A crowd of about 100 had gathered, including curious tourists who had wandered over the road from the National Museum of Scotland to watch the spectacle. Salmond shook hands with a supporter who had arrived with his three terriers clad in saltire-patterned dog jackets. Another, Dave Llewellyn, who streamed footage of Salmond's arrival to a pro-independence website, said that he had come to court 'to support Alex against the weight of the British state'. He blamed the arrest on Theresa May, then Prime Minister.

Seven police officers in high-vis jackets cleared the path for Salmond, Anderson and Gunn as they walked the barrier-lined route from the car to the court entrance, and less than half an hour later Salmond, with Anderson representing him, appeared in a private hearing in Court Two. It lasted under five minutes, with two police officers posted outside the door to ward away any would-be observers. Sheriff Frank Crowe put the fourteen charges that had survived the night to Salmond, who made no plea or declaration, as is common in such cases.

Salmond returned to a jury room set aside for his team before stepping away to phone Moira, his wife, in his first act after the hearing.

The written statements were handed out to journalists and then Salmond, wearing a long dark overcoat, a light blue shirt and a tie emblazoned with saltires, announced that he had 'great faith in the court system of Scotland. I've got recent cause to have great faith in the court system of Scotland. That is where I'll state my case.' He added:

> Now, I am informed that the rules are that your questions and my answers might breach court rules. You know me well enough to know that I'd love to say a great deal more, but I've got to observe the rules of the court and it's in court where I will state my case.

Salmond then returned to the court building, where he consulted his legal team, before the waiting car took him, Anderson and Gunn back to the George. Client and lawyer held a debrief session while the media adviser left for Glasgow. He told Salmond in the days that followed that he would not work for him again during the criminal case.

Gunn says that while Salmond never appeared rattled during the court appearance he was less certain of his ground than he had been during the civil proceedings:

> Obviously he was now taking this very seriously indeed because now he was on the back foot whereas the entire time of the judicial review he had been on the front foot because he knew he was right and he had the bits of legal evidence he was going to propose.

Salmond was not the only one caught off-guard by the scale of the charges he was facing. Nicola Sturgeon first learned that her former mentor had been arrested when she read Mackay's tweet in her office on the fourth floor of the Scottish Parliament. The First Minister walked out and silently held her mobile phone out to an aide to show them the news. 'She was genuinely, as we all were, taken aback,' the civil servant recalls. 'Just like, God, what the hell is going on? It came as a shock to Nicola. It came as a shock to all of us.'

The fourth floor of Holyrood's ministerial tower is dominated by a large open-plan office with banks of tables for special advisers and senior civil servants. It was here that many government aides discovered the full extent of the allegations from news broadcasts on a large TV screen in the corner of the room. The mouths of those in attendance hit the floor as broadcaster James Matthews read out the charges one by one live on Sky News.

A number of those present had worked for the SNP both in and out of power before gaining jobs in government, while some of the officials had served in senior positions under both Salmond and Sturgeon. The news stopped all of them in their tracks, with the situation made all the more disturbing by the fact that the dates accompanying the charges all related to Salmond's time in office. 'It was almost like something from a movie: you can imagine that office scene where people are standing around gawping at the screen,' says one person present. 'Many of us worked for Alex for a number of years. And you're thinking, "This is unbelievable, this is awful, horrible." It was of a magnitude of something that you never expected, you'd never experienced before in the job.'

Deputy First Minister John Swinney had been chairing a Brexit meeting alongside Constitution Secretary Mike Russell in St Andrew's House when the news came through. As various policymakers and other attendees filtered out of the conference room, Swinney noticed that Russell was looking distractedly at his phone. When it was passed to the Deputy First Minister, he struggled to process the words in front of him, such was the scale of what was being revealed. Both men had known and worked closely alongside Salmond for decades and the charges had come like a bolt from the blue.

The atmosphere also dramatically altered elsewhere in the

building as news of the charges emerged. Senior civil servants who had been closely involved in the judicial review were said to look more relaxed than they had done for weeks. 'I've never experienced how things could go from tragedy to vindication and celebration in such a short period of time because that really was how it felt,' says a government source sympathetic to Salmond.

It is certainly true that senior figures in government had felt hemmed in during the sixteen days between the former First Minister winning his civil case and being criminally charged. They felt they had been dealing with what one official calls 'the full Salmond fury unleashed, uninhibited, unshackled by any legal constraints'.

The previous two weeks had seen numerous attacks from the Salmond camp on those closest to Sturgeon, although rarely with the First Minister herself the direct target. They ranged from politically serious issues such as how the March and April meetings about the harassment investigation were arranged to the bizarre, including claims that Salmond had been 'airbrushed' out of the SNP's website. Responding to the revelation that it now had fewer than a dozen mentions of his name, he told the *Scottish Sun*: 'Nicola should stop rewriting history and concentrate on making history by taking Scotland to independence.'

After Sturgeon's camp accused Salmond of launching a smear campaign against her and her allies, including her husband, SNP chief executive Peter Murrell, and chief of staff Liz Lloyd, he moved to publicly draw a line under the feud. In an interview published three days before his scheduled meeting with Police Scotland, he told the pro-independence *Sunday National*: 'It takes two to tango and I'm just not playing this game. I have told my team that we are not getting involved. This "uncivil war" stops now.'

* * *

The process that would eventually lead to Salmond being charged had been put in train six months earlier. Although no official decision had yet been made by the Scottish government about the claims against him, Judith Mackinnon, the investigating officer for the civil service, contacted Ms A and Ms B on 1 August 2018 to ask whether they would cooperate in a police investigation if officials referred their cases to detectives.

Both women raised concerns over the weeks that followed about the implications for their anonymity of this course of action.

Ms A told Mackinnon she was torn about suggestions the police should investigate and raised concerns about the impact and fallout of such a case. 'There is a part of me that feels if law enforcement agencies are of the view that something should be pursued as a criminal case then that is what should happen (and indeed that a decision on how it's handled isn't for me to take),' she said.

'However, my motivation in reporting this has never been to seek criminal consequences, and as things currently stand I don't feel comfortable committing to a process that would culminate in me – or anyone else – being required to "face off" against FFM in court.'

Ms B was stronger in her response, saying she felt her identity had been protected by the government's process. She added: 'However, if the police were to become involved, I would no longer be afforded this level of anonymity – particularly if this went to court. I feel that to me, the risk of police involvement outweighs what could be achieved.'

Nevertheless, Permanent Secretary Leslie Evans set the ball rolling just four days after being told of the complainers' fears about a criminal investigation. On 17 August, she spoke to David Harvie, who as the Crown Agent is the third most senior figure in Scotland's prosecution service, about the case. Harvie, who first came to prominence due to his involvement in the Lockerbie bombing trial, would later become a lightning rod for Salmond's anger at how the Crown handled the case. A note in Harvie's biography that he was 'seconded to the Foreign and Commonwealth Office' between 2001 and 2004 is taken by the former First Minister's allies as a euphemism for him working as a spy for Britain's security services.

The Permanent Secretary and Crown Agent spoke again on 19 August and 20 August, when Evans sent Harvie information relating to the complaints before getting a hard copy of the government material to him the following day. Wasting no time, Harvie met Police Scotland's Chief Constable Iain Livingstone and Detective Chief Superintendent Lesley Boal, who went on to lead the criminal investigation, on 21 August, the same day he received the now completed report. His attempt to hand over a copy of the material was swiftly rejected by the senior officers, who also raised concerns about the government's plans at that time to make the findings public given they were now being handed over for an investigation of potential criminality. 'Harvie was in possession of a copy of the Scottish government's internal conduct conclusion report and offered to provide [me] with a copy,' Boal said in a witness statement released to the Holyrood inquiry. 'I refused this offer and neither I nor the chief constable viewed this document.'

Civil servants had already been warned about trying to play detective during the government probe. Fiona Taylor, the deputy chief constable of Police Scotland, said in a written statement to the Holyrood inquiry that officials had been reminded they were not trained to investigate potentially criminal conduct or engage with complainers. The discussions had taken place in relation to the drafting of the new harassment policy, but she said it became clear the civil servants were asking about a 'specific set of circumstances' rather than general procedure when they asked about how to involve the police.

Taylor said police advised at a meeting on 6 December 2017 'that where criminality was suspected, individuals should be directed to support and advocacy services' so they could make informed decisions about whether or not to take their issues further.

Despite the previous chiding, there was agreement at the meeting between Livingstone, Boal and Harvie. This included the need for a 'proactive approach' to identify other potential complainers against Salmond, including by contacting people in similar roles to the women who had already come forward.

This attitude would infuriate supporters of the former First Minister, who believe the size of the operation was disproportionate to the allegations. 'The scale of the team was absurd,' said one Salmond ally.

Codenamed Operation Diem, the tight-knit investigation team initially comprising seven officers was launched in the days following the meeting with Harvie. Based out of Fettes, which was Police Scotland's Edinburgh headquarters, the unit would double in size by February 2019, the month after Salmond first appeared in court, before dwindling to a group of five by September. Only three officers were attached to it by the time of the trial. At a total cost of £834,000 – including £24,000 spent on 'non-staff costs' – detectives would take 386 witness statements over the course of the nineteen-month investigation. These included regular visits to St Andrew's House to speak with any officials who had worked closely with Salmond. Interviews were arranged in advance, but this did not stop the staff involved 'shitting themselves' in the words of one witness as they waited for the building's reception desk to call and tell them that detectives had arrived and wanted to speak to them.

Those being questioned were given the option of going to Fettes, but most chose to book out private rooms in St Andrew's House to speak to the plain-clothes officers. A similar approach was taken with witnesses from outside the government, with detectives driving to people's homes if they did not want to attend the police station.

In often multiple sessions, each of which lasted around two hours, officers would note responses in long-hand, with one writing and the other leading the questioning before they swapped roles to give weary hands a break. At the end of each discussion the interviewee had to decipher the officers' handwriting then sign the bottom of the notes to confirm it was an accurate representation of what was said.

In some cases, rumours and apocryphal stories ended up being probed as if they were fact. An official who had worked as a senior press officer for Salmond but is now employed in another part of the civil service was asked during his interview about a fist fight he had apparently had with the former First Minister in the basement of St Andrew's House. It turned out he had in fact only told colleagues that he briefly fantasised about punching Salmond after one particularly vociferous and lengthy tirade of abuse over the rejection of an interview on BBC News 24. No violence had ensued despite the fleeting thought crossing the official's mind while Salmond was taking part in a hastily arranged piece for radio in the broadcast suite, which is in the bowels of the government's headquarters.

The investigation of Salmond came with a lot of political pressure and while this may have been on a different level, Police Scotland had grown used to being placed under intense scrutiny by elected officials since its inception in 2013. The merging of the country's eight regional forces had caused controversy in itself, which resulted in a greater spotlight being shone on early problems. These included bad press about armed officers responding to routine calls with their guns visible and high levels of stop and search. But both of those controversies paled into insignificance when compared to the deaths of two people by the side of the M9 near Stirling in

July 2015. John Yuill, twenty-eight, and his partner Lamara Bell, twenty-five, were left trapped in their car by the roadside for three days despite a call being made to Police Scotland. Yuill died at the scene of the crash and although Bell was transferred to hospital, she did not survive. At the time of writing, legal action was expected against Police Scotland over the case.

Sir Stephen House was the first chief constable of the new single force and as such bore the brunt of the criticism for the scandals, which quickly dwarfed the credit he had received at the start of his tenure for transforming Scotland's approach to tackling domestic abuse and a large fall in knife crime. He apologised for the M9 deaths and was publicly backed by Sturgeon, but in private the situation was markedly different. At a meeting in the First Minister's office at Holyrood in August 2015, House was effectively dismissed despite the employment of police officers, even those at the top of the force, not being a matter for politicians as part of efforts to maintain operational independence. Noel Dolan, who at the time was Sturgeon's closest adviser, says:

> Stephen House essentially was sacked. He resigned but he essentially was sacked for a pretty poor reason. The main thing was the two people who died on the M9. Stephen House was held responsible for the behaviour of some junior call centre respondent because the police in central regional had fucked it up. So there was a lot of pressure on him.

Sources close to House say he 'burns with hate towards Nicola' because his time in Scotland ended in such ignominy. In February 2018, House was appointed as an assistant commissioner to the Metropolitan Police before being promoted to deputy commissioner seven months later. 'He hasn't forgiven or forgotten what happened and he is now deputy chief of the Met,' Dolan adds. 'He will rue the day that he ever had anything to do with Scotland or the SNP.'

*   *   *

This was not the press release the Scottish government had envisaged sending out about Alex Salmond.

'We can confirm that final settlement of £512,250 has been made to Mr Salmond for legal costs arising from his petition for judicial review.'

The pay-out, which covered 87 per cent of Salmond's legal fees, was made on the punitive 'agent and client' basis because of the shambolic way the government had handled the civil case.

There had been bitter negotiations between the former First Minister's lawyers and the government over the size of the pay-out until officials finally conceded in August 2019. A further £118,523 was spent on external legal fees, taking the public purse's total bill to at least £630,773 for the court battle against Salmond.

Despite the outlay and humiliation, there were few signs of many lessons being learned in St Andrew's House.

By September, in an extraordinary move, the Crown Office had served a warrant on the Scottish government in a bid to obtain documents as part of the criminal case after an initial request for material in June. Civil servants say the warrant was requested and 'agreed with the Crown', but prosecutors were less certain of the situation.

On 21 November, the day of Salmond's first preliminary hearing, a court date used to make sure that the defence and the prosecution are ready for the case to go to trial, principal procurator fiscal depute Liz Ramsey sent a letter asking for confirmation if it was 'now the Scottish Government's position that it is not required to comply with the warrant'. She was pushing officials after 'considerable latitude' had already been given to turning over documents and now raised the prospect of detectives combing St Andrew's House. The letter added:

> If the Scottish Government's position is that it would now wish Police Scotland to seize and independently search all material held by Scottish Government potentially covered by the terms of the warrant (extraordinary though that may seem), then I would be grateful if the Scottish Government make clear that is the position.

When the letter was made public four months later, the government said it had undertaken 'a rigorous process to ensure compliance with the warrant and the transfer of all relevant documents to the police. The warrant process included oversight by an independent commissioner, appointed by the court.'

A small unit of civil servants who had not previously had involvement with any aspect of the Salmond investigations was indeed set up inside St Andrew's House and tasked with sifting information for the criminal case. Details were kept extremely tight, with multiple sources sympathetic to each of Sturgeon and Salmond describing the set-up as 'Chinese walls' – where a barrier is created to prevent information being shared that could lead to conflicts of interest. The team had its own secure room with an encrypted filing system, with external lawyers brought in for advice because Sturgeon's team had lost trust in the Scottish government's legal department after the judicial review. The same software used by the Serious Fraud Office to carry out forensic audits was bought to comb the Scottish government's systems as around 250 million emails, files and electronic calendar entries were searched. 'Come hell or high water, we were not going to mess this up in the way that happened with the judicial review,' says one official.

At its largest, the unit comprised eight people and was headed by a Scottish government director. The work was gruelling and rolled over to carry out the same job during the Holyrood inquiry. Multiple members of the team suffered health problems. It will never be known how much the stress of the job contributed to this, but there is no doubting the intense burden on the team.

'The timings of the deadlines for this information were just incredibly demanding,' says a government source. 'The people in that unit were under such pressure to try and turn around that work. They were decent people put in a very difficult position to try and fulfil the parameters of the request.'

Salmond would later claim under oath during his committee appearance that the government failed to hand over about forty documents to the criminal case which subsequently surfaced in the course of the Holyrood inquiry.

Following the warning letter from the Crown, a memory stick was handed initially to prosecutors and then to Salmond's lawyers at the first preliminary hearing. Its contents – an array of text, WhatsApp and other messages – would further fuel his claims there was a 'plot' against him. He would manage to have some led as evidence during the criminal hearings but, despite repeated attempts, has not been able to make the full cache public because of legal restrictions.

The November court date was also where the full indictment against Salmond was revealed for the first time. The details of the charges – particularly of an attempted rape at Bute House where he was accused of removing a woman's clothes, pinning her against a wall and pushing her on to a bed before lying naked on top of her and trying to rape her – further horrified the Scottish public. He would ultimately be acquitted of all charges.

Salmond arrived at Edinburgh High Court more than ninety minutes early for the 10 a.m. hearing, after which, flanked by his sister Gail Hendry and other supporters, he stopped to address the press. He said:

> I am innocent and I will defend my position vigorously but the only place, the only proper place, to answer criminal charges is in this court, and that is what we intend to do.
>
> As you'll understand, I am not permitted to say too much save that we have lodged our defence statement with the court. It pleads not guilty to all charges and explains some of the circumstances in which they have come about. I am conscious we are in the middle of a general election. I'm not going to say anything that would influence that democratic process.

Sturgeon's decision to back the snap 2019 general election was not uncontroversial within the SNP. Murmurs of discontent about the possibility of the nationalists losing the influence they then enjoyed in the hung parliament quickly broke out into the open.

Angus MacNeil, the MP for Na h-Eileanan an Iar and a Salmond ally, told *The National* the move was a gift to Prime Minister Boris Johnson. He also condemned the SNP leadership's push for a second referendum on Britain's membership of the EU, which he said came at the expense of a focus on independence. Salmond's later analysis would echo MacNeil's criticism.

The Scottish campaign for election to the UK Parliament largely focused on a mixture of the constitution and attempts by opposition parties to home in on domestic issues reserved to Holyrood. Despite polls showing falling faith in the SNP's stewardship of Scotland's public services, the First Minister's popularity was increasing as Sturgeon's personal rating, which had sunk dramatically compared to her early days in office to become decidedly mixed since mid-2017, rose into positive territory in the days before the election.

When the result came through – complete with MacNeil's predicted Conservative majority that allowed Johnson to 'get Brexit done' – it was another resounding victory for the SNP north of the border. The nationalists picked up many of the seats they had lost two and a half years previously to return forty-eight MPs with 45 per cent of the vote.

Predictably, the Prime Minister ignored the First Minister's renewed demands for another independence referendum as each waved competing democratic mandates at the other. Privately, some in Whitehall believed Salmond's upcoming criminal case could prove politically bruising for Sturgeon, particularly when combined with a growing unhappiness with the SNP's domestic record, and allow Downing Street to play a waiting game on the constitution.

Little did they know an unprecedented crisis was about to change everything. On 31 December, as Alex Salmond celebrated his birthday with his mind on the upcoming legal proceedings, a cluster of cases of pneumonia was reported in Wuhan, Hubei Province, China.

The year had started with everyone in Scotland expecting the Salmond verdict to be the biggest story in decades; as it turned out, it wasn't even the biggest story of the day.

The most eagerly anticipated trial in Scottish legal history would be overshadowed by a public health crisis that changed the lives of everyone on the planet.

CHAPTER 12

SALMOND ON TRIAL

23 MARCH 2020, 2.55 P.M.

Nicola Sturgeon leaned down and scooped the distraught Scottish government official into her arms. The woman had been a complainer in the case against Alex Salmond and had collapsed sobbing on the floor of an empty office in St Andrew's House after hearing that he had been acquitted of thirteen counts of sexual assault. Sturgeon had only recently learned of the woman's involvement in the case and had been blindsided. She walked into the room, picked her up and immediately began hugging and consoling her.

Just a few moments earlier, the First Minister had been told the verdict of the eleven-day trial at the High Court in Edinburgh. She was sitting in her mahogany-walled office in the Scottish government's headquarters with her principal private secretary John Somers and special adviser Colin McAllister, who was reading the jury's ruling on each charge as they were live-tweeted by journalists in the court. There was no explosion of emotion, but the mood was sombre. Unlike some in the government, Sturgeon had always been privately measured about the potential outcome of the trial. Every time one of her officials speculated about the prospect of Salmond being found guilty on the back of a single day's headlines or chatter from some present in court, she would remind them of the conviction rates for sexual assaults. In the year running up to Salmond's trial, 43 per cent of prosecutions led to a guilty verdict.

The court case was not the only major event weighing on the First Minister's mind, though. Far less personal but equally traumatic were the projections of the potential Scottish death toll from coronavirus that she was now being briefed on by government experts. The agreed solution was to impose draconian restrictions on citizens unlike any in living memory by going into lockdown in a bid to slow the surge.

Sturgeon moved almost straight from the verdict and its tearful aftermath into a meeting of the emergency Civil Contingencies Committee, known as Cobra, the acronym for the Cabinet Office briefing room where they are generally held. She discussed with Boris Johnson how they would announce the news that citizens were no longer allowed to leave their homes for more than an hour a day.

The staff in St Andrew's House were in a daze after the court verdict, with some civil servants 'stunned into inaction' according to one present, but there was no time to dwell on what was happening elsewhere. A BBC camera crew was quickly called in so that Sturgeon could make a televised address to Scottish viewers immediately after Johnson had spoken to the whole of the UK. The plan was agreed between London and Edinburgh in the hope that, between them, the First Minister and Prime Minister would each speak to the parts of Scotland that the other could not reach because of the public's polarised views on the constitution.

Sturgeon's ability to put the Salmond trial into the back of her mind and focus on the health crisis impressed even long-standing allies. One aide says:

Nicola, like proper political leaders in times of extremis are able to do, had that clarity of thought, purpose and strength to say,

'I'm going to have to deal with a world of shite over the fallout from this trial and I know what's coming at me in the fullness of time but right now the only thing that I need to do – the only thing that I can do – is to focus on Covid and the pandemic and the lockdown announcement that I have to make tonight.'

Salmond also focused his attention on the pandemic as he stood on an eerily quiet Royal Mile and made a statement outside the court following his acquittal. Journalists were crushed up against a rectangular barrier in a manner that would soon become illegal, waiting with anticipation to hear whether he would launch an attack on his successor and her allies at the top of the SNP. Instead, he delivered a carefully controlled two-minute speech that even some of his critics within Sturgeon's administration admitted was 'first ministerial' and showed his ability to capture the public mood at key moments.

Salmond thanked the court system, the jury, his 'exceptional' legal team, his friends and family 'for standing by me over the last two years', and well-wishers who had sent him messages. He hinted at the revenge he was plotting but put it into perspective as he gave the assembled media a light ticking-off for behaving in a manner likely to spread the virus:

As many of you will know, there is certain evidence that I would have liked to have seen led in this trial but for a variety of reasons we were not able to do so. At some point that information, those facts and that evidence will see the light of day. But it won't be this day and it won't be this day for a very good reason. And that is, whatever nightmare I've been in over these last two years, it is as of nothing compared to the nightmare that every single one of us is currently living through. People are dying, many more are going to die. What we are doing just now – and I know you've got a job to do – is not safe. I know it's your job but it ain't safe and my strong, strong advice to you is to go home, those who can, who are able to, take care of your families and God help us all.

After making the sombre speech, Salmond appeared visibly flushed with relief. It had been 747 days since Leslie Evans had written to him to reveal the Scottish government's investigation. The final fourteen had been extraordinary as the highest-profile trial in Scotland's history coincided with the emergence of the largest threat to public health in living memory.

* * *

9 MARCH: DAY 1 OF THE TRIAL; 5 NEW CONFIRMED COVID CASES IN SCOTLAND

Lady Dorrian looked down to her right from her position on the bench of Court Three as she told the jury that whatever they might have read about the 'well-known public figure' sitting opposite her was irrelevant. All that mattered was the evidence that would be presented before them. Four weeks had been set aside for the trial, but it would be truncated to half that time.

Before each of the nine women and six men was finally selected, they were told they should withdraw if they had 'strong feelings in support or in animosity' about the man who had divided the country in two on the constitution five and a half years earlier. All stayed and agreed to reach a 'fair and unbiased' verdict on the fourteen charges facing Salmond, who had lodged special defences of consent to four and one of alibi.

Advocate Depute Alex Prentice QC was low-key in his demeanour, but he opened the prosecution with its most shocking allegations. Standing behind a screen, as each complainer did so they could not see Salmond, a former Scottish government official told the court she had been assaulted twice in Bute House during the independence referendum campaign of 2014. The woman was the first to testify but was publicly described as Woman H because each complainer had been given an alphabetic pseudonym that followed the chronological order of when the crimes were alleged to have been committed.

On the first occasion she claimed to have been assaulted, in May 2014, Woman H said Salmond had invited her to drink shots of a Chinese white wine spirit after they had discussed the day's events following a dinner. She claimed he then tried to 'grope' her and laughed when she protested but she was able to leave.

The following month, she alleged, he tried to rape her following a reception at the First Minister's official residence. Woman H told the court Salmond had blocked her path and tried to grope and kiss her as she attempted to leave. She said he followed her with a bottle of wine in hand to the 'Connery Room' – which the movie star had stayed in during his 2007 visit – but appeared to have calmed down and apologised.

The woman alleged Salmond then 'full-on pounced' and started pulling off her clothes and stripping himself naked. She said: 'I felt like I was being hunted. He was physically all over me, kissing me, just taking my clothes off.'

She claimed Salmond pushed her onto the bed then lay naked on top of her but fell asleep, allowing her to execute an 'escape plan' that involved her shutting herself in a bathroom. As the sun rose, she left the building by the back door, she told the jury.

* * *

10 MARCH: DAY 2 OF THE TRIAL; 4 NEW CONFIRMED COVID CASES IN SCOTLAND
It was not the evidence of the day that had the most significant long-term impact on Salmond or the women who had accused him of criminality. James Doleman of the Byline Times website

accidentally named a complainer to his more than 30,000 followers on social media as he live-tweeted the trial. He swiftly deleted it, but the damage had already been done and it was being taken extremely seriously by the court. Unlike in England, in Scotland it is a convention rather than a legal requirement not to name women who have made allegations of sexual assault. That changed in the Salmond trial when a visibly irritated Lady Dorrian told Doleman he had committed an 'egregious breach' of protocol, banned him from tweeting for the rest of the trial and passed an anonymity order making it illegal for anyone to do anything that could identify the women in the case. The strict legal enforcement effect of the rule would have a significant bearing on the fallout of the case.

Doleman had tweeted an exchange of messages between Woman H and another complainer, Woman J, where H said: 'I have a plan. And means we can be anonymous but see strong repercussions.' Woman H told the court that the repercussions were to do with the SNP and police taking action. She said she had made contact with the SNP in November 2017 to raise her complaint for the first time, having been influenced by the #MeToo movement. She had started to experience 'what I could describe as flashbacks', she added.

She said she had spoken to SNP compliance officer Ian McCann that month but revealed only 'the top line' about the alleged assaults without giving explicit details. On 6 November, an exchange with Mr McCann ended with him replying: 'I appreciate how difficult that must have been. Will sit on that and hopefully never need to deploy it.'

Woman H was being cross-examined by Shelagh McCall QC, who opened Salmond's defence by challenging the complainer over her attendance at the event after which the attempted rape was alleged to have taken place. The truth was, McCall suggested: 'You were not at the dinner at all.' The complainer replied: 'I wish on my life it wasn't true. I wish I wasn't there … I wish the First Minister had been a nicer and better man and I wasn't here.' The 'better man' motif would later be echoed as a cornerstone of Salmond's defence.

*　*　*

11 MARCH: DAY 3 OF THE TRIAL; 9 NEW CONFIRMED COVID CASES IN SCOTLAND

'It's hardly groping. Would you call that groping?' Gordon Jackson had taken to the floor in Salmond's defence. He was cross-examining Woman A, the complainer he was trying to suggest was part of a coordinated effort to have Salmond imprisoned. She had told the court that Salmond 'ran his hands down the curve of my body, over my hips, commenting, "You look good, you've lost weight,"' in Edinburgh's Ego nightclub. She further alleged that during a by-election campaign in 2008, he had planted 'sloppy' kisses on her mouth and touched her bottom. Jackson said 'trivial things' had been turned into criminal charges after the *Daily Record* story in August 2018 and questioned why the alleged nightclub incident had not been mentioned in six police interviews. Woman A said she was surprised that it had not come up because she thought she had told the police. Pressed on her contact with other complainers in the case, she said some had come to her for advice. 'I would not be encouraging people to make a complaint. In every case I made it clear it was a decision for them to take.'

The court also heard from an SNP politician, Woman C, who alleged that Salmond had his hand on her leg in the back of his ministerial car while her husband was sitting in the front. McCall put it to her that Salmond 'says he never touched your leg', to which she responded: 'I wish that was the case because then I would not have to be here today.'

The former First Minister's team also continued to cross-examine Woman H, who denied having a previous 'consensual' sexual

231

encounter with Salmond following a function at Bute House in August 2013. In a sign of how coronavirus was affecting proceedings, one prosecution witness on the attempted rape charge was unable to attend the court because he was confined to Italy. Instead, jurors were shown a video of a police interview with the celebrity, who cannot be named for legal reasons, which was conducted over Skype in June 2019. The fact that he could not be cross-examined by the defence meant the jury was advised to treat his evidence with greater caution than that of other witnesses.

The first case of community transmission of coronavirus in Scotland unrelated to travel had been identified and Sturgeon urged people to stay at home for a week if they had a fever or persistent cough.

*   *   *

12 MARCH: DAY 4 OF THE TRIAL; 24 NEW CONFIRMED COVID CASES IN SCOTLAND

Cross-examining Ms A, who was designated Woman F in the trial, Jackson showed the jury a series of emails sent in the hours after the December 2013 Bute House incident. It included a message that said a bottle of the Chinese spirit Maotai was 'now all gone' and that 'there may be one or two sore heads in the morning'. She rejected the suggestion that she had been drinking heavily and told the court she had been trying only to 'wet my lips' with the alcohol.

Woman G gave evidence on her allegations of sexual assault at both the Ubiquitous Chip and Bute House. Her mother also gave evidence, telling the court her daughter had been upset during a phone conversation between the pair. The mother said that she thought Salmond had murdered his wife after the government official said she knew 'something that's going to change everything' that involved the First Minister. The mother told the court: 'I said, "Oh my God, has he killed Moira?" She said no.'

Speaking at a press conference in St Andrew's House following a Cobra meeting, Sturgeon announced that events hosting more than 500 people would be cancelled from the following Monday but the government had decided to keep schools open. Care homes were advised to shut to all but essential visitors, but the measure did not prevent the virus sweeping through elderly residents to devastating effect.

*　　*　　*

13 MARCH: DAY 5 OF THE TRIAL; 25 NEW CONFIRMED COVID CASES IN SCOTLAND

An SNP worker told the court that Salmond imitated a zombie before trying to kiss her on both cheeks and the mouth. Woman J said the incident happened when the pair were alone late at night in Bute House after a stressful day in the run-up to the independence referendum. She said:

> Out of the blue he said, 'Have you seen that zombie movie?' I didn't have a clue what he was talking about. He straightened his arms … and did an impersonation of a zombie walking towards me. He put his hands on my shoulder and leant in to kiss me on one cheek … then the other, then leant in to kiss me on the lips.

McCall told the court that Salmond denied the encounter had happened.

Woman D, a civil servant, told the court that Salmond stroked her hair and face in a lift, prompting a colleague to push his hand away and tell the First Minister to behave himself. The alleged incident was one of a number said to have occurred between 2011 and 2013 where Salmond was alleged to have left the woman feeling 'demeaned' and 'humiliated' after touching her. She told the court that she considered the behaviour to be 'small fry in the grand scheme of things' and never made a formal complaint because she feared doing so would harm her career.

Ms B, who was designated the title Woman K in the trial, also outlined her allegations against Salmond.

In a statement issued by the Scottish government at 4.01 p.m., around the time proceedings at the High Court were finishing, then chief medical officer Catherine Calderwood confirmed she was 'saddened to report that a patient in Scotland who has tested positive for coronavirus has died in hospital'. It was the first tragedy, but it would be far from the last. The person was described as 'older' with 'underlying health conditions' and the Scottish government was showing little appetite to impose heavy restrictions and instead aiming to let the virus spread through the population in a controlled manner. National clinical director Jason Leitch said: 'The best science available says that if you allow the growth at a certain level, we will control the rising of the peak and we won't create a second peak. We fear that in other parts of the world that's what they're doing.'

In court, Jackson had to apologise during cross-examination because of a recurring hacking cough he said had been dogging him for 'about six weeks'. Lady Dorrian replied: 'I'm sure the ladies and gentlemen of the jury would be comforted by that.' Asked about the coughing and spluttering, Prentice joked to reporters outside court: 'I'm hoping he will self-isolate.'

*   *   *

16 MARCH: DAY 6 OF THE TRIAL; 18 NEW CONFIRMED COVID CASES IN SCOTLAND
A civil servant known as Woman B revealed concerns had been raised about Salmond's behaviour in Bute House as early as 2010. She told the court he had tried to recreate a 'sexualised' image which was being proposed for his official 2010 Christmas card.

She said trying to escape his embrace during the incident in Bute House had been like 'wrestling with an octopus'. The picture, Ae Fond Kiss by Jack Vettriano, shows a woman dressed in a short, silky Santa dress looking up into the eyes of a dominant male lover, as if about to kiss him. It was considered inappropriate for the card. Woman B said she raised the alleged incident with a colleague the following day but decided not to lodge a complaint 'because of the relationship between the civil service and the First Minister'. She feared she would be 'removed' from her job.

She agreed with McCall when asked if Salmond 'appreciated your work and professionalism' but rejected the suggestion that the alleged behaviour could be described as 'high jinks', saying: 'I think restraining someone by the wrists and trying to kiss them is more than inappropriate.'

Salmond was formally acquitted of removing a shoe from Woman E, stroking her foot and trying to kiss it at Bute House in October 2013 after the prosecution dropped the charge without leading any evidence. The Crown closed its case having told one witness who was on their way to Edinburgh by train to turn around and go home because their evidence would not be required.

Letting the virus spread was no longer an option. Scientific advisers to the UK government had warned that 'social distancing' by the whole population was the only way to stop the death toll from coronavirus hitting 260,000. People were told to stop socialising, including staying out of pubs, clubs, theatres and cinemas, and start working from home. Every member of a family or household with Covid symptoms was told to stay at home for two weeks, while those with serious underlying health conditions were told to isolate for at least twelve weeks. Would-be holidaymakers were told to cancel their trips.

The increasing restrictions created an even more bizarre atmosphere in the High Court. Everyone who entered had to clean their hands using bottles of sanitiser provided by staff. Yet observers crushed together in the public gallery to watch the Salmond trial, and journalists sat beside each other in the overspill room, where a live stream of proceedings was beamed in both to compensate for the lack of capacity in the court itself and to limit the number of people watching the complainers give evidence. One reporter used his woolly hat as a makeshift mitt to try to limit the chances of picking up the virus from door handles. The decision by a group to file their copy from the nearby Edinburgh Hilton Carlton hotel rather than the crushed media room in the court seemed wise. It later emerged that a Nike conference at the establishment in late February was the venue for Scotland's first outbreak of the virus.

* * *

17 MARCH: DAY 7 OF THE TRIAL; 24 NEW CONFIRMED COVID CASES IN SCOTLAND

At long last, it was Alex Salmond's time to mount his defence. After six days of listening intently to the evidence against him, the former First Minister was going to give his side of the story. His evidence to the court outlined the plot he believed was constructed against him. He said:

> I'm of the opinion, for a variety of reasons, that events are being reinterpreted and exaggerated out of all possible proportion. Some – not all – are fabrications, deliberate fabrications for a political purpose. Some are exaggerations taken out of proportion and I think that the impact of some of the publicity of the last eighteen months might have led some people, quite innocently, to revise their opinions and say, 'Oh well something happened to me' and it gets presented in a totally different way. People get into the sausage machine and can't get out even if they want to.

He claimed he had a consensual sexual encounter with Woman H where 'neither party were naked but in a state of partial undress, in terms of buttons or whatever' and they had 'parted good friends with no damage done'. He denied any sexual contact with her during the two incidents listed in the charges from 2014 and said she was not at Bute House on the night of the alleged attempted rape. Salmond said Woman H had remained one of his biggest 'cheerleaders' until he failed to endorse her in a political project. He also told the jury he had received a 'friendly warning' from Kevin Pringle in January 2018 that if he put his name forward as a candidate again 'there would be a complaint against me' from Woman H, which he claimed was his 'first inkling' of any allegation from her.

Salmond accused Woman A of exaggerating 'just as she encouraged at least five people to exaggerate or make up claims against me'.

He also denied having 'sexual contact' with Woman D and said Woman B had 'misremembered' the Christmas card incident, which he said was not 'entirely inappropriate but I wouldn't do it again'. Salmond admitted he wished he had 'been more careful in people's personal space but there was no intention whatsoever to offend'.

The former First Minister described the atmosphere of working in his team as 'quite unlike anything else in government', involving as it did 'working 24/7 and living out of their pockets, with people knitted together and more informal than the civil service or any other environment'. Spreading out his arms, he talked of the 'blurring of the normal boundaries between social and professional life' and the pressure that went with the job.

His successor was at the same time telling MSPs that Scotland was on the cusp of a 'rapid acceleration' in the spread of coronavirus, with another death being confirmed and the total number of cases rising to 195. Scotland's NHS was formally placed on an emergency footing.

In a rare moment of cross-party consensus far removed from what would follow in the coming months, then Scottish Conservative leader Jackson Carlaw praised Sturgeon's abilities, saying: 'I have every confidence in her leading the country's response to the crisis.'

* * *

18 MARCH: DAY 8 OF THE TRIAL; 32 NEW CONFIRMED COVID CASES IN SCOTLAND

The witnesses called by Salmond painted a more positive picture of life working for him in government than the narrative up until that point. Former private secretary Lorraine Kay said her time in his office was 'the highlight of my career', agreeing that the 'tactile' former First Minister was 'touchy-feely, an old-fashioned man' but maintaining that he never crossed the line into inappropriate behaviour with her. Karen Watt, who was his principal private secretary from 2009 to 2012, said working with him was a 'privilege and a penance', adding: 'He could be quite fierce if things weren't as they should be.'

Businesswoman Samantha Barber also gave evidence, saying Woman H was not at the Bute House dinner after which she had alleged Salmond attempted to rape her. Barber told the jury the woman had told her she was 'not going to be there' and had asked her to go instead. One defence witness's insistence on wearing a face mask inside the court drew ridicule from some observers not yet used to the sight.

Sturgeon's Constitution Secretary Mike Russell wrote to his UK counterpart Michael Gove to say the Scottish government would pause its work on holding an independence referendum in 2020. It was also announced that all schools in Scotland would close, while panic buying left many supermarket shelves empty and online shopping services crashed.

*   *   *

19 MARCH: DAY 9 OF THE TRIAL; 39 NEW CONFIRMED COVID CASES IN SCOTLAND

When Moira Salmond accompanied her husband into court for the first time, fevered speculation started that she would testify in his defence. It was a false alarm – and the man who did give evidence did not provide the sort of character reference Salmond would have hoped for. Former special adviser Alex Bell confirmed he had seen nothing untoward on entering the drawing room where Salmond was said to be recreating the Christmas card pose with Woman B. However, asked why he had returned to the room, he told the court he wanted 'to ensure that the welfare of my colleague was OK'.

More full-throated support for Salmond came from Roger Cherry, who was his permanent driver from 2007 until 2013. He told the court he saw nothing inappropriate during the journey with Woman C.

Aileen Easton, who was head of news in Salmond's office during his time as First Minister, told the court she had 'no concerns' about her staff working with him during that period.

In a ninety-minute closing speech, Prentice prodded his notes as he urged the jury to consider the evidence as a whole rather than each case in isolation. He wanted them to consider whether there was a pattern to Salmond's behaviour. Using the former First Minister's full forename, as he had done throughout the trial, the prosecutor said:

I suggest Alexander Salmond's conduct over the span of the charges was intimidating, humiliating, degrading and created an offensive environment ... There is a further common theme running through this case and it is that these ladies effectively had no one to turn to. They felt they couldn't speak out and expose what had been taking place. They didn't consider that they had any real option.

As Salmond took notes, Prentice also rejected any suggestion of a conspiracy and questioned what the motive would be for the mix of SNP members and politically neutral civil servants with 'impressive CVs', who 'loved their jobs' and had 'great careers ahead of them' to devise such a plot.

Salmond's defence was forced to cancel the appearance of another witness after they were advised to self-isolate because of coronavirus.

New criminal trials were to be stopped in Scotland and school exams were also cancelled. Sturgeon admitted in Holyrood that the day's tally of thirty-nine recorded new cases was 'likely to be an underestimate of the true prevalence of the infection' as the number of people who died with the virus increased to six.

*   *   *

20 MARCH: DAY 10 OF THE TRIAL; 56 NEW CONFIRMED COVID CASES IN SCOTLAND

The strategy put forward by Gordon Jackson was two-track. First, rather than argue Salmond 'always behaved well or couldn't have been a better man on occasions', he insisted his client's actions had been blown out of proportion. He said evidence given relating to more 'trivial' charges revealed 'the same pattern over and over' of 'revisionism' about the seriousness of what took place. He said: 'You're supposed to be satisfied beyond reasonable doubt that the former First Minister was, not an eejit or inappropriate, it was criminal – serious matters.'

Secondly, he wanted to convince the jury there was something fishy about the complaints against his client. 'There's something that doesn't smell right about the whole thing,' he told them.

> I don't know what's going on. I'm not suggesting you can work it out either. But I do know this – every single complainer brought to this trial is in the political bubble. This has gone far enough, gone on long enough, too long maybe, and it's time, I say to you, quite bluntly, to bring this to an end.

Lady Dorrian told the jury they 'must not hypothesise or theorise' as she sent them out.

A nearby branch of Pizza Express that was giving away free food that would otherwise be thrown out as restaurants shut down kept reporters and photographers fed before the wait began in the upstairs space outside Court Three. After two and a half hours of deliberation, where journalists debated amongst themselves and tried to draw informed speculation from Prentice or Jackson as they walked through the hall, it was announced that the fifteen-strong jury had failed to come to a conclusion and the court would reconvene on Monday.

That evening, Sturgeon made a televised address to the nation telling all cafes, pubs, cinemas and gyms to shut immediately. She warned that Scots were facing the 'biggest challenge of our lifetimes' and issued an emotive plea to families, particularly older people who are most at risk from the virus. The First Minister said: 'We are asking you to stay away from your grandkids, from the people you love. That's hard. But it is for your protection – so you can stay around to see them grow up.'

The thought crossed the minds of those watching: would the court even be able to reconvene for a verdict?

* * *

23 MARCH: VERDICT IN THE TRIAL; 83 NEW CONFIRMED COVID CASES IN SCOTLAND

Edinburgh was a ghost town. A striking exception was the High Court, where, for the final time, Salmond was dropped off by a car around the corner from the main doors and walked along the barriers that protected the entrance in his dark overcoat and saltire tie. He arrived to the news that the jury had been reduced by two members but the case could continue. A woman had been discharged with a justifiable reason, while a man had been removed from the group following a complaint. Lady Dorrian said the reasons for the removals could not be disclosed and the Crown Office later decided not to take further action against the male juror. Although the jury now had only thirteen members, the original bar for conviction had not altered. Lady Dorrian told those who remained: 'There must be eight of your present number in favour of such a verdict.' It meant a 7–6 majority of the remaining jurors could find Salmond guilty and he would still be acquitted. The voting breakdown of all juries in Scotland is secret.

The deliberation, which took place in a larger room so the jurors could distance themselves from each other, carried on through the morning, past a lunch break and into the afternoon. Finally, at around 2.45 p.m. news filtered out that verdicts had been reached. Members of the public and the media in attendance showed their security passes and took their seats. In front of them in the dock, flanked by two white-shirted security guards, sat Salmond. A former First Minister of Scotland was about to find out if his peers had deemed him guilty of sexual attacks on women he worked with.

Tension overwhelmed the silent room as the foreman of the jury stood to read out the verdicts. A celebratory clap rang out from one of Salmond's supporters as the first was pronounced, causing a police officer to rush over to the person responsible.

CHARGE ONE: sexual assault of Woman A. Not guilty by majority.

CHARGE TWO: sexual assault of Woman A. Not guilty by majority.

CHARGE THREE: sexual assault of Woman B. Not guilty by majority.

CHARGE FOUR: sexual assault of Woman C. Not guilty by majority.

CHARGE FIVE: sexual assault of Woman D. Not guilty by majority.

CHARGE SIX: acquitted during the trial.

CHARGE SEVEN: sexual assault of Woman F. Not guilty by majority.

CHARGE EIGHT: sexual assault with intent to rape of Woman F. Not proven by majority.

CHARGE NINE: sexual assault of Woman G. Not guilty by majority.

CHARGE TEN: sexual assault of Woman G. Not guilty by majority.

CHARGE ELEVEN: sexual assault of Woman H. Not guilty by majority.

CHARGE TWELVE: attempted rape of Woman H. Not guilty by majority.

CHARGE THIRTEEN: sexual assault of Woman J. Not guilty by majority.

CHARGE FOURTEEN: sexual assault of Woman K. Not guilty by majority.

Salmond remained impassive and stared straight in front each time he heard he had been cleared. After being told by Lady Dorrian he was free to go, he replied: 'Thank you, m'lady,' before thanking the guards and slowly walking out of the dock to convene with his legal team. Twenty minutes later, he emerged to the media and a small group of onlookers to make his statement on the Royal Mile.

A car was waiting, as it had been at the end of each day, on St Giles Street. As he walked around the corner to the vehicle, Salmond waved at a man who shouted: 'We knew you were not guilty,' and spotted Jackson. Smiling broadly, the pair touched elbows in celebration. The former First Minister was vindicated and heading home.

The good news would not last for Jackson. The weekend after the trial, a video emerged in the *Sunday Times* of the lawyer talking about the case on the Edinburgh to Glasgow commuter train service. He had made derogatory comments about Salmond being 'a bully' and said part of his tactics in court was to 'put a smell' on one of the complainers. He added: 'We thought that eventually people might think she's a flake and not like her.' Jackson, who also appeared to name complainers in the covertly recorded video, was referred to the Scottish Legal Complaints Commission. The investigation had not concluded at the time of writing.

Jackson said he was the victim of a 'deliberate set-up' but stepped down as Dean of the Faculty of Advocates. He was replaced by Roddy Dunlop, who had represented the Scottish government in the judicial review against Salmond.

As Sturgeon prepared to tell the country it was going into lockdown, officials in St Andrew's House struggled to process the magnitude of all that had happened in a mere six hours. One source present says: 'It was the weirdest of days because of the juxtaposition of the trial result and imminent lockdown. It was like the world was ending. I probably wasn't the only one who was thinking I just can't cope with a combination of all these things.'

At 8.30 p.m., Johnson told people they were only permitted to go outside to buy food, to exercise once a day, or to go to work if they absolutely could not work from home. Anyone breaking the rules would face police fines.

The Prime Minister's announcement was echoed by Sturgeon as she said: 'The advice should not be considered optional. It should be seen instead as a set of rules to be followed ... I appeal to everyone across Scotland to do the right thing – for yourselves, for your loved ones and for your community.'

As Scotland entered lockdown, Alex Salmond was a free man with even more time to plot his revenge on the people he believed had tried to have him wrongly imprisoned.

CHAPTER 13

WOMEN ON TRIAL

18 FEBRUARY 2021, 4.34 P.M.

The MSPs knew that what they were about to do carried a high risk of identifying an alleged victim in a sexual assault trial. The Scottish Parliament's own lawyers had warned it could amount to contempt of court. Rape Crisis Scotland had begged them to change their minds as it would put the woman's safety at risk.

They did it anyway.

Under normal circumstances it would be inconceivable that Holyrood would publish information it knew could illegally breach the anonymity afforded a complainer in a sexual assault trial when the document in question had been written by the man acquitted of the crime. Yet that is exactly what happened with Alex Salmond's evidence to the committee inquiry set up to examine how the Scottish government botched its investigation into Ms A's and Ms B's sexual harassment claims. A combination of the febrile atmosphere whipped up by pro-Salmond bloggers, astute media manipulation by the former First Minister, a Crown Office that had allowed the information to sit elsewhere in the public domain for six weeks, and a looming election that looked certain to return Nicola Sturgeon for another term as First Minister meant opposition members were willing to cast legal norms aside. Yet the people they ended up hurting were those they had repeatedly claimed were their top priority: the women who had spoken out against Salmond.

The complainer whose anonymity was put at risk had even called the Parliament's chief executive David McGill ten minutes before the planned publication in a desperate bid to get them to stop. The chastened public servant could only apologise and tell her he had to do as instructed by the elected politicians.

Sandy Brindley, chief executive of Rape Crisis Scotland, believes the way this episode was handled was the 'greatest betrayal' of the women in the whole sorry saga. 'They knew that publishing this information would pose a significant risk of identifying one of the complainers and they just did it anyway,' she says. 'What that told me was that they viewed the women as collateral damage in the pursuit of their political agenda. I was genuinely so disillusioned that they would act in that way.'

But the publication of evidence which could identify a complainer was just one of a number of decisions made by the committee inquiry that made the women feel that, in the words of one, they were victims of a 'witch hunt'. Two of the women who testified in the criminal trial also had personal communications seized by the committee against their will. They felt their motives were constantly being questioned and their integrity impugned. Several of the women involved said living through the fevered climactic weeks of the parliamentary inquiry had taken a heavier toll on them than giving evidence in the criminal trial.

An interview conducted at the time with another of the women gives an insight into this burden. 'I am honestly tearing my hair out,' she said.

I don't understand how we are in this situation where we are being essentially attacked by an institution that is supposed to represent and protect the people of Scotland. It just feels like everyone is a pawn in Salmond's game. I think it is sad more than anything that you can't have a Parliament that rises above party loyalties and actually does some good. I don't know if it would have been different if we weren't so close to an election, but I doubt it. I genuinely struggle sometimes to process that this is real life, and the hardest thing about it all is that you feel silenced. You can't really speak up for yourself.

The committee had been set up two years earlier with much nobler intentions. It was established in January 2019 shortly after the conclusion of the judicial review but was put on pause until after the conclusion of the criminal trial. Its official remit was to 'consider and report on the actions of the First Minister, Scottish government officials and special advisers in dealing with complaints about Alex Salmond'. The group underwent personnel changes during its life, but the final line-up consisted of nine MSPs, four belonging to the SNP – one of whom, Deputy Presiding Officer Linda Fabiani, acted as convener – as well as two from the Scottish Conservatives, one from each of Scottish Labour and the Lib Dems, and independent MSP Andy Wightman, formerly of the Greens.

Committee members had originally thought the remit would mean investigating whether Sturgeon had helped cover up sexual misconduct allegations against Salmond during her time as his deputy. But the jury's verdict in the criminal case and Salmond's very public anger at the First Minister's refusal to intervene in the government investigation meant this was no longer a credible scenario. Instead, the focus shifted to an even more extraordinary possibility – whether the First Minister had been part of a plot to fabricate allegations against her predecessor for political gain. Salmond's public stance on how he had come to be accused of multiple sexual assaults had changed subtly but significantly from that laid out by his defence lawyer in court the year before. He was no longer someone who, while denying criminality, acknowledged that he had behaved unacceptably and should have been a 'better man'. He was now the wronged party – an innocent man fighting valiantly to expose a wide-ranging conspiracy that had nearly seen him falsely imprisoned.

To the horror of the women involved in the criminal trial, this new version of events began to gain traction with an element of the public. This was partially because of the success of bloggers peddling pro-Salmond conspiracy theories, partially because Scotland's poisonous political culture encouraged it and partially because so many lifelong Scottish nationalists so badly wanted to believe it.

* * *

The emotional rollercoaster endured by long-standing SNP members over the Salmond affair was personified by Maureen Watt. She had been an MSP since 2006 and served as a minister under both Salmond and Sturgeon. Her father, Hamish Watt, was part of the first mini-nationalist surge in 1974 when he was elected as the MP for Banffshire, and her son, Stuart Donaldson, worked in Salmond's constituency office before serving as the MP for West Aberdeenshire and Kincardine from 2015 to 2017.

Sitting in a snug corner of the Scottish Parliament's bar in the days after criminal charges had first been levelled against Salmond in 2019, Watt broke down in tears in front of two political journalists. She was struggling to comprehend – or believe – the seriousness of the allegations and made it clear as she wiped her eyes that she desperately wanted to know the identities of the women involved. What was striking for those present was how hard it appeared for Watt to accept what was happening, as if the allegations themselves were a direct attack on everything she held dear, personally and politically. The visceral reaction underlined the deep psychological investment many members of the SNP felt in Salmond – particularly the generation that had been part of building the party from struggling opposition to all-conquering government. For someone inside the movement to break ranks with such damaging claims against the man who came closer than anyone to leading the cause to victory in the 2014 independence referendum appeared unthinkable.

That sense of grief appeared to have turned to anger two years later when Watt took a markedly different tone as she questioned Salmond at the Holyrood inquiry. In terse exchanges, she repeatedly returned to her former leader's behaviour and explored lines of questioning that were not part of the committee's remit. After one pointed question about the 2013 Bute House incident with Ms A, Fabiani told Salmond he did not have to answer. Sides had been taken and Watt was now firmly part of Team Sturgeon. Of course, as an SNP MSP Watt was in the privileged position of knowing many of the key players in the case and had insider knowledge about what had gone on. Those without such direct access were relying on what they heard and read.

By this point, Team Salmond had been mounting a sophisticated spin campaign casting him as the victim for almost two years. Even while hampered by legal constraints in the run-up to the criminal trial, emissaries for the former First Minister had been telling any political journalist or newspaper editor who would listen about 'collusion' between the women who made the allegations. Salmond deliberately never used the word 'conspiracy' in public, but he certainly did in private. In an email to aides, sent in October 2018 while his civil case against the Scottish government was gathering momentum, he said a media enquiry was beneficial because 'it gets us closer to where this sordid little conspiracy comes from'.

The extent of the alleged scheme against Salmond varies depending on who is telling the story and whether they have to put their name to it. The 'full-fat' version involves the complicity of most of the instruments of the Scottish state and begins with a panic in SNP headquarters that Salmond was considering running to replace Mark McDonald if the former minister had quit Holyrood in the wake of his 2017 scandal.

With the Scottish government's new harassment policy being developed just days after McDonald resigned, the suggestion was that its retrospective aspect was designed to entrap the former First Minister as part of a bid to stop him returning to public life. In the wake of the judicial review defeat, it's theorised, the conspirators moved on to ramping up pressure on the police and potential complainers to increase the likelihood of having him jailed. In this extraordinary version of events, SNP and government officials were assisted by the Crown Office in actively trying to imprison the man who just a few years previously had led the country.

Before the case began, senior figures in the prosecution service had been concerned they would be accused of pursuing a political vendetta, but they feared parts of the independence movement would accuse them of working for the British state to stunt the push for separation. Nobody anticipated they would be seen as working on behalf of Sturgeon's administration to have her predecessor and former mentor put behind bars.

In addition to its lack of political logic, the theory offered no credible explanation as to why several of the complaints had originally been made against Salmond years prior to the alleged conspiracy being cooked up. This was accounted for in the scaled-back 'diet' version of the conspiracy, in which a picture is painted of incompetence and back-covering that spiralled out of control as events began to run away from those at the top of both government and party. The panic-stricken officials are accused of mounting a cover-up amid the dawning realisation that Salmond was going to win the judicial review. They put pressure on witnesses, police officers and prosecutors to secure a conviction that would justify the civil service investigation despite the outcome in the Court of Session.

Salmond stated during his appearance before the Holyrood inquiry that the plot against him only materialised once the police investigation was under way. But this account was contradicted during the same session when he referenced the fact that complaints against former ministers were made part of the policy in the days after the Scottish government was contacted by Sky News about the Edinburgh Airport incident. He also pointed to Permanent Secretary Leslie Evans becoming the ultimate arbiter of any investigation after she was made aware of the prospect of complaints being made against him.

Salmond told MSPs under oath:

I believe that the motivation for furnishing complaints to the police was initially to defeat the judicial review by having it postponed. I think that it came to be believed among some people that the loss of the judicial review and the loss of a court case would be cataclysmic, not just for Leslie Evans, senior officials in the Scottish government and special advisers, but for Nicola Sturgeon. Unfortunately, I think that people came to the belief that the police process would somehow assist in, first, not losing the judicial review and, thereafter, making sure that the loss of the judicial review was swept away in the inevitable publicity of the criminal trial. If I had been convicted of any offence in the criminal trial, that would have been the case.

This would seem to suggest he in fact believed forces were at work against him before detectives got involved. Some MSPs on the committee soon became attracted to this unlikely possibility as they realised it was fast becoming their best hope of damaging Sturgeon. Investigating the merits of a conspiracy was not part of the inquiry's remit but, with the election on the horizon, they smelt blood in the water around the SNP and pushed the issue. Back-channels had opened up between members of the group and allies of Salmond, with Scottish Labour deputy leader Jackie Baillie particularly well-informed of the Scottish government's pressure points.

An inevitable result of the committee's decision to pursue this new line of inquiry was that doubts would be cast on the characters of the women who had made complaints against Salmond. All the women were already being fiercely demonised on the internet, with bloggers who dubbed them 'the alphabet women' attacking them on a daily basis and their identities regularly published on social media, with one man eventually jailed for breaching the court order by deliberately tweeting their names.

A sobering insight into the trauma caused by this online abuse was provided by Ms A's husband when he gave an interview to the *Daily Record* on 8 May. 'The social media attacks were like a black hole we were sucked into,' he said.

> It felt like watching my wife self-harm when she was glued to a screen reading abusive comments. She has been bullied by thousands of people she has never met who are hiding behind the shield of the internet. The anonymity rightly afforded to my wife in law has been both a blessing and a curse. I shudder to think of the consequences that would be caused by a fraction of the online abuse reaching our actual doorstep. But the anonymity has also meant my wife is just a silhouette, a concept, a fictional character to many, whose motives and storyline can be picked apart without real knowledge or empathy.

Ms A and Ms B had been keen to engage with the Holyrood inquiry to provide context to their experience but hesitated due to a growing suspicion at how the committee was operating. 'It felt like the committee members were feeding Salmond's conspiracy theories,' says Brindley. 'It made it really, really difficult for the women to feel safe to participate in the process.'

When Ms A and Ms B eventually did give evidence in private, someone within the committee promptly leaked the details to the press.

* * *

To back up his claims of a plot against him, Salmond pointed to letters circulated by both the Scottish government and the SNP once the police had started their investigation. In some cases, former government officials received notes from both their old employer and the party, which they had never worked for. The government told people their contact details had been passed to detectives, noting the move may be 'unsettling' for those involved, and provided the investigation's dedicated telephone number 'if you wish to speak to Police Scotland'. During his evidence session, Salmond said one of Sturgeon's special advisers told a civil servant what to write in the letter as he clearly suggested its contents were designed to try to ensnare him.

The author of the SNP's email was one of the main targets of the former First Minister's ire. As the party's chief operating officer, Sue Ruddick works closely with Sturgeon's husband, the SNP's chief executive Peter Murrell. During the police investigation, she told officers Salmond had pushed her against a wall on a flight of stairs in a fit of temper while campaigning in the Glenrothes by-election in 2008. The claim was listed in the twenty-one charges initially put to Salmond by police but didn't make it to court. Anne Harvey, who works in the SNP's Westminster group, later swore an affidavit saying 'categorically' there was no physical aggression on the part of Salmond and that he had only 'brushed past' Ruddick on a stairway.

Sent five days after the first complaints against Salmond were reported, Ruddick's note did not mention the former First Minister by name but highlighted that the party was 'firm in its belief' that allegations of harassment 'must be taken seriously' and 'anyone who considers that they have been subject to such behaviour must feel able to come forward'. Individuals could confidentially report 'any matter' to compliance officer Ian McCann, it added.

Ruddick was also a member of a WhatsApp group which Salmond claimed contained messages that proved the plot against him. The 'Vietnam' group was used to discuss the case by several SNP figures and was named in an apparent belief that the police investigation was called Operation Diem in reference to Ngo Dinh Diem, the final President of the State of Vietnam, who was deposed and assassinated in a military coup. A series of texts, WhatsApps and emails between SNP and Scottish government officials, some of whom were complainers, formed the cornerstone of the conspiracy. They had been passed to Salmond's lawyers in the build-up to the March 2020 criminal trial as part of usual disclosure procedures and their discovery had a profound effect on the former First Minister. 'The day I read those messages was one of the most distressing days of my life,' he told the committee. Salmond's lawyers had failed to have all of the messages led during the criminal trial and were desperate for them to be disclosed through the committee.

One eyebrow-raising series of messages sent by Murrell, who as the most senior unelected member of the SNP is in a position of huge influence in Scottish public life, were leaked under mysterious circumstances. On 25 January 2019, the day after Salmond first appeared in court and the full scale of the charges against him became public, Murrell wrote to Ruddick: 'Totally agree folk should be asking the police questions … report now with the PF [procurator fiscal] on charges which leaves police twiddling their thumbs. So good time to be pressurising them. Would be good to know Met looking at events in London.'

Murrell added: 'TBH [to be honest] the more fronts he is having to firefight on the better for all complainers. So CPS [Crown Prosecution Service] action would be a good thing.' The mention of the Metropolitan Police referred to complaints that had been passed to them by Police Scotland in January 2019. Statements from four women that related to alleged incidents in London were examined by detectives in the capital, who recorded one allegation of crime before deciding it was 'not appropriate to begin any criminal investigation'. Once the trial in Scotland was finished, officers at the Met looked at the claim again and spoke to the woman involved 'to ensure there was no additional information that could impact on the decision to take no further action'. The complaints only became public when they were revealed by *The Times* the day after Salmond was cleared.

Six months after the conclusion of the criminal trial, Kenny MacAskill had obtained Murrell's messages, which hadn't been led in evidence during the proceedings. MacAskill claimed they had arrived anonymously through the post in an envelope which misspelled his name. He initially passed them to the Crown Office and the inquiry committee, but when the former Justice Secretary heard nothing back, he forwarded scans to the *Daily Record* in advance of Sturgeon's husband's appearance at the inquiry. The episode sparked another police investigation on the instruction of the Crown Office. It is illegal to publicly reveal any evidence disclosed as part of a criminal trial that is not led in court, under laws brought in by MacAskill during his time in government to try to prevent witness intimidation by gangsters.

After he was interviewed by detectives, MacAskill, who by this time had written several newspaper columns calling for Murrell to resign and was publicly backing Salmond, accused the Crown Office of 'abusing its powers' in directing Police Scotland to investigate. The source of the leak had not been discovered at the time of publication and the police investigation was ongoing.

In its report, the committee unanimously dismissed any malign motive on Murrell's behalf and accepted his explanation that his intention had been to advise that SNP members with 'specific, personal questions' about the criminal case against Salmond should address those queries to the police rather than to the party.

Salmond was desperate for the full cache of messages that had been disclosed to his legal team to be made public and was banking on the Holyrood committee securing their release during the inquiry despite the legal restrictions. During his appearance before MSPs, he alluded to exchanges already in the public domain that he believed backed up the idea of a conspiracy. These included text messages from Ruddick about the importance of getting another complainant 'back in the game' and another that if the police could not find the required evidence 'I will get it for them'. Salmond also read out Woman H's text message from the trial that said: 'I have a plan by which we can remain anonymous.'

Under pressure from Salmond, the committee used powers never deployed by Holyrood before to compel the Crown to hand them over. McGill wrote: 'It has been asserted to the committee that the documents include evidence that elements of the Scottish Government (including special advisers) used the Scottish Government's harassment complaints procedure and complaints considered through the same to damage the reputation of Alex Salmond.' He added that it was 'in the public interest to establish the veracity of these claims'.

Once they were handed over, the MSPs unanimously determined they were the private messages of women supporting each other through a traumatic experience and dismissed any notion that they proved a conspiracy. However, this did not stop them asking for a second tranche amid suspicion that the Crown hadn't handed over everything that was relevant. Again, on reviewing the messages, they decided they did not illustrate what Salmond had suggested.

In a statement released through Rape Crisis Scotland, the women said they were 'deeply disappointed' that the committee had requested the messages at all and 'deeply disturbed' that the Crown had handed them over. They added:

> Not a single one of these messages relates to the remit of the Committee or the Committee's published approach to the inquiry ... Each individual in the messages requested by the Committee experienced behaviour from Alex Salmond that was unacceptable and which either Police Scotland or the Crown Office considered potentially criminal...
>
> There is no manual as to what happens to you when you speak to the Police and they inform you that the actions you describe could be criminal. There's no handbook that sets out whether or how you'll be protected, what your rights are and what happens to your identity. There's no immediate offer of support from a third party, someone who can help guide you through the process. That simply isn't there. So you turn to your friends and colleagues for support.
>
> And when the person you have been asked by Police Scotland to give evidence about is someone who was and is a hugely powerful figure, there is comfort in knowing that you are not the only one going through that experience, you find support in solidarity.
>
> It is impossible to counter claims of conspiracy by those who selectively choose messages, without any context. These are private and personal communications which should not need to be in the public domain to prove a theory false or for complainers to be believed.

Looking back at the incident, one of the women says the prolonged uncertainty of not knowing if the Parliament would publish the messages had caused serious distress.

> We just felt completely powerless because they were being completely irrational about what they wanted and why. They had lost all sense of boundaries and sense of what their actual remit was. It had turned into a complete witch hunt and we felt like we were being targeted for something and had no idea what we were supposed to have done to deserve it.
>
> They were coming after us like we had done something wrong because [Salmond] told them to. And all the while they were saying that the women were their top priority, those absolute hypocrites.

Sturgeon became increasingly belligerent the longer the inquiry wore on, accusing her predecessor of pedalling 'false, damaging conspiracies that have no basis in fact'.

Having initially decided to treat the claims of a plot with quiet derision in the hope that they would not gather any momentum through the oxygen of publicity, allies of the SNP leader now believe it was an error not to aggressively rebut the theories as soon as they began to appear.

A senior government source says:

> Why did we want to do this to Alex Salmond? A man who has a minor cable show that three times a year causes an embarrassment to the Scottish government in the pages of the *Daily Mail*, and that is the provocation for a conspiracy involving everyone from the Lord Advocate [to] the Chief Constable, the First Minister, the Permanent Secretary? It doesn't bear the slightest bit of scrutiny.

I must confess I think one of the mistakes we made is that for a long time we didn't give it much serious thought because we just took the view that this is so obviously ludicrous that we don't really need to fight that argument very hard and we shouldn't dignify it with a response. We should have been more alive to that because in these post-Trump times if you are not actively shooting this shit down it will just grow in a way I don't think was true five years ago.

Committee members insist they were right to explore the credibility of Salmond's claims. Conservative MSP Murdo Fraser says it was 'important from the point of view of everybody involved, including the key players, including the women who made the complaints, that we tried to understand where the truth was'. Yet he is equivocal on whether that was fully achieved. He says: 'My conclusion in the end was we did not find compelling evidence to support the conspiracy theory. That doesn't mean to say it wasn't true, but it was not proven.'

Alex Cole-Hamilton, the Liberal Democrat MSP, is certain that Salmond was wrong. He says:

Salmond kept saying, 'Look under these rocks here and you'll find this massive conspiracy against me,' the messages in particular. As opposition members we didn't really have any skin in that game as to whether there was a conspiracy or not, but because an allegation had been made we felt duty bound to test it.

The government members consistently pushed back on that, which is odd because actually, when we did see the messages we discovered there really wasn't any substance to what he was saying. You could understand that they would be pretty devastating for him to read, and very bruising for his ego, but they didn't amount to conspiracy at all.

*   *   *

Salmond's claim that the conspiracy was cooked up to protect senior figures in the SNP administration fuelled the committee's desire to publish his evidence despite the risk of it identifying a complainer. One of the women who had accused him of sexual assault was a senior official in the Scottish government and was referenced in his written submission. Opposition MSPs were desperate to publish it as they hoped it would get them closer to damaging Sturgeon's reputation. Salmond was also ramping up the pressure on the committee by threatening to refuse to appear if he was not satisfied with the evidence that had been produced by the Crown. But there was a problem – a big one. The Parliament's legal advice was clear that publishing the submission risked breaching the court order because of the identification issues.

Setting aside the moral climate in which breaching the anonymity of a sexual assault complainer had come to be seen as a justified political tactic, MSPs were balancing the risks. They knew they were potentially breaking the law, but would Scotland's beleaguered prosecution service have the stomach to pick a fight with a parliamentary committee?

The MSPs had only got to this point due to Salmond's extraordinary ability to manipulate the media. Attention-grabbing stories that furthered his narrative increasingly appeared across the printed press and on television, while Scottish journalists who had not received a personal phone call from the former First Minister at some point during the drama were rarer than unsigned copies of his referendum diaries. Sometimes he did not even have to bother engaging with the media directly to shape the agenda. Leaks from the committee had been a running source of frustration and rather than follow the usual protocol of simply emailing his written submission – which doubled up as his evidence to the separate James

Hamilton inquiry into whether Sturgeon had broken the ministerial code – to Holyrood clerks, he sent the explosive document to every MSP on the group in the knowledge that it would be unlikely to stay under wraps for long. He was not wrong. Scotland's political journalists found their Friday nights ruined as *The Times*'s website published a story at 5 p.m. headlined: NICOLA STURGEON IS ACCUSED OF 'UNTRUTHS' BY ALEX SALMOND.

The former First Minister had gone on the record, through his evidence, to accuse his successor of a series of breaches of the ministerial code and of giving 'simply untrue' accounts of the March and April 2018 meetings at which the government investigation was first discussed. Although he would continually refuse to say his former protégée should resign, if even some of his accusations were found to be true, her position would be politically untenable. Sturgeon's response to the leak was bracing. Her spokesman said:

> We should always remember that the roots of this issue lie in complaints made by women about Alex Salmond's behaviour whilst he was First Minister, aspects of which he has conceded. It is not surprising therefore that he continues to try to divert focus from that by seeking to malign the reputation of the First Minister and by spinning false conspiracy theories.

Aware of the legal risks, *The Times* did not publish the full submission and reported on it in such a way as to maintain the anonymity of the complainer involved. Other outlets were less responsible. Full versions of the evidence, with minimal redactions, quickly appeared on both *The Spectator*'s website and the Wings Over Scotland blog. When the Crown Office voiced its concern at the potential contempt of court, the nationalist blogger withdrew the document entirely, but the London-based magazine was prepared to dig deep into its pockets and fight its corner.

When the Holyrood committee initially voted against publishing Salmond's submission, or even a redacted version of it, *The Spectator* decided to go to court to ask for the anonymity order to be changed. In a move which raised eyebrows in the Scottish media, they used Ronnie Clancy QC and Levy & McRae to ask for an exemption to the order for all evidence passed to the Holyrood inquiry including 'submissions submitted by the First Minister, by Alex Salmond and by Geoff Aberdein'. It effectively meant the magazine had employed Salmond's own lawyers to go to court to ask permission to identify one of his alleged victims.

The Aberdein evidence had been a long-running source of frustration for opposition members of the committee. Salmond's former chief of staff had submitted a written account of the 29 March and 2 April meetings with Sturgeon, as well as other relevant information, but legal advice meant it could not be published or referenced as part of questions to any witnesses. The material was deemed so sensitive that the MSPs were only allowed to view it during an hour-long 'reading room' session, with no notes or photographs allowed to be taken of the evidence.

Frustrated members considered alternative ways of getting the information into the public domain. Discussions took place about the prospect of the material being leaked either to the right-wing Guido Fawkes blog, which is registered in the Caribbean tax haven of Nevis as part of a move the website's owner Paul Staines has called 'a litigation shield', or to an MP who would read it out in the House of Commons under the protection of parliamentary privilege. The talks were short-lived, with MSPs both balking at the moral implications of such a move and realising they needed Aberdein to provide the hard evidence. Salmond's former chief of staff was not asked about the plans but had repeatedly made clear he wanted no involvement in the unfolding political drama beyond submitting evidence to the inquiries.

When it came to the *Spectator* hearing, Lady Dorrian, the Lord Justice Clerk who had imposed the order while in charge of Salmond's trial, did not agree to the change but instead added a few words to the original ruling to clarify that it prohibited any identification of the women as complainers in the criminal proceedings. In reality, it changed nothing about the rule itself but was touted as a victory by both the magazine and Salmond's supporters. The episode further cemented the odd alliance of one of Scottish nationalism's most famous proponents with Andrew Neil and Fraser Nelson, the fiercely pro-Union Scots who run the publication. They had been brought together by their now shared animosity towards Nicola Sturgeon.

One of the most important parts of the virtual hearings and subsequent written decision by Dorrian was what was not included. There had been no move by either the court or the Crown to force the magazine to remove what remained on its website – the slightly amended version of Salmond's evidence – which was taken as tacit approval of its publication. It was argued in some quarters that this meant the committee could publish the submission in the same form without censure and the former First Minister quickly resubmitted his evidence so it did not contain any of the redacted material. But, as with everything relating to the inquiry, it would not be as simple as first imagined.

Lawyers for Scottish media outlets were confused by the Crown's inaction because they believed the version on *The Spectator*'s website still posed problems when read in conjunction with other material already in the public domain – so-called jigsaw identification.

The ultimate decision on publication by the committee was passed to the Scottish Parliamentary Corporate Body (SPCB), which is tasked with making sure Holyrood runs properly. The group, which includes representatives of every party as well as the Presiding Officer, received legal advice from both Holyrood's in-house lawyers and Ruth Crawford QC setting out the risks of publishing the evidence.

The full advice presented to MSPs on 17 February 2021 can now be revealed for the first time. The confidential document from the Parliament's legal services department said:

> Standing that 'likelihood of identification' is not a high bar and applying the test of the reasonably informed observer with an interest in the matter, we conclude that publication … risks undermining the purpose of the Order which is to protect the anonymity of those who were complainers in the proceedings of HMA v Salmond. Undermining the purpose of the Order would in our view amount to a contempt of court. Whether or not proceedings would be brought is a matter for the Crown Office. As discussed previously it is for the Committee to consider its approach to risk.

Similar concerns were raised by Crawford.

Meanwhile, charities that work with survivors of sexual violence were horrified that the Parliament was even considering publishing the evidence and deeply concerned about the impact the high-profile case would have on potential victims considering reporting their experiences. Brindley wrote to Presiding Officer Ken Macintosh on 18 February:

> I cannot stress how important it is that the Parliament fulfils its obligations in respect of not identifying – either directly or in combination with other documents in the public domain – complainers from the criminal trial.
>
> The treatment of the complainers from the trial has been intolerable, particularly online. They have been hounded, identified

online and had threats made against them. I am clear that if the Parliament publishes anything which could lead to the identification of any of the complainers you will be directly responsible for putting their safety at risk.

After two meetings to discuss what to do, the SPCB voted to publish the evidence with the same redactions as the magazine. They had gambled that even though the material was risky, the Crown would not object, especially when it was already in the public domain. They were wrong.

Prosecutors almost immediately raised 'grave concerns' with the Parliament. They warned the material could breach the court order and identify one of the women and said they were considering what steps could be taken to initiate action. In a vivid illustration of how Scotland's political norms had disintegrated, the Crown Office was threatening to prosecute the Scottish Parliament. In the chaos that followed, there were questions about why there had been no consequences for *The Spectator* publishing the same material. An emergency SPCB meeting the following morning agreed to redact the submission 'in line with presentations from the Crown Office'.

Salmond's 36-page account was then removed from the website before being reissued with five of its thirty-three sections redacted by purple bars. The Parliament's humiliation was made complete when it was noticed that one of the blanked-out paragraphs was unrelated to the criminal trial. In an act of staggering and unexplained incompetence, it instead contained an allegation that Sturgeon had breached the ministerial code by making an 'untrue' statement to Holyrood in 2019.

Members of the committee were unanimously angered by the decision of the SPCB, but, as with almost every other issue facing the inquiry, their reasons split according to their political allegiances. Fraser now calls the decision to back down 'astonishingly lily-livered' and says the Speaker of the House of Commons would never agree to a similar demand from England's Director of Public Prosecutions. He adds:

> The idea that the Crown Office would prosecute the Presiding Officer of the Scottish Parliament and members of the corporate body is just extraordinary. This is not Zimbabwe, a tinpot dictatorship where the Crown is prosecuting Members of Parliament. It is astonishing. I thought they were incredibly weak in backing down.

Others were simply dismayed at the original decision to publish. Fabiani says:

> I was seriously shocked. I don't know how it came about, but somewhere there should absolutely not be party politics at play is in the corporate body of the Parliament, who have liability for everything that happens. And I think the fact that they had to change their mind, take it down, just made them look really stupid.

Brindley is equally damning about the overall impact of the committee inquiry on experts working with victims of sexual violence on a daily basis. 'There is no doubt it has set the public conversation about sexual harassment back,' she says.

> It has promoted so many myths about sexual crime and about what a not guilty or a not proven verdict means. It has sent a clear message to women thinking about reporting sexual harassment about how they might be treated. It was a real low moment for us in Scottish politics.

Reflecting on the experience of potentially having her anonymity breached, the woman involved now says: 'This is meant to be a Parliament and they were willing to put aside the protections given to victims of sexual offences for some political vendetta. I have never been more ashamed of the Parliament.'

However, Salmond was incandescent at the decision to remove, edit and then republish the evidence and issued a statement that said:

> The blocking of the Committee in this matter and others is nothing whatsoever to do with protecting the anonymity of complainants, which I support and have upheld at every stage in this process. Rather, it is a matter of the shielding of some of the most powerful people in the country who are acutely aware of how exposed they would become.

The shambles only increased his fury with the Crown Office and added to suspicions in his camp about the motivations of some at the top of the prosecution service.

Securing Salmond's appearance was thought essential for the credibility of the committee and the decision to withdraw the evidence almost scuppered it entirely. His reasons for non-attendance included Covid restrictions, demands for immunity from prosecution if he said anything that breached the court orders from his trial, and the fact that he could not refer to the redacted parts of his evidence. These were met with varying degrees of sympathy from opposition members who were convinced the SNP MSPs in the group did not want their old boss to attend given the potential embarrassment for Sturgeon. The suspicions were fuelled during arguments in private sessions where the nationalist members accused Salmond of failing to cooperate and insisted the committee could not allow him to derail their timetable.

Baillie almost quit twice over what she saw as blockages by the government, particularly a refusal to release key legal advice and the slow delivery of documents, and a feeling of futility of finishing the inquiry without hearing from Salmond. Although she believed the former First Minister and his lawyers were manipulating proceedings – having done some of their bidding herself – the veteran politician feared the committee's conclusions would have less weight without having questioned the man at the centre of the case.

Cole-Hamilton confirms that opposition members 'actively discussed resigning from the committee' during the stalemate with Salmond. Fraser adds: 'People thought, "What is the point of us continuing with this if one of the key players is not prepared to come and give evidence?" So I think it was pretty close to collapsing.'

Had the group folded, it would have been an existential crisis for the Scottish Parliament. As it was, the toing and froing only added to Sturgeon's frustration with the drama. The inquiry was unanimous that the First Minister should be the final witness, but she saw her appearance delayed on three occasions while negotiations took place, often in public, with Salmond.

Ironically, it was Sturgeon appearing to lose her cool in the Holyrood chamber that opened the door for a resolution to be found. Under pressure from Baillie at First Minister's Questions, she said: 'I still hope the committee will perhaps use the powers that are available to it to ensure that everybody relevant sits before this committee.' With Sturgeon's explicit backing for the move, the SNP members suddenly had no justification for objecting to Salmond's appearance. The stage was set for the two most significant figures in modern Scottish nationalism to set out their competing versions of history.

CHAPTER 14

STURGEON ON TRIAL

22 MARCH 2021, 12.02 A.M.

Working long hours is part and parcel of running the country, but this was different. John Swinney was up after midnight in his Perthshire home awaiting the email that would decide the fate of Nicola Sturgeon.

Three hundred and sixty-four days after Alex Salmond was cleared of thirteen sexual assault charges at the High Court in Edinburgh, James Hamilton, the former Director of Public Prosecutions in Dublin, was ready to reveal whether he believed the First Minister had broken the ministerial code. The previous twelve months had seen the SNP fall into a bitter civil war as any pretence of a relationship between the two titans of Scottish nationalism was dropped.

Hamilton's findings were sent first to Swinney because, as Deputy First Minister, he had formal responsibility for the investigation into his boss. The reason for its earliest of early hours arrivals was because of a promise by Sturgeon that it would be published on the same day it was received by the government. This would now happen while still allowing time to prepare for the fallout. Swinney had known both Sturgeon and Salmond for decades. His relationship with the former First Minister had broken down irrevocably in the wake of the sexual harassment scandal and they had not spoken since July 2017, when Swinney had delivered the eulogy at the funeral of Gordon Wilson, whom Salmond had succeeded as SNP leader in 1990.

Sturgeon's trusted deputy would be able to sleep more easily after reading the Irish barrister's conclusion: 'I am of the opinion that the First Minister did not breach the provisions of the Ministerial Code in respect of any of these matters.'

The 25-word summary was a clear vindication that saved Sturgeon's job, even if the 62-page document painted a more complex picture of how she and her officials handled the Scottish government's harassment investigation of Salmond.

Four days earlier, she had been at her lowest ebb. The leaking of some of the conclusions of the separate Holyrood inquiry, which found by majority that she had misled Parliament, had shaken the First Minister. The most headline-grabbing aspect of the committee report had been briefed on the evening of 18 March, a Thursday, which meant its most damaging findings would hang in the air over the weekend before Hamilton's investigation was published on the Monday.

During that period of limbo, Sturgeon was taking counsel with her closest allies. These included Swinney, whom she told to 'be ready' for what might come at the start of the week. In effect, she was preparing him to step up and take over as leader of the government and try to reunite a fractured SNP just weeks before a crucial Holyrood election. Her popularity had soared back to levels not seen since the 2015 election campaign as the public showed their approval of her daily coronavirus press briefings, but it was Sturgeon's view that the office of First Minister was more important than her personal survival, and she would have resigned if Hamilton had been overtly critical or found that she had broken the rules. Such a move would have caused chaos both for a Scottish government still in the grip of the pandemic and for the nationalist cause. It was to this end that Swinney was seen as the safe pair of hands to provide some calm amid the potential storm.

'For those seventy-two hours – from the Thursday night until five minutes past midnight on Monday – things were up in the air because we didn't know what was going to happen,' says one long-standing aide.

The report's vindication meant Sturgeon was sure to survive. Hamilton's judgment, rather than that of the Holyrood committee, had long been accepted as the key verdict that would decide Sturgeon's future.

Having been cleared, she now found herself in a much stronger position to contest the upcoming election with a renewed push for a second referendum and she duly unveiled a draft independence bill the same day Hamilton's report was published.

* * *

As Salmond and Sturgeon's bitter war had come to its high-profile climax over the previous month, a gripped audience was reminded why their partnership had been such a success. The two most talented politicians Holyrood had ever seen once again showed themselves to be head and shoulders above their parliamentary peers as they effortlessly danced around any awkward questions during their appearances in front of the committee.

Both politicians impressed throughout their marathon evidence sessions, which clocked in at eight hours for Sturgeon and six for Salmond. Even a nasty chest infection, which led to an unscheduled break as a cough dogged him throughout proceedings, didn't hinder the former First Minister's performance. He had been driven the majority of the 170-mile journey from Strichen by SNP councillor Chris McEleny before swapping cars into his lawyer

David McKie's Range Rover in Linlithgow, his home town, for the final furlong into the Scottish Parliament.

He was thirty minutes early for his 12.30 p.m. appearance on 26 February in the Robert Burns room. Otherwise known as Committee Room One, the space where the inquiry had held all of its evidence sessions was deep cleaned before the nine MSPs sat down socially distanced from each other. In stark contrast to Salmond's trial at the very start of the pandemic, breaks were scheduled so the venue could be ventilated and wiped down as part of efforts to minimise the risk of a Covid-19 outbreak.

Wearing a dark blue suit, light blue shirt and navy tie emblazoned with saltires, Salmond was dressed in almost exactly the same outfit as when he had been cleared of all criminal charges at the High Court in Edinburgh. His demeanour was also similar. He chose to eschew the bombastic attack some had expected and instead approached proceedings in a calm, controlled manner. But he maintained a flair for the dramatic.

In a lengthy opening statement, he attacked Sturgeon's conduct as First Minister and suggested she had abused her position to criticise him during a televised coronavirus briefing the previous day. Asked if the 'tools of the state' had been used to protect her reputation, she had accused him of 'creating an alternative reality' because that was 'easier than just accepting that at the root of all this might just have been issues in his own behaviour'.

Repeating himself for impact while speaking slowly and deliberately, Salmond told the committee: 'I watched in astonishment on Wednesday when the First Minister of Scotland – the First Minister of Scotland – used a Covid press conference – a Covid press conference – to effectively question the result of a jury. Still, I said nothing. Well, today, that changes.'

He said there was 'no incentive or advantage for me in revisiting the hurt and shock of the past three years, from a personal perspective – nor, indeed, from the perspective of two complainants who were failed by the government and then forced, directly against their express wishes, into a criminal process' but added that no one could move on 'until the decision-making that is undermining the system of government in Scotland is addressed'.

Salmond then delivered a withering verdict on how the country was being governed under Sturgeon:

> Some people say that the failures of these institutions – the blurring of the boundaries between party, government and prosecution service – mean that Scotland is in danger of becoming a failed state. I disagree. The Scottish civil service has not failed; its leadership has failed. The Crown Office has not failed; its leadership has failed. Scotland has not failed; its leadership has failed.

The only irritation shown by Salmond towards the questions from opposition members was an early exchange with Alex Cole-Hamilton in which the former First Minister refused to apologise for any of his past behaviours. Instead, he pivoted to his often-repeated phrase that 'over the past three years there have been two court cases, two judges and a jury, and I am resting on the proceedings of those cases'.

With traditional political rivals happy to be handed ammunition to fire at Sturgeon, it was SNP MSPs who drew Salmond's contempt. He told Alasdair Allan, a former minister who had worked in Salmond's parliamentary office before being elected to Holyrood: 'You're a committee of the Scottish Parliament, not a sort of Joe Bloggs, you're there to find out and investigate.' Allan did not contribute to the meeting again after the put-down as Salmond demonstrated his ability to find people's pressure points without needing to raise his voice.

As he recalled being shown the memory stick containing the

messages between senior SNP figures, Salmond said attitudes and behaviour were revealed to him that he would not have expected from people he had known for thirty years.

The exchanges proved, in Salmond's view, the 'pressurising' of and 'collusion' with witnesses, as well as 'the construction of evidence because the police were somehow felt inadequate in finding it themselves'. He added that detectives 'do not need assistance from Inspector Murrell, Sergeant Ruddick, [or] Constable McCann'.

Crucially, he said there was no evidence of Sturgeon being involved in any attempt to malign him, but he repeated his assertion that her closest political allies tried to destroy his reputation to the point of having him imprisoned.

While Sturgeon herself was not directly being pursued, Salmond's supporters were well aware of the destabilising effect of their goal of taking out her closest allies. 'You can only sacrifice so many pawns before the queen is in danger,' one said in advance of the pair's committee appearances.

There was near-universal agreement that Salmond's performance was an impressive moment of political theatre from a man who batted away any attempts to undermine him with ease, but there was next to no new evidence or revelations that unduly troubled Sturgeon. Nevertheless, the very fact he was making damaging allegations horrified senior SNP figures. Humza Yousaf, then Justice Secretary, told comedian Matt Forde's *Political Party* podcast that he found the fallout of the inquiry even more upsetting than the original allegations. He said:

> It's not that I looked to Alex Salmond as any kind of moral compass – that's not the point. But the fact that since then he has frankly engaged in a campaign that has been so obviously directed towards the First Minister, towards Nicola personally, has

been saddening and really upsetting because it could have done our cause a hell of a lot of damage – it still might do our cause a hell of a lot of damage.

We have not processed it, but it has been deeply upsetting on a personal level, on a human level, but you've got to just deal with that.

Ultimately, as a government we failed two women – at least, that we know about – and we've just got to make sure that that does not happen again.

The momentum did appear to be against the First Minister in the run-up to her long-delayed appearance on 3 March. The day before, some of the most damaging legal assessments by Roddy Dunlop and Christine O'Neill, the government's external counsel in the judicial review, were published showing their mounting, and repeatedly ignored, concerns about the case.

One of the questions in the minds of multiple committee members during their investigation was why the Scottish government seemed intent on withholding information if it had nothing to hide. Not long after the group formed, Sturgeon had promised to 'fully cooperate with the committee and its inquiry', but it had become clear that was not the attitude of her administration.

SNP ministers often talk about respecting the will of the Scottish Parliament when it comes to its backing for a second independence referendum. The phrase was thrown back in their faces after two earlier votes by MSPs demanding the legal advice from the judicial review be released to the Holyrood inquiry had simply been shrugged off. Tensions boiled over as opposition parties threatened a vote of no confidence in Swinney over his continued refusal to provide them with the requested information.

With defeat looming and the fate of Sturgeon's most trusted minister on the line, the legal advice was belatedly dripped out.

However, it happened in such a piecemeal fashion that it proved almost impossible for the committee, which did not shine when it came to cross-examining witnesses at the best of times, to properly question the First Minister about the crucial evidence.

Opponents think the holding back of key material until the last minute was a calculated move by the SNP to either suppress it entirely or blunt its impact at the start of the election campaign.

But senior figures in the government insist the delay in releasing the material was caused by trying to convince the Lord Advocate, who is both Scotland's most senior prosecutor and a member of the government, to agree to its publication. Legal advice to ministers remains confidential in all but the most extreme circumstances to allow free and frank discussion to take place. If James Wolffe, who initially believed the inquiry's request was not enough to break this convention, had rejected a request for release, he would have had to resign on the spot as he would be breaking the collective responsibility all members of the Cabinet are bound by, and consideration was given to sacrificing the minister.

A source closely involved in the talks says:

> If we couldn't get the law officers over the line then we were facing a simple choice: are we going to have to turf the law officers – probably more than just the Lord Advocate – overboard in order to get this done?
>
> Can you imagine the sense of crisis at that point? If the opposition thought they needed to send signals to us about how serious this was, yeah cool, but we were still sitting there between a rock and a hard place. We didn't have a way forward until we got the Lord Advocate to agree to it.

What eventually convinced Wolffe, who by this point had already told Sturgeon he would quit after the election, was that confidence in the justice system was being undermined as a result of petrol being poured on the conspiracy by the refusal to publish the evidence.

The deck was further stacked against Sturgeon by the publication of written evidence that contradicted her claim that she had rejected Salmond's request to help with the government investigation during the 2 April 2018 meeting.

A statement by the advocate and former SNP MSP Duncan Hamilton said Sturgeon offered to intervene 'if it comes to it'. Hamilton, who was Salmond's lawyer, said he was willing to make his written submission an affidavit, meaning it would be confirmed by oath, in a move that underlined his confidence in the veracity of his own evidence. Both he and Kevin Pringle, the SNP's former director of communications, also said Geoff Aberdein was 'in no doubt' that Ms A's name had been 'shared with him' by a senior Scottish government official.

In what was the first of many evenings of high drama over that single month, the Scottish Conservatives called for Sturgeon's resignation before she had mounted her defence to the committee. The First Minister's political allies thought the Tories had overplayed their hand, but the personal stress was clearly showing within her family. That evening, Gillian Sturgeon, her sister, wrote on social media that a 'hard-working, caring individual [is] being pushed to her limit' and that the man who had helped her to 'reach her dream has helped destroy her'.

Although generally just as polished as her former mentor when she finally made her appearance, emotion crept in when Sturgeon was asked by Murdo Fraser if she would apologise for telling people to 'trust' the former First Minister during the 2014 independence referendum. Her voice cracked and she appeared close to tears as she said:

I trusted him. I am not going to apologise for the behaviour of somebody else. If I have things in my behaviour to apologise for, I will apologise. But I do not think it's reasonable to ask me to apologise for the behaviour – some of which he'll deny of course – of Alex Salmond.

Throughout the gruelling session, Sturgeon tried to switch the focus back to her predecessor's behaviour at every opportunity as, like him, she controlled the narrative no matter what questions were put to her by committee members, who were out of their depth. As well as multiple arguments between convener Linda Fabiani and Conservative Margaret Mitchell, the deputy convener of the group, SNP members delivered a series of meandering interventions that added little to proceedings except to give their boss a breather from any challenging enquiries. Grandstanding with little end result was not confined to the party of government, however, with Mitchell taking five and a half minutes to ask the final question of the session. It is unclear what point she wanted answered.

Sturgeon rejected all of the allegations against her individually as they were raised: that she had known about complaints earlier than she had originally admitted; that she failed to report them to civil servants; that she breached the ministerial code; that she or her inner circle were out to 'get' Salmond by encouraging evidence against him, a claim she dismissed as 'absurd'. She also suggested her predecessor was motivated by 'anger' against her.

She was less convincing when pressed on whether she had been told of the investigation into Salmond on 29 March, but her attack on his failure to apologise for his 'deeply inappropriate' actions towards women captured many of the headlines. She said: 'That he was acquitted, by a jury, of criminal conduct is beyond question. But I know, just from what he told me, that his behaviour was not always appropriate. Yet across six hours of testimony, there was not a single word of regret, reflection or even simple acknowledgement of that.'

Those close to Salmond were far from convinced by the sincerity of Sturgeon's emotion even as they realised she had emerged unscathed from the session. 'The ice queen disnae greet,' one said privately in the hours after her appearance.

It is certainly true that Sturgeon's controlled persona rarely cracked under intense pressure, with allies able to recall only two occasions when emotion ruled her reactions.

The first instance was during a fraught interview with Sophy Ridge on Sky News in October 2020 in which she became visibly frustrated in response to questions about when she first learned of allegations against Salmond. This was the first time Sturgeon had publicly attacked her predecessor, saying he wanted to 'shift the story and make a big conspiracy'. She also suggested he was 'angry' with her because 'I didn't cover it up, I didn't collude with him to make these allegations go away'. Sturgeon then read out WhatsApp messages between the pair live on air. It had been reported the previous day that allies of Salmond believed the First Minister had not released all of the relevant exchanges in her written evidence to the inquiry. After telling Ridge she was 'happy to read to you right now' to demonstrate that the messages contained no relevant evidence, Sturgeon detailed the missing messages, although the sheet of A4 paper she held up while doing so suggested the eyebrow-raising move was not entirely spontaneous.

The second time the situation got the better of her was on a subject much closer to home. Murrell's first appearance before the committee in December 2020 had been strikingly unimpressive – one ally conceded it showed why he was a 'backroom operator', while SNP staffers told him he had to appear 'less arrogant' in his follow-up session. It had certainly caused problems for his wife. He told MSPs the key meeting at their home on 2 April 2018 'was a Scottish government matter and Scottish government business is not for me' as the SNP's chief executive. According to Sturgeon, she had met Salmond in her capacity as party leader, which was why she did not have to inform the Scottish government of the meeting. When she was pressed on this contradiction by then Scottish Conservative Holyrood leader Ruth Davidson, the First Minister's voice audibly trembled in the Scottish Parliament's debating chamber. She accused her opponent of wanting to 'attack my husband and use him as a weapon against me'. Sturgeon had visibly lost control as she added: 'I do not gossip about [government business], even to my husband. I am the First Minister of the country, not the office gossip.' Davidson had clearly got under her skin. Sturgeon failed to answer the substantive point about the contradiction between her and Murrell's statements. It was widely agreed that Sturgeon was on shaky ground on this point and she did not produce a convincing explanation at any point during the inquiries. In his report, Hamilton said that although he accepted that Sturgeon's 'motivation for agreeing to the meeting was personal and political … it could not in my opinion be characterised as a party meeting'. He added: 'Members of political parties do not ordinarily attend party meetings accompanied by their lawyers, and when the First Minister's husband, who is chairman of the SNP, arrived home, he did not join the meeting.'

Hamilton did not make any ruling on whether that breached any rules and stated only that 'the First Minister did not seek to make any case to me that this was a party meeting' despite her having told Parliament on 10 January 2019: 'I have responsibilities as leader of my party and I took part in meetings in that capacity.' Perhaps Sturgeon's reaction to Davidson was so visceral because her husband had inadvertently exposed her weakest point.

The emotional intensity would only increase during an extraordinary eight days that would decide the fate of the First Minister.

* * *

David Davis and Alex Salmond became friends while both were serving MPs and their closeness remained over the coming years despite their differing political views. Indeed, the then Conservative Brexit minister was the inaugural guest at the former First Minister's Edinburgh Fringe Festival show in 2017. When briefings from Salmond allies started to buzz around the Westminster and Holyrood political bubbles that Davis had an adjournment debate in the House of Commons that 'would be worth watching' on the evening of 16 March 2021, it became clear a significant move was being made.

Sturgeon found out about the speech around an hour before it took place, after her aides picked up chatter from journalists. The First Minister stepped out into the open-plan ministerial tower office on the fourth floor of the Scottish Parliament, the same spot where shocked civil servants had watched as the charges against Salmond were read out live on television, to follow proceedings alongside her special advisers.

A feeling of anger grew in the room as Davis revealed that a 'whistleblower' had sent him a new tranche of messages downloaded from Ruddick's phone by the police as well as a series of texts between government officials. Although he admitted the exchanges were not clear proof of a criminal conspiracy, he said they showed 'a very strong prima facie case that demands further serious investigation' and supported Salmond's claim of a concerted effort by senior SNP figures to encourage complaints against him.

Potentially most damaging was an email exchange he read out between Judith Mackinnon, the civil servant who led the investigation into Salmond, and Barbara Allison, then head of HR, in which Mackinnon complained 'Liz interference v bad'.

The message suggested that 'the First Minister's chief of staff is interfering with the complaints process against Alex Salmond', Davis claimed. He added:

If true, this suggests the chief of staff had knowledge of the Salmond case in February, not in April as she has claimed on oath. The First Minister has also tied herself to that April date ... She was of course aware earlier than that. The question is, just how aware and how much earlier.

All of the material read out by Davis was then sent to the Holyrood inquiry, with the exchange between Mackinnon and Allison made public. In their full context, far from corroborating Davis's claim that Lloyd was pursuing a vendetta against Salmond, they actually showed the civil servants were worried she was trying to hush up the complaints in an attempt to protect the Scottish government.

Mackinnon wanted to speak to the government official who sent the emails from the Eurostar and who was known as Woman G in the criminal trial, but she was strongly against taking part in the probe. The woman, who was referred to as Ms X throughout the parliamentary inquiry, sought advice from Sturgeon's chief of staff on how to excuse herself.

Mackinnon wrote that the woman

did not tell us she didn't want to tell her story or participate. She told us she was concerned and needed to consider. Liz interference v bad – promoting a climate that doesn't encourage people to be supported to speak out. This contradicts the FMs own public statements about sexual harassment and doesn't allow Perm sec to fulfil her duty of care.

Ms X also released a statement in which she described Davis's allegations as 'fundamentally untrue' and insisted she 'did not tell Liz who the complaint was from, who it was about or the nature of the complaint'. She added: '[Lloyd] offered to convey my concerns and what I wanted to happen to an appropriate senior civil servant, who was the most appropriate person to discuss the issue with. I agreed to this course of action. This was not "interfering" but acting in line with my wishes.'

Sturgeon's team was furious at the 'misrepresentations' of evidence, which were publicly rejected by the First Minister as she attacked Davis and Salmond for being part of an 'old boys' club' during a particularly combative Thursday FMQs session. The tone of the response had been part of an attempt by the SNP leader to be on the front foot and she was finishing the day in a relatively positive frame of mind.

As she left the Scottish Parliament shortly before 7 p.m., James Matthews, the Scotland bureau chief of Sky News, sent a tweet that turned the situation on its head: 'EXCLUSIVE: First Minister Nicola Sturgeon misled Parliament, concludes Holyrood harassment committee'.

The broadcaster duly had a camera crew waiting at Sturgeon's home when she arrived back in Glasgow around an hour later amid a scramble amongst government and SNP aides to find out what was going on. 'It was a shitty way to end the day, put it that way,' says one aide.

The most significant leak of the inquiry had taken place before the decision had actually been signed off. It was the fourth meeting of the committee that week and tempers were already frayed amongst the exhausted politicians, who had also met on the Monday – when they took evidence in private from Ms A and Ms B – as well as the Tuesday and Wednesday as they tried to write and agree a report in record time.

A Holyrood official showed Fabiani the tweet from Matthews and the convener duly informed the group, who erupted with fury. SNP MSP Stuart McMillan stormed out of the virtual meeting, declaring he was going for a walk before logging off, but unionist members were only concerned about the reaction of one man. Andy

Wightman was the swing vote on an inquiry otherwise equally balanced between entrenched unionist and nationalist MSPs. He had come to the conclusion that Sturgeon had failed to tell the truth in her written evidence and had penned the amendment that had just passed by majority in the committee. With the meeting ongoing and all of the decisions still reversible, there was concern that the incandescent and independently minded politician would change his mind. Wightman did not alter his vote and at 7.50 p.m. the meeting wound up – with some MSPs keen to watch the BBC *Panorama* 'Salmond v Sturgeon' programme in which they featured – and the report was finally signed off.

The following day, with television crews outside her home and concerns building in her team that the First Minister would look embattled and under siege, it was decided that the best form of defence was attack. The committee itself was the target. First, her spokesman released a statement that questioned the integrity of its members, saying they had resorted to 'baseless assertion, supposition and smear' then, in an extraordinary move, three of the four SNP MSPs on the inquiry trashed its findings. In lines issued by the SNP press office, Alasdair Allan, Maureen Watt and Stuart McMillan accused the opposition of making '11th-hour predetermined political assertions that have no basis in fact'. They added: 'For the opposition, this was never about the truth. It was never about the evidence and, shamefully, it was never even about the women. All of these are being sacrificed in pursuit of political ends. This is the politics of desperation by the opposition members.'

Private briefings also went on to try to undermine the personal integrity of Wightman, who was seen across the chamber as someone who approached issues with an open mind; suggestions that he would have been pursuing a vendetta were widely ridiculed.

Salmond was watching the unfolding chaos from afar with a sense of satisfaction. He had by this point spoken to James

Hamilton on multiple occasions for evidence sessions and was convinced the investigator would find something amiss with Sturgeon's conduct, while the leaked committee decision further seemed to turn the tide in his favour.

In fact, the early disclosure of the finding against the First Minister allowed her team to seize the narrative ahead of the Hamilton report being published and undermined the Holyrood inquiry's credibility. 'To be honest, the leak was the stupidest thing I've ever seen,' says one senior figure in the government.

Fraser agrees and thinks the Holyrood findings could have had an impact had they been made public after the Hamilton report, even though it cleared Sturgeon, as they would have been the final pieces of evidence published on the saga. He says: 'Instead, the government spent all weekend trashing the committee and then Hamilton came out with his report on Monday afternoon and they could say, "Well, Nicola is in the clear, it's all over." And the story became a leak. So I was really cross about that.'

Various finger-pointing has since taken place about who briefed the material, with one MSP going as far as to phone broadcast journalists to deny responsibility for the disclosure, but in truth by that point the committee had become a sieve of confidential information.

The most shocking leaks were not the conclusions to the report but the evidence from the private session with Ms A and Ms B, which was disclosed first to the *Scottish Daily Mail* and then to the *Sunday Times*. Both newspapers reported similar findings, with the *Mail* stating that the woman had described Salmond's behaviour as an 'open secret' in government while the *Sunday Times* said MSPs were told the atmosphere was 'like the Wild West', with staff expected to tie the former First Minister's shoelaces, straighten his tie, apply hand sanitiser to him and comb his hair and remove dandruff. The tension, sense of betrayal and downright anger between all involved escalated once again over the weekend. In a statement at the time, the women said: 'It is extremely upsetting that this confidentiality has been breached – particularly after we had impressed on the committee our concerns about some members' politicisation of our experiences. To selectively comment on our evidence also risks misrepresenting it.'

The anger still burns with members of the committee. Fabiani says:

> I was disgusted at that leak, absolutely disgusted. That was horrible. How must these women have felt? We let them down, yet again. Everywhere they've turned they've been let down and it's just awful. Who is going to come forward now in the civil service to say 'I've got an issue' when they see what happened to their colleagues?

* * *

After months of relentless pressure and the prospect that she might have to resign, Sturgeon should have felt huge relief on learning that she had been cleared by Hamilton. While that was the case for her inner circle, the First Minister herself was hesitant and full of questions for the aide who broke the news to her by telephone at around 12.20 a.m. on 22 March. She pushed and probed with a series of questions about the detail of the report, looking for any opening that could be used to undermine her. 'One thing you've got to appreciate about the First Minister is she is a pessimist by nature,' says a close ally.

It had also been a particularly gruelling period for Sturgeon, who as well as having the prospect of damaging findings emerging from the various inquiries lurking at the back of her mind was dealing with the impact of the coronavirus pandemic in Scotland. In a year that involved near-daily televised briefings, lockdown had eased over the summer before tightening again in winter and she had been part of a screeching U-turn along with the UK government to cancel a planned relaxation of the rules over Christmas. Allies of Salmond had been scathing about the original proposal to let people travel and families mix as the second wave of the virus approached its peak and were happy to let their scepticism of the First Minister's judgement on the issue be known. By this point, the number of deaths linked to coronavirus in Scotland had reached almost 10,000.

While Sturgeon was stress-testing her vindication, her PR machine was hammering home the good news. It relentlessly pushed the top line of the Hamilton report and the view that it was an impartial, credible document and as such the only report into the First Minister's conduct that mattered.

Its conclusions had flatly rejected Salmond's claims against his successor, but it was not uncritical of her. Hamilton cast doubt over Sturgeon's version of events around the March and April 2018 meetings and said it was 'credible' that a senior Scottish government official had leaked the name of Ms A to Aberdein. An internal civil service investigation into the alleged leak is ongoing at the time of writing.

Hamilton did share one frustration with Salmond, which was around the inability to tell the whole story of his investigation because of legal restrictions. Redactions made to prevent jigsaw identification meant the report could not be 'properly understood' and could present an 'incomplete' and 'misleading' version of events, the lawyer said in an accompanying letter. With 'certain particular individuals' who had a 'significant role in certain events' unable to be identified, Hamilton said: 'I am deeply frustrated that applicable court orders will have the effect of preventing the full publication of a report which fulfils my remit and which I believe it would be in the public interest to publish.'

In a line that delegated responsibility for a key finding to the committee, Hamilton said it was 'for the Scottish Parliament to decide whether they were in fact misled'. At 8 a.m. the following day, the Holyrood inquiry confirmed it believed that was the case, but the momentum had gone and its credibility was shot. As well as the previously leaked finding, its full report included criticisms of Sturgeon – all of which were voted against by the SNP members – about her unminuted conversations with Salmond and the 29 March meeting, with opposition MSPs concluding they were 'not in a position to take a view on whether the First Minister's version or Geoff Aberdein's is more persuasive'.

The committee also said the Hamilton report 'is the most appropriate place to address the question of whether or not the First Minister has breached the Scottish ministerial code', leaving the two inquiries passing key issues to each other.

The group's unanimous verdict on the civil service was damning, particularly for Permanent Secretary Leslie Evans, who had endured a torrid time during evidence sessions and was recalled on multiple occasions as well as being one of numerous senior officials who had to correct their evidence given under oath. The fact that officials performed so poorly in front of MSPs was particularly galling given that £54,378 of public money was spent hiring external assistance to help them prepare for their evidence sessions.

The committee found there was an 'individual failing' by Evans over the unlawful handling of complaints against Salmond and her behaviour had 'left her open to accusations of having had inappropriate contact' with Ms A and Ms B. The group said the 'entirely avoidable' concession of the judicial review was 'unacceptable' and 'those responsible should be held accountable'. With an increasing bunker mentality developing that no one in the Scottish government could be sacrificed, a spokesman instead said: 'The First

Minister retains her confidence in the Permanent Secretary.' The process of Evans's departure would not start until after the Holyrood election.

The upcoming contest meant entrenched battle positions were being stuck to on all sides, no matter the evidence. The committee report had been published at 8 a.m. on the Tuesday and by 4 p.m. a vote of no confidence in Sturgeon, tabled by the Conservatives after the legal advice was published, went ahead but was comfortably defeated. Fraser says:

> Everybody knew there was an election coming, everybody knew that a major asset to the SNP was Nicola Sturgeon as an individual and her performance during the Covid-19 pandemic. Therefore, anything that damaged trust in Nicola Sturgeon would be very damaging for the SNP, and conversely helpful to the opposition. But then by the time we got to the vote of no confidence I was like, 'What's the point?' There's no point going on with this because it just looked like a hopeless cause.

The motion fell by sixty-five votes to thirty-one with the combined twenty-seven Labour and Liberal Democrat MSPs abstaining, as Sturgeon said she would not be 'bullied' out of her position.

Attacks on the First Minister over the inquiries halted almost as soon as the initial feeding frenzy over their findings had passed and Holyrood shut down for the election. Some opponents think this was in part due to the Conservatives overplaying their hand. Baillie says: 'The minute somebody survives a motion of no confidence it's all gone, you move on.'

Salmond was privately seething at Hamilton's findings, particularly as he felt the report ducked making a decision on Sturgeon's failure to correct the record at Holyrood about the 29 March 2018 meeting. Publicly he said the outcomes of all the inquiries 'despite their manifest limitations … must be accepted, just like the verdicts of juries and the judgments of courts'.

Speculation was building about whether he would mount a political comeback. The previous July he had declined an early opportunity to return to frontline politics when former SNP MSP Dave Thompson asked him to lead his new Alliance for Independence party. Allies of the former First Minister said at the time there was 'not a snowball's chance in hell' of him signing up as they played down the chances of him re-entering the electoral fray.

In a written statement issued on 24 March, shortly after Holyrood had broken for the election, Salmond gave little hint of such ambitions. Instead, he expressed his disgust at Evans remaining in post despite the damning criticism of her and said he would 'shortly be instructing my lawyers to bring proceedings in the Court of Session arising as a direct result of the conduct of the Permanent Secretary'. At the time of writing, it is still unclear what these are. Salmond also made a complaint to Police Scotland about the August 2018 leak of the sexual misconduct allegations to the *Daily Record*, which at the time of writing was still being assessed by officers. He said:

> I intend to make no further public comment on these issues and will leave the police and the courts to do their job. Instead, I intend to move on, just as Scotland should now move on to debate the key election issues before us all, principally economic recovery from the pandemic and the future independence of our country.

Some commentators picked up on the last sentence as a suggestion that Salmond intended to have a voice in the upcoming campaign, but with just six weeks until voters went to the polls, the general consensus was that the moment had gone for him to launch a bid to return to the Scottish Parliament.

Not for the first time, Salmond was about to catch people off-guard by taking an audacious political risk.

CHAPTER 15

ALBA

26 MARCH 2021, 2.10 P.M.

Alex Salmond was smiling, but the people who had worked most closely with him during his political career knew he was furious. A video teed up as part of the launch of the Alba Party had cut off abruptly, briefly flashing to a computer screen showing the virtual 'backstage' area where journalists and bloggers were waiting to ask questions. The technical glitch left the former First Minister – who was wearing his trademark dark suit, saltire tie and matching pin badge – standing at a poorly lit podium staring mutely down the barrel of a camera. Over his right shoulder was his new party's logo; to his left was the slogan 'for the Independence #Supermajority'.

In an unprecedented move, a new party was being launched six weeks out from an election. But this was not the smooth start the former First Minister had been hoping for. He briefly glanced off to his left before readjusting his eyes towards the viewers, where he held their gaze before breaking into a grin. Salmond kept his composure for the seventy-seven seconds of dead air, but technical gremlins would continue to blight the event.

The media – mainstream and otherwise – had been invited to the virtual event, but no one watching the YouTube live stream could initially hear what was being put to the party leader. It was almost halfway through the two-hour event before the sound came on from the virtual green room.

When they became audible to the public, journalists' questions were every bit as bruising as those at the Champany Inn when Salmond first set out his stall against the allegations that had appeared in the *Daily Record*. After repeated questions about his conduct, including if he was 'discredited' and whether he thought women would feel uncomfortable with his return to frontline politics, it was Tom Gordon of *The Herald* who went for the jugular: 'Are you still a bully and a creep or have you reformed?' The former First Minister – who had consistently retorted that the results of 'two court cases, two judges, one jury, three inquiries' should be accepted – said that judgement would be made by voters. He added: 'This is an argument that's going to the people, and on the people's hands that argument will rest. Either Alba will be successful, and many people will rally to our standard, or it won't, and we will find out over the next six weeks.' Salmond, who kept both hands gripped on the lectern throughout proceedings and was being fed the questions through a bluetooth headset in his right ear, added: 'The ultimate judgement will be one for the people to make and on that judgement will the success or not of Alba depend.'

Salmond was having trouble pronouncing his new party's name. 'It's "Al-a-buh",' he would later tell anyone who would listen, having pronounced it 'Al-bah' during the launch. He also confirmed he would pause his RT show for the duration of the election campaign.

Long-term observers who were used to Salmond demanding the highest standards for his set-piece events were struck by the low-rent production values of the launch.

There was a kinder reception from the bloggers chosen to appear, which was a roll call of the cranks and misfits of the online independence movement. They included Stuart Campbell of the notorious Wings Over Scotland blog; Denise Findlay, a former member of the SNP's conduct committee who quit the party amid an antisemitism row after she tweeted 'Israel is a Nazi state'; and Gareth Wardell, who goes by the name Grouse Beater and was expelled from the SNP after writing a critical blog about a Jewish trade unionist which referred to Hitler 'accusing "the Jew" of gradually assuming leadership of the trade union movement'.

Contributions by Campbell, Findlay and Dave Llewellyn were muted by the technical problems. After asking his question, Llewellyn, a former chemist who sold and shipped psychoactive substances known as zombie drugs to the UK from his base in Antwerp, Belgium, before they were banned in 2016, walked around his home smoking a roll-up cigarette in full view of the others on the call.

One of the bloggers who could be heard was Roddy MacLeod, who goes by the name Barrhead Boy online, and he offered support to Salmond by attacking broadcast and print journalists. He said: 'I am horrified – horrified – at some of the media questions you have had to suffer today. Someone mentioned that character matters but obviously not when you work for the right-wing media.'

Salmond resisted the urge to join the pile-on, instead saying that journalists were 'entitled to ask me questions'. He added: 'We have an open press conference. People can ask me what they like. That's part of the engagement of politics and I make no complaint whatsoever about that. That's up to folk how to frame their questions and I'll frame the answers.'

Despite his reluctance to help whip up a frenzy at his first press conference, Salmond's decision to prominently include these controversial figures illustrated the extreme nationalists who were now his core audience. The zoomer wing of the independence movement had become increasingly hostile towards Sturgeon, particularly as the fallout between the First Minister and Salmond seeped into the public domain. The attacks on the public figurehead of the independence movement became more and more personal as the belief grew that she was both dragging her heels in the push for Scotland to leave the UK and aligned with a campaign to destroy her predecessor.

Wings Over Scotland in particular, which had once been enthusiastically promoted by the SNP hierarchy, was a conduit for much of the pro-Salmond conspiracy theorising that contaminated public discourse throughout the Holyrood inquiry. While far from a household name in Scotland, Campbell had deep reach into the grassroots of the SNP, with many party activists avid readers. This audience was helpful to Salmond's new mission because many of the most devoted nationalists were increasingly discontented with Sturgeon and were beginning to glow with nostalgia for the heady days of the 2014 campaign and the man who spearheaded it. This led to resentment from some within the party who were unhappy with Sturgeon's focus on Salmond's behaviour in the run-up to and during her committee appearance. An influential figure who defected to Alba says: 'There probably was a correlation between the people that were aggrieved by how nasty Nicola was towards Alex and the people that thought the SNP was being soft on independence.'

Some of those who made the leap might have already been looking over their shoulders nervously, as allies of Sturgeon urged her to purge malcontents from the party after she was cleared of breaching the ministerial code. One plan would have seen any elected official who contributed to Wings Over Scotland, which by this point included former SNP Cabinet Secretaries Kenny MacAskill and Alex Neil as well as the MP Angus MacNeil and councillor Chris McEleny, lose the whip.

Suspicions had been growing amongst what was quickly becoming known as the SNP's 'awkward squad' that Salmond supporters were being quietly pushed aside after Tasmina Ahmed-Sheikh, the former SNP MP who co-hosts *The Alex Salmond Show*, failed vetting for the 2019 European elections. Doubts had also been briefed about the suitability of McEleny, who was one of three other Alba candidates announced by Salmond at the party's launch, to stand for high office. He later accused the SNP of being worse than a 'banana republic' in how it created its candidate list for the European elections.

In the weeks before Alba launched, Joanna Cherry, a vocal supporter of Salmond, had been sacked from her frontbench role at Westminster. She had previously indicated she planned to stand against Sturgeon loyalist Angus Robertson as a candidate in the forthcoming Holyrood election and was forceful in her public criticism of a rule change by the party's National Executive Committee that banned dual mandates as an MP and MSP, which she blamed for her decision to withdraw and thought was targeted at her specifically. Further questions had recently been raised about how the SNP was governed by Sturgeon and Peter Murrell when three members of its finance and audit committee quit after being denied access to the party's full accounts. Douglas Chapman would later quit as party treasurer, citing similar concerns.

Speculation had been building for months about whether Salmond would attempt to secure a third stint in the Scottish Parliament, but many expected he would not want to put himself through what would be a bruising campaign that focused on his past behaviour.

Senior figures close to Sturgeon admit there was a 'nervousness' at the top of the SNP when they heard the news because of the potential electoral impact. However, they quickly came to see Alba as a poultice that would draw out disenchanted members who were causing the leadership problems. One source says:

Rather than going through a process that could have been much messier, a lot of them voluntarily went, so there was at least an element of relief. I remember being told a list of people that went from my constituency and I must confess I heard the names and I thought, 'Good.' These were the people that were difficult and who were not on board.

The fear amongst some in the SNP that Salmond would sweep into Holyrood was not shared by Sturgeon. One senior campaign source says:

> She saw it as more of a nuisance. For a good two weeks all any-body asked her about was him, which wasn't what she wanted to talk about, what anybody in the party wanted to talk about, because we wanted to set the narrative. So when he came out of the woodwork it was more annoying than anything else.

The initial response from the SNP was not nearly so calm. In keep-ing with the shambolic feel of the Alba launch, a confused Peter Smith of ITV News was thrust back onto the screen for a second question while he was on another phone call. The quick-thinking broadcast journalist simply read out the SNP's recently issued press release which launched a personal attack on its former leader:

> This is perhaps the most predictable development in Scottish politics for quite some time. At this time of crisis, the interests of the country must come first and should not be obscured by the self-interest of someone who shows no sign whatsoever of reflecting on serious concerns about his own conduct – concerns which, to put it mildly, raise real questions about the appropri-ateness of a return to public office.

Throughout the event, Salmond had insisted his new party would run 'a positive campaign and we shall not rise to any negative debate', but he could not resist a wry barb at his former colleagues:

> I would just comment that if this was the most predictable development in Scottish politics, then as far as I know, very few, if any people have actually predicted it. It's somewhat easy to say something is predictable after the event. The challenge of a prediction is to make that forecast before the event.

Salmond's more traditional opponents were also fearful of the impact Alba could have on the election given that the new party's success relied on gaming Holyrood's voting system. As well as a traditional first-past-the-post constituency ballot, there is a regional list vote which is an attempt to make the Scottish Parliament more proportional. Every constituency seat a party wins makes it more difficult for them to return a regional MSP. With the SNP so dominant in constituencies, Alba was only standing on the lists, in the hope of boosting the number of pro-independence MSPs. If this plan worked, it would be at the expense of the Conservatives, Labour and Greens, whose representation largely relied on what has been termed the 'second vote'.

Labour was about to put a private poll into the field when Salmond made his announcement, so quickly added a series of questions about Alba. When the results came back a week later, they placed the party at 4 per cent, which was consistent with most surveys carried out during the campaign. This meant it was borderline whether any of its candidates would be returned as MSPs, as it is generally assumed the threshold is 6 per cent. Internal focus groups were also asked about the former First Minister and the results heartened Labour strategists, some of whom had been panicking that they would suffer severe losses as a result of the new dynamic. A source in the party says:

The reaction to Salmond in the focus groups was almost totally negative, including amongst the groups you would consider to be his core support, like men aged thirty-five to fifty. There was a real lack of warmth. For about a week after they launched, Alba featured pretty heavily in our morning strategy meetings every day. Within two weeks they were gone and we barely talked about them.

Public polls consistently showed that Salmond was hugely un-popular, often coming beneath Prime Minister Boris Johnson, although Alba strategists hoped that the proportion of Scottish voters who felt favourability towards their leader, between 8 and 14 per cent, would be enough to secure MSPs. There is now an accept-ance that as well as being one of the very few people who could have gathered significant attention for the launch of a new party, the former First Minister ended up also being a drag on its ambi-tions. Multiple figures in Alba believe that Sturgeon ramped up personal attacks on Salmond during the campaign in a deliberate effort to further discredit her predecessor.

Former Justice Secretary MacAskill, who announced his defec-tion the day after the launch event, says:

> Alex was a factor. He is tainted, but I think he's been grossly besmirched. He did things that he maybe shouldn't have, but equally his lawyer had to say that. I would have said that if I was his lawyer. If you were to take forty years of my private life, I wouldn't want them paraded before a court. And he was acquit-ted by the jury, so I think that a lot of what was thrown at him was a smear.

Others in the party believe that Salmond would have boosted sup-port if he had been more prominent when voters were casting their ballot. One says:

We had the nuts and bolts of a successful campaign, but we drastically lacked profile. And you can't get the level of profile needed to get 6 per cent in an election in a six-week window. If Alex had been planning this all along, you would have put 'Alex Salmond's Alba Party' on the ballot paper. Everyone was obsessed, particularly the SNP, with Alex's personal ratings, but he had about 14 per cent that felt really favourable towards him. That's enough to win. If we had 'Alex Salmond's Alba Party' on the ballot paper, I think we would have won seats.

By the time Salmond was unveiled as the leader of the party, it was too late to add his name to the ballot paper, as they had missed the Electoral Commission's cut-off date for changes. The SNP continued its aggressive response to Alba when MacAskill announced his move. Westminster leader Ian Blackford issued a statement calling him 'an increasing embarrassment to many in the SNP' and claimed to be relieved about losing one of his MPs. Blackford added: 'That he is joining a party with serious questions to answer about its leader's suitability for public office is no surprise.'

Around the same time, Sturgeon gave her first public reaction to Salmond's new party, telling reporters: 'I take no pleasure whatsoever in saying this, but I think there are significant questions about the appropriateness of his return to public office given the concerns that have been raised about his behaviour previously, but that's for voters to judge and decide.'

Then the SNP machine went quiet on Alba as suddenly as it had exploded. A collective decision was taken over the weekend that engaging with Salmond and his campaign would only enhance their standing through the oxygen of publicity. It is probably no coincidence that Kevin Pringle, the party's former director of communications under both Salmond and Sturgeon, wrote in his *Sunday Times* column that his 'strong advice to the SNP is to largely ignore Alba, as far as is possible, and concentrate on its own campaign'. However, multiple figures in the party's headquarters said the shift in tone was a strategic decision by Murrell, despite him being a target of Salmond's fury over the previous months.

A senior figure in the SNP's election campaign says: 'Peter's mode is to speak to the voters, give them something, tell people why they should vote for you, and don't bother with the rest of it because it's all just needless noise and distraction.'

The launch also had a major impact on the women who had made complaints against Salmond. Ms A's husband told the *Daily Record* that Salmond's return to the political arena had left his wife 'incapacitated by depression'. While walking with his children in Edinburgh in the run-up to the election, he saw a group of Alba supporters but refused their leaflet. In a conversation that caused his 'stomach to lurch and heart to pound', he told them his wife had been one of the women to accuse Salmond of sexual assault:

> There I stood, holding my children's hands. No questions were asked of me, just defensive line after defensive line. The power that Salmond wields horrifies me. It's a power that makes people who have never met him jump to his defence. It's a power that lets him twist the narrative to suit his ends. It's a power that has been a fog over my family's life for years. It's a power that comes from what Alex Salmond represents to many – Scottish independence, no matter what it takes.

* * *

Alba was registered with the Electoral Commission by the multi-award-winning journalist Laurie Flynn on 8 February, the same day that Murrell gave an awkward evidence session to the Holyrood inquiry. About 150 miles north of the Edinburgh address to which the party is registered, Salmond was overseeing the finishing touches to a broadcasting unit in Ellon, Aberdeenshire. He was considering using the venue to broadcast a press conference if his own appearance before MSPs, then still under negotiation, fell through, but it was missing crucial hardware from Vodafone that would allow the venue to be connected to the public. Instead, it would serve as a hub for Alba events, including the launch, during the election campaign.

Salmond had been approached by at least three other new pro-independence parties, but Flynn was seen as being the most credible and Alba offered a blank canvas because, unlike the other start-up groups, its existence had not been made public, even if its registration had been noted by some figures in SNP headquarters.

The coronavirus pandemic helped keep the plan a secret, with regular Zoom meetings soon taking place involving some of the senior figures in the operation. Salmond asked MacAskill to join in early March and the pair took part in a series of video calls with Ahmed-Sheikh, former Yes Scotland director of operations Mark Shaw and the ex-SNP digital guru Kirk Torrance. The calls quickly shifted from weekly to nightly affairs in the run-up to the launch.

Cherry was aware of the conversations and was sounded out early on about the prospect of leaving the SNP but made it clear she was not interested. The only other parliamentarian who swapped parties ended up finding out about Alba by chance. Neale Hanvey had a controversial career in Westminster, having won Gordon Brown's old seat of Kirkcaldy and Cowdenbeath in 2019 despite being suspended by the SNP during the election campaign after it emerged that he had previously shared a Facebook post which included an image of billionaire George Soros as a puppet master controlling world leaders, an antisemitic trope. He was readmitted to the party after apologising and working with the Jewish community. Hanvey was even made the party's vaccines spokesman before being quickly sacked for donating to a crowdfunder to enable barrister Sarah Phillimore to sue his fellow SNP MP Kirsty Blackman.

During a Westminster group meeting held just three days before the Alba launch, MacAskill had been subjected to heavy criticism over comments he had made to the media about the party leadership. Hanvey thought the treatment was unfair and texted his fellow MP to offer support, adding that he was finding the situation 'intolerable'. Sensing an opportunity, MacAskill told him there was the option of another party and Alba duly had its newest recruit, with the defection announced over the party's launch weekend.

The election campaign was unlike any the UK had seen before due to the pandemic, and the First Minister was visibly tired and irritated during a number of media appearances. This was perhaps not surprising given the preceding fourteen months facing both the ongoing coronavirus crisis and the threat to her political future posed by Salmond. Sturgeon's interactions with the media were limited as aides took full advantage of pandemic restrictions, which stopped reporters simply turning up at events to ask awkward questions. Allies insist her overriding concern was maintaining public safety as she began to ease Scotland's lockdown restrictions.

One campaign source says:

> There was always Covid just at the back, always there. She never fully immersed herself in the politics of the election. She never went full attack dog, full political mode because there was still Covid and there were still people dying and there were still people in hospital or sitting at home and not able to go anywhere or hug their families.

Although the SNP press office was keeping its vow of silence on all things Alba, the party leader was still being asked about her former mentor whenever she appeared in public. At an event with the Scottish Parliamentary Journalists' Association, one of just three online 'huddles' she held with the media during the six-week campaign, Sturgeon called Alba a 'hindrance' to the independence movement and said she would not be picking up the telephone to Salmond after the election, before opening up about the personal impact of the disintegration of their relationship. She said:

> I look at him now and won't always recognise the person I was close to all these years ago. That's something I have had to come to terms with over the past couple of years and I've probably come to terms with it more now than I have in the past.

In words that political observers noted as being significant, Sturgeon said she was 'no longer accountable or answerable to Alex Salmond' and was 'no longer obliged to explain things he says', adding: 'Not that I ever blindly went along with what he said.'

Former SNP MSP Andrew Wilson suggests that the end of the friendship had in some ways given Sturgeon the confidence to plough her own furrow:

> If you are in the shadow of someone as substantial as Alex with as razor-sharp a brain, you want to give yourself the space to have your own thoughts. It was quite telling after the Alba announcement that Nicola said she no longer had to think about what Alex was thinking. That is the shadow out of which she has stepped.

Another relationship Sturgeon had seen break down was that with Noel Dolan. The man who had been her closest adviser for twelve years had spoken out in support of Salmond when the allegations first emerged and publicly stated he would be voting for Alba. When she was asked about the severing of ties with people such as

Salmond, MacAskill and others, the First Minister separated her former aide from the rest as she tried to build a public bridge. She said:

> I love Noel and will always love Noel. He is entitled to his opinion, but I don't consider my relationship with Noel to have broken down. I've not spoken to him for a wee while but that's circumstances more than anything else, but I still hold him in the highest of regard.

The view is different from the other side. The day Dolan's initial comments on the Scottish government investigation appeared in the *Sunday Herald*, he says he received two phone calls, one from Salmond thanking him and another from a special adviser in the Scottish government asking him not to speak to the press. He sent Sturgeon a text in October 2018 praising a policy in her conference speech but did not receive a response and the pair have had no contact since.

He says now:

> She loves me. Well, I love her too. It's nice that she would say such things although it was the politic thing to do. I genuinely do not understand what happened with Nicola and I do think her behaviour over this matter and her involvement in the vilification of Salmond has been fairly unpleasant. It's not the person I left in 2016, unfortunately.

* * *

The pandemic meant the election campaign largely spluttered along without ever truly coming to life, which suited Sturgeon if not Salmond. Alba tried to create momentum through a series of photo opportunities that pushed the spirit of the rules about mass gatherings and occasionally backfired. One instance saw Salmond and three of his candidates line up in front of Stirling Castle with giant posters that combined to spell out the party's name. Unfortunately for them, as they struggled to organise themselves into the correct order, a photographer snapped the confused-looking group spelling 'Abla'. After rearranging the letters, Salmond attacked the BBC and STV for not including him in their leaders' debates. The struggle to secure primetime broadcasting slots was a source of frustration for the former First Minister, who knew how important visibility was to achieving any kind of breakthrough. Perhaps more than featuring in the big set-piece events, he wanted regular slots on the evening news bulletins, which are still vital to parties getting their messages out. Threats of legal action, a tactic long deployed by Salmond and still used by the SNP when trying to muscle in on Westminster election coverage, failed to alter the dynamic.

The other opportunity to grab voters' attention is social media, and an Alba campaign video went viral in a wave of controversy. As a camera swooped over crowds of independence supporters draped in saltires, the voice of actor Angus Macfadyen described the Scottish 'forces of freedom' who defeated the armies of the English 'oppressor' at the Battle of Bannockburn in 1314. This 'demonstration of people power by the sma' [small] folk of Scotland was the straw which broke the spine of English superiority', he added. The video was quickly condemned as stirring up anti-English sentiment, a claim Salmond dismissed as he accused critics of having 'scant regard for the history of Scotland'.

The rhetoric again showed that Salmond was targeting hardline nationalists, many of whom might have just stayed at home rather than voting given their disillusionment with the SNP. The messaging was simple on the surface, but Alba's manifesto delved deeper to address specific concerns within parts of the online Yes movement around wedge issues such as trans rights and Brexit. In an attempt to win over the sizeable minority of independence supporters who do not want to rejoin the European Union, the party proposed instead applying to be part of the European Free Trade Association. This would mean fishermen were not bound by rules set in Brussels, and it was expected that the policy would play well in the harbours that are central to Salmond's old constituencies. Alba also weighed into the very live debate about gender self-identification by stressing its commitment to 'women's sex-based rights' – a move designed to capitalise on anger in the SNP base over Sturgeon's position on the issue but also to help detoxify Salmond. The party pushed a five-point plan to alleviate child poverty which included large investment in local communities.

The mix of culture war flashpoints, heavy nationalism, pragmatic solutions to complex problems and promises to help those in need was similar to that deployed by populists across the world. The offer to voters highlighted both Salmond's strengths and his weaknesses. He was able to see political opportunities and was prepared to be bold and take risks to capitalise on them in a way that few others would dare. The Alba manifesto was carefully targeted and did not lack depth despite being hastily assembled. In his new party, however, the former First Minister's excesses and desire to push things to the edge were not tempered by the allies and advisers, particularly the likes of Sturgeon, Pringle and Geoff Aberdein, he had both in government and as SNP leader.

One former aide says:

Salmond has an undoubted political genius, or had an undoubted political genius. That genius was partnered with people who could take that and turn it into something actually useful. There were always people who were able to take that and grow it into something. Throughout this story over the last few years, we've seen Alex in a more raw form. Take the machine away from Alex and what he does doesn't actually work. That's been revealed.

Now Salmond's most fervent fans had become his advisers. Many revered him uncritically and, rather than being assets behind the scenes, were public drags on the campaign. This applied to party candidates as well as the bloggers who fought with SNP activists, supporters of unionist parties and, ultimately, themselves. Champion boxer Alex Arthur was criticised for calling Romanian beggars 'over-fed pigs' and economist Jim Walker was found to have branded Nicola Sturgeon a 'cow' as would-be Alba MSPs' social media feeds came back to haunt the party.

Salmond was also struggling to maintain the positivity he promised at the party's launch and it was during appearances away from the mainstream media that he let his guard down and played up to his new hardline audience. Speaking to the pro-independence podcast *Twa Auld Heids*, he slated the quality of politician at Holyrood: 'Unfortunately, with one or two honourable exceptions, and some good, gifted parliamentarians who are in the Scots Parliament, we've ended up in many cases with a parliament of numpties.'

Such comments struck a populist tone that would elicit chuckles and nods of agreement from the public at large but also undermined the institution Salmond was arguing should be running all matters of state in Scotland. It was also an unsubtle attack on the SNP, which would not go down well with many of the party's supporters who might have been tempted to vote for Alba.

In campaigning only for list votes that would be unlikely to see any SNP MSPs elected because of Holyrood's electoral system, he had also identified a gap in the market for nationalist parties. However, he was unable to fill that void, with the pro-independence Scottish Greens picking up two additional MSPs after increasing their share of the vote by 1.5 percentage points. SNP strategists acknowledge that Salmond's argument had merit, but the stumbling block was the new party itself.

Her votes may have been leaking to other pro-independence parties on the regional list, but Sturgeon was beginning to enjoy the campaign as coronavirus restrictions eased and she was able to take part in more events. Like the rest of the population, she had been living in her own tight bubble for the previous fourteen months and for the vast majority of the time had only seen the inside of her home, the ministerial car that took her to and from Edinburgh and the largely empty St Andrew's House. She was also exceptionally paranoid both about catching the virus and about being 'pinged' by Scotland's Test and Protect service, which would have meant a period of self-isolation. As such, Sturgeon was far more cautious than the other party leaders at the beginning of the campaign and largely confined herself to online events. When she did venture around the country, she chose the events and constituencies carefully, returning to those where she had been given a particularly warm welcome. That was more common than not, with the First Minister telling aides she was receiving the best doorstep feedback from voters since the 2011 campaign. That anecdotal evidence was about to be put to the test.

* * *

Nicola Sturgeon woke up on Thursday 6 May 2021 knowing she would win the election. The crucial question was whether she could win a majority to both match the high point set by Salmond a decade earlier and turbo-charge her case for a second independence referendum. It being Scotland, many of those casting their ballots had to brave snow, hail and torrential rain to reach their local polling stations. Voters formed socially distanced queues and were given hand sanitiser and disposable pens as they made their way through one-way systems, while staff sat behind screens as part of efforts to protect people against coronavirus. Perhaps it was the pandemic effect of people just looking for any excuse to leave their homes, but turnout increased by 7.7 percentage points to 63.5 per cent, the highest level for any Holyrood election in the Scottish Parliament's history.

After casting her ballot, Sturgeon was confronted by the convicted racist and former Britain First deputy leader Jayda Fransen, who was also standing in Glasgow Southside. In an exchange that was captured on video by an onlooker, the SNP leader was flanked by activists as she stood her ground and called Fransen a 'fascist' and a 'racist' who would be rejected by the electorate. The 'independent' candidate received forty-six votes.

Another pandemic-enforced change to the election saw votes counted over the two days following the polls closing, rather than the traditional overnight count, to give time and space for deep cleaning.

On 7 May, a small team of SNP strategists, including Sue Ruddick and party lawyer Scott Martin, set up in a rented boardroom of the Radisson Red hotel in Glasgow to crunch the numbers but did so without the party leader or chief executive. Instead, Sturgeon and Murrell watched most of the results come in from their home. In the afternoon, the First Minister made her way to the Emirates Arena in the east of the city, accompanied only by Liz Lloyd, to hear the result in her own constituency. She comfortably won with a majority of 9,456, despite a 4.8-point swing to Scottish Labour leader Anas Sarwar, who was standing against her.

Sturgeon returned home to watch the rest of the results come in on both the BBC and Twitter while also using her iPad to follow an online spreadsheet of data about the shape of the new parliament, which was being updated by party staff with each new declaration.

Even though no regional list results would be announced until the following day, Alba candidates headed to their polling stations to watch the initial votes being counted and collect intelligence about the likely outcomes. As the day wore on, it became clear the news was not good. Being second top of the ballot paper made it easier for activists to spot the party name as votes were counted, even allowing for social distancing. What was missing in most cases were crosses to indicate support and, with information being exchanged via text and WhatsApp messages, the dismal showing quickly made its way around the group.

In the 15,000-capacity P&J Arena in Aberdeen, Salmond stalked the counting tables with a pen and clipboard in his hands. He was sporting a blue and white Alba rosette and wearing a disposable face covering, which served the dual purpose of complying with the coronavirus rules and disguising his reaction to the result.

Not even the bag of Marks & Spencer's treats brought by his sister Gail, who was one of a small group of supporters joining him in the cavernous venue, could sugar-coat the numbers that were being returned. Alba took just 743 votes, 2.1 per cent, in Aberdeen Donside and only 3.4 per cent, 1,135 votes, in Banffshire and Buchan Coast, which had previously been fertile territory for Salmond. In an image that captured a diminished figure, the former First Minister was photographed sitting on his own at a table looking downcast as he examined his mobile phone. In front of him was a litter of Lucozade bottles and empty disposable coffee cups as well as scattered papers and folders. He fronted up to reality, telling BBC Scotland he did not think Alba would win any seats, going by the data he had collected that day.

Sturgeon's Saturday schedule closely resembled that of the previous day, exchanging messages and phone calls with strategists and watching television and social media as more results came through. The SNP had suffered a severe blow to their chances of winning a majority on the Friday when Jackie Baillie, Holyrood's greatest survivor, once again retained Dumbarton for Labour. Two other key target seats – Galloway and West Dumfries, and Aberdeenshire West – were held by the Conservatives, meaning that Sturgeon had fallen one MSP short of overall control of the parliament. With campaign staff feeling slightly deflated through a combination of the result and the prolonged counting process that sucked some of the adrenaline from the day, the First Minister gave a defiant televised speech saying there was 'simply no democratic justification whatsoever for Boris Johnson, or indeed for anyone else, seeking to block the right of the people of Scotland to choose our own future'. She added:

> Let me be very clear about this: if the Tories make such an attempt, they won't be placing themselves in opposition to the SNP; they will be standing in direct opposition to the will of the Scottish people, and they will demonstrate conclusively that the UK is not a partnership of equals.

She then phoned the team still in the Radisson Red to thank them and chat to staff, which one person present says 'geed everybody up' about the result, particularly when combined with the speech.

Salmond did not attend the Saturday count in Aberdeen as it was confirmed that Alba had won just 2.3 per cent of the votes in the north-east of Scotland, far short of what was required to see him return to Holyrood. The party secured an even more meagre 1.7 per cent of the vote nationwide, but Salmond proved he hadn't lost his touch for spin. He said: 'I think our success is registering as a political party and registering on the political spectrum. To form a political party in a six-week period, to publicise it, to get the activists and the members and the candidates and the programme – I don't know if it's ever been done before.'

He then joined some of the bloggers who had backed Alba for

a 34-minute discussion on the three-hour *Through A Scottish Prism* video podcast. His demeanour was upbeat as he lashed out at the people he blamed for the result, including television and newspaper journalists, who, he told the bloggers, resembled 'weirdos and cranks', before adding: 'We have reached a total counterpoint in journalism where the mainstream media are insane and the online community is sane, forward-looking and thoughtful.'

Salmond also attacked the SNP, accusing its 'graceless' leadership of 'grand old Duchess of York behaviour' by leading activists up to the top of the hill on the prospect of a second referendum on multiple occasions. This included turning his fire directly on Sturgeon as he said: 'Nicola will prevaricate. Nicola lost her nerve on independence back in 2017 and has never recovered it. It's as simple as that.'

In an obscure corner of the internet, surrounded by new allies considered too unsavoury for the SNP, the former First Minister remained fixated on the protégée who had forsaken him.

CONCLUSION

BECAUSE OF THE PRIZE

Ms A's and Ms B's sexual misconduct complaints against Alex Salmond remain unresolved. It is unlikely they will ever be properly dealt with.

The women who dared to speak up have been ignored, vilified and abandoned. They deserved better.

Salmond did not act in a criminal manner. Nor did he act in a manner befitting a First Minister.

In his closing speech at the High Court, Gordon Jackson summed up the defence of his client simply: 'I'm not dealing with whether or not he could have been a better man, because he certainly could have been. I'm in a court of law dealing with whether he's guilty of serious criminal charges.'

The behaviour admitted to by Salmond should not be excused just because he was acquitted.

Bosses can be demanding and running a country is a high-pressure environment where it would be remarkable for the person in charge not to lose their temper on occasion. It should not happen so often that it becomes a running joke between the staff forced to use humour as a defence mechanism. It should not happen so often or be so ferocious that other employees feel unable to cope. It should never involve situations where women feel uncomfortable.

Much of politics involves, as Salmond put it in court, the 'blurring of the normal boundaries between social and professional life'. Yet why people working in Salmond's office were 'knitted together' in a way that was 'more informal than the civil service or any other environment' remains unclear. Civil servants have a duty to be politically neutral. They should work hard and serve their ministers professionally. They should not be carrying out political projects or be involved in late-night drinking sessions in hotel rooms and bedrooms with the First Minister. Given the power dynamic at play, he should not be pressuring them into such situations. He certainly should not be partaking in 'sleepy cuddles' with a member of staff.

A more complex man than the caricature he is often now presented as, there was an opportunity for Salmond to reflect after he walked free from court. Kevin Pringle, who knows his former boss better than almost anyone in Scottish politics, perhaps including Nicola Sturgeon, gave good advice in his *Sunday Times* column the weekend after the verdict. He wrote: 'Gordon Jackson QC, the senior defence lawyer, said that Salmond could have been "a better man". But I also know him to be a kind man, both to me and others I care about. Perhaps he will emerge from this nightmare to be that better man.'

The plea fell on deaf ears. Having cut a contrite if defiant figure in public during both the judicial review and the criminal trial, all pretence of self-reflection disappeared as he pushed his conspiracy theory and tried to overthrow Sturgeon's closest allies.

Launching Alba and renouncing the gradualist approach to securing Scottish independence he has espoused for his entire political career further tarnished his reputation. The Holyrood election result showed a descent from lauded national statesman to discredited has-been which was as rapid as it was dramatic. In the summer of 2014, Salmond almost brought the British establishment to its knees as, against all the odds, he convinced 1,617,989 Scots to vote for independence. Less than seven years later, his new party could win the support of only 44,913 people across the country. Shortly after this book is published, Alba will hold its inaugural party conference and the coming months and years will show whether or not he can once again defy political gravity and expectations. There is space for another pro-independence force in Scottish politics that pushes the SNP hard on a series of policy positions, not least to be bolder in the pursuit of a second referendum, but in May 2021 the electorate overwhelmingly rejected the party fronted by Salmond.

* * *

There is little about the Salmond affair which enhances the reputation of Scotland's institutions – or its most senior figures, past and present.

Under the leadership of Sir Peter Housden, the Scottish government first failed women by sweeping complaints about the former First Minister under the carpet. It then failed not only the two civil servants who came forward to raise the complaints but also Salmond himself by conducting an unfair and unlawful investigation into the allegations. Having turned a blind eye to unacceptable behaviour until it was years too late, the government was then deaf to repeated warnings from its own lawyers about the shambles it had made of the eventual investigation. With Leslie Evans now installed as Permanent Secretary, it followed an unlawful process and referred complaints to prosecutors against the express wishes of the women involved. It bent and broke rules and left itself open to accusations of even worse behaviour. Most damagingly of all, it undermined public trust in Scotland's most important institutions' ability to deal with the misbehaviour of powerful figures.

Yet what were the repercussions for those to blame? For more than two years after the Court of Session eviscerated the probe into Salmond, nothing changed. The discredited sexual harassment procedure remained in place. The people in charge of implementing it were the ones who had botched it so badly before. The Permanent Secretary who oversaw it had her contract extended. A review was not even commissioned into the inadequacies until nineteen months after Salmond's victory in the judicial review.

The effects of the limbo were perhaps best summed up by Dave Penman, the general secretary of the FDA union which represents civil servants, when he gave evidence to the Holyrood inquiry:

> Part of the point of such processes is to prevent people from being bullied in the first place, rather than simply to catch people out. That is an issue about the culture, the approach of those with responsibilities in the process and how the process is applied. We would not say that people still have confidence in the process for dealing with complaints. We would indicate that the issues that we talk about are not historical; they are current. That can only be due to a failure in how the policy has been applied, whether that is about individuals, a broader culture or the responsibilities of those who are ultimately in the most powerful positions and set a tone for how such things will be dealt with.

In his written evidence, Penman revealed that the union was aware of around thirty complaints, whether formal or informal, against at least five different ministers during the SNP's time in power.

He added: 'However, many of those who approached FDA did not want us to pursue the matter as the perception was that their concerns would not be handled sensitively or in confidence and they were concerned that raising the issue could impact on their career.'

The Salmond saga will undoubtedly have made this worse.

In 2014, when he left office, the Scottish government's 'people survey' found that 8 per cent of officials felt they had been bullied or harassed. In 2019, that number was 11 per cent. The figures suggest the culture in government has in fact worsened in recent years, no matter how much some senior figures want to point the finger at the former First Minister as the sole culprit.

Scotland not only failed its first #MeToo test; it failed to learn its lessons as all of its institutions were pulled into a sideshow of high political drama that was easier to deal with than the deep-seated issues and cultures that remain in place, no matter the willing rhetoric. This was all supposed to change, but what has been the effect of the ensuing circus? Ms A and Ms B were clear when speaking to the Holyrood committee. One said:

The handling of these complaints has been quite damaging – unsurprisingly, perhaps – to the prospect of other people coming forward. I was really hoping that if you raised a complaint … you would be helping to set a healthy precedent that, actually, no minister is exempt from the standards and policies that should regulate appropriate behaviour. I would hope that you can bring forward complaints against even the most powerful people and they will be taken seriously, and that, through that precedent, a culture can be built that makes people feel that things are possible. Unfortunately, I suspect that that has been hindered rather than helped by the way that things developed.

The other woman added:

A procedure gets you only so far. Even if you have the most perfect procedure that provides all those assurances and support to people who make complaints, you also need a culture that enables people to feel that they can use that procedure. Maybe things have changed significantly, but from what I have seen, I do not feel reassured that there has been a meaningful change in culture. I think that the government has given itself a bigger hill to climb because of the failure of the process. I presume that, if anything, that will deter people from coming forward.

How recommendations proposed by Laura Dunlop QC in a report published in March 2021 are implemented will be vital to turning around that public impression. A commitment has been made to have any future complaints investigated externally, a decision made three years after trade unions advised just that during the truncated consultation on the procedure that was used to investigate Salmond.

A new team will be set up 'to ensure the highest standards of propriety and integrity across the civil service in Scotland', while improvements have also been promised on how information is stored and retrieved following the courtroom humiliations. The challenge will be to ensure these systems lead to more effective investigative processes and change the culture of secrecy so often on display throughout various inquiries. The appointment of a new Permanent Secretary will also be key, as is the amount of influence Evans is allowed to have over the changes before she leaves office at the end of her contract in March 2022. Will the person who oversaw the failings of the last attempt to bring in a new procedure be allowed to shape its replacement?

A new broom has also swept into the Crown Office following the election, with James Wolffe replaced as Lord Advocate by Dorothy Bain, and the prosecution service will want to move on from a bruising period that saw its very integrity questioned. As with so much of this episode, it was more a case of cock-up than conspiracy. It undoubtedly made a series of flawed decisions, particularly around the handling of *The Spectator*'s publication of Salmond's evidence. The rationale for allowing the material to stay online and in the public domain for six weeks before threatening to take legal action against the Scottish Parliament remains unfathomable.

That does not mean that Holyrood's deficiencies should be excused. The greatest test of the very structures of devolution highlighted numerous shortcomings, notably the Parliament's tribalism, toothlessness and lack of talent. The committee was weak in the face of government obstruction and too easily manipulated by Salmond. MSPs of all stripes were unwilling to set aside party loyalties for the greater good. Much of their final report is valuable, but the group itself is tainted by conduct unbecoming of what was supposed to be an independent inquiry. Holyrood often pats itself on the back when looking at goings-on in Westminster, but it is difficult to imagine a House of Commons committee presiding over such a fiasco.

As two journalists, we must also acknowledge the media's failings. A largely understaffed and under-resourced newspaper industry often failed to interrogate the spin being put to it – mostly by allies of Salmond but also by Sturgeon's supporters – because of a keenness to secure attention-grabbing headlines. Meanwhile, the BBC barely did a worthwhile piece of original reporting on the whole affair.

The limited scrutiny of a complex case left the field open for hyper-partisan bloggers to plug the gap. The likes of Wings Over Scotland and former diplomat Craig Murray, who was later jailed for breaching the court order put in place to protect the women's identities, gained greater influence partially because of the lack of depth in the reporting elsewhere. But their hero worship of Salmond, extreme hostility to the female complainers and bad faith merely highlighted the desperate need for more investment, bravery and diversity in mainstream outlets. The dire gender balance within the media – particularly on the Scottish politics beat – also raised questions about the framing of the reporting during the various inquiries. For obvious reasons, this is a criticism that could also be levelled at this book.

* * *

Nicola Sturgeon had long known about Salmond's bullying behaviour but was knocked sideways by the realisation that his conduct towards women had also fallen short. The guilt she still feels about this lack of awareness is key to understanding her attitude towards subsequent events. The First Minister feels betrayed by her mentor and neglectful of those she had a duty of care towards. One of the reasons there have been no repercussions for the failures of government in this affair is her conviction that Salmond should show contrition first. This ultimately resulted in a grave risk to her political career as he set out to gain revenge.

Sturgeon survived that bitter war with her predecessor and then shrugged off her tired government's mixed domestic record to win another handsome victory in the May 2021 election. More importantly, she vanquished internal enemies who had backed Salmond in the process.

Yet she fell short of the majority that would have piled pressure on Boris Johnson to agree to another referendum. The Salmond investigation forced Sturgeon to choose between the two central pillars in her political life: her nationalism and her feminism; her loyalty to her mentor and her commitment to social progress.

There is an argument that she has been more successful in the fight for women's freedom than in the fight for Scotland's freedom. With the prospect of a second independence referendum looking remote, perhaps her greatest achievement will be as an inspiration to young women entering politics.

Yet serious questions remain about how her party continues to handle harassment complaints. During the fateful meeting of 2 April 2018, Salmond told Sturgeon of concerns raised about the behaviour of Patrick Grady, but she did nothing. He was still the SNP's Chief Whip at Westminster until March 2021, when the allegations that he behaved inappropriately towards two young men were finally made public by one of the complainers. Even then, Grady only left the post because he resigned. Patricia Gibson, another SNP MP accused of harassment at the same time, is still part of the frontbench team in the House of Commons. She strongly denies any wrongdoing.

When Derek Mackay quit as Finance Secretary in February 2020 after it emerged that he had sent hundreds of messages to a schoolboy on social media, including telling him he was 'cute', the party launched an investigation that dragged on until Mackay relinquished his membership. Indeed, when the *Scottish Sun* first put the allegations to the Scottish government, they were initially met with an attempt to erect barriers to publication. Sturgeon also gave greater ministerial responsibility to Fergus Ewing in February 2020 despite being aware of an investigation into allegations of bullying, which he denies, by two civil servants. That inquiry is ongoing following Ewing's post-election sacking from the Cabinet.

Promising to create a 'culture where bullying and harassment is not tolerated and where there is trust in how matters will be handled if things go wrong' – as Sturgeon did when announcing the Scottish government's response to the Dunlop review – only carries any weight if it is backed up by action when it is political allies under the microscope.

A functioning system of accountability also depends on the shared understanding that some things are more important than political advantage. All sides of Scotland's constitutional debate have failed in this regard. The dream shall never die, Salmond famously said as he announced his resignation as First Minister, and the nationalist movement has been guilty of placing greater value on avoiding damaging the cause than on the welfare of others.

Humza Yousaf inadvertently made the point when he described Salmond's actions towards Sturgeon following the trial verdict as being 'really upsetting because it could have done our cause a hell of a lot of damage – it still might do our cause a hell of a lot of damage'. He quickly added that women must not be failed in the way Ms A and Ms B had been, but he had already let slip the true priority of many in the SNP, including those at the top of the party.

Others are more blunt. One senior figure who has been central throughout both Salmond's and Sturgeon's leadership says now:

> I have asked myself, 'Was I blind?' We are talking about people – some of whom are good, close friends of mine – who have since said things about behaviours they have experienced that have horrified me that I was unaware of at the time. And do I have a sense of guilt over that? Of course I do. Do I have questions that I ask myself over whether I'm blameless or not? Of course I do. These are my friends. But set that aside – the bullying and the horrible human being that he was – why did we tolerate it? Because of the prize.

The complaints against Alex Salmond date back to a time when Scotland was in the grip of a fevered constitutional debate. They came to light at the height of the intense scrutiny of #MeToo. The aftermath splintered Scottish nationalism, with Salmond and Sturgeon's relationship now broken beyond repair.

What has the impact been of this ugly episode on tackling sexual harassment? The verdict from one of the original complainers to the Holyrood inquiry was bleak:

> It went from feeling that we had made people feel able to speak up – when they thought that they would never be able to – to feeling that we had just created a position that left them open to so much often personally directed abuse and misrepresentation on social media, so it has been completely crushing.

TIMELINE

3 September 2004: Alex Salmond is elected as leader of the Scottish National Party (SNP) for the second time, with Nicola Sturgeon as his deputy.

3 May 2007: Scotland elects its first SNP government and Salmond becomes First Minister.

5 May 2011: The SNP breaks the electoral system and wins a majority at Holyrood.

18 September 2014: Scotland votes 'no' to independence by 55 per cent to 45 per cent.

20 November 2014: Sturgeon is sworn in as First Minister, replacing Salmond.

7 May 2015: The SNP records a historic landslide general election victory in Scotland, winning fifty-six out of fifty-nine seats and Salmond is returned as an MP.

5 May 2016: The SNP loses its majority at Holyrood, but Sturgeon is comfortably returned as First Minister.

23 June 2016: The UK votes to leave the European Union by 52 per cent to 48 per cent, but 62 per cent of voters in Scotland back Remain.

8 June 2017: Twenty-one SNP MPs lose their seats in the snap general election, including Salmond.

7 November 2017: The issue of possible complaints against former ministers is proposed as part of a new Scottish government sexual harassment policy in the wake of #MeToo.

9 November 2017: Salmond launches his chat show on RT.

16 January 2018: Ms A makes a formal complaint against Salmond under the new procedure.

24 January 2018: Ms B makes a formal complaint against Salmond.

7 March 2018: Salmond is told of the complaints.

29 March 2018: Sturgeon meets Geoff Aberdein in her Holyrood office to arrange a meeting with Salmond.

2 April 2018: Salmond travels to Sturgeon's home in Glasgow and the pair discuss the Scottish government's investigation. He asks her to intervene, but she does not.

22 August 2018: Ms A, Ms B and Salmond are told the decisions of the inquiry. Criminal complaints are referred to Police Scotland.

23 August 2018: Salmond successfully stops the government publishing the outcome, but it has already been leaked to the *Daily Record*, which publishes the story.

8 January 2019: Salmond wins a judicial review, which rules the government's investigation was 'unlawful', 'unfair' and 'tainted by apparent bias'. He was later awarded £512,250 in costs.

24 January 2019: Salmond appears in court charged with fourteen offences, including two counts of attempted rape.

12 December 2019: The SNP wins an additional thirteen seats to return forty-eight MPs in the snap general election.

23 March 2020: Salmond is acquitted of all charges following a two-week trial at the High Court in Edinburgh. Scotland goes into lockdown because of coronavirus.

22 March 2021: Sturgeon is cleared of breaching the ministerial code by independent investigator James Hamilton.

23 March 2021: Sturgeon is found to have misled Parliament by a majority of MSPs on a Holyrood committee set up to examine the Scottish government's botched investigation.

26 March 2021: Salmond launches the Alba Party.

6 May 2021: The SNP falls one seat short of a majority as Sturgeon is again returned as First Minister. Salmond fails to win a seat at Holyrood as Alba wins just 1.7 per cent of the vote.

APPENDIX

THE DECISION REPORT

Decision Report summary excerpt
Formal complaints against
Former First Minister, **Alex Salmond**

Decision Report by
Leslie Evans, Permanent Secretary
Scottish Government

....

Summary of conclusions on Causes for concern A–I
Complainer A (Causes for concern A, B, C and D)

....

Cause for concern A. In [redacted] in a hotel room, FFM placed his hands over the eyes of Ms A who was present in the room on official business, from behind and without warning, and spun her round apparently in order to make her feel dizzy.

Conclusion: Well founded. The conduct was unwanted and had the effect of violating Ms A's dignity and occurred because of her sex.

Cause for concern B. In [redacted] in FFM's hotel bedroom, FFM asked Ms A, who was present in the room on official business, to turn off the lights. FFM instructed her to remain with him alone in the room. FFM then proceeded to have a long conversation with her about matters personal to him which continued until 3am.

Conclusion: Not well founded in itself. However, when taken with other incidents it may demonstrate a course of conduct which would appear to a reasonable person to amount to harassment.

....

Cause for concern C. Around November 2013 in Bute House when Ms A was alone in FFM's company late in the evening on official business on FFM's instruction, in a private part of the building, FFM kissed her on the lips as she was leaving the room. This was 'more than a peck'.

Conclusion: Well founded. The conduct was unwanted and of a sexual nature. It had the purpose or effect of violating Ms A's dignity and creating an intimidating, degrading, humiliating and offensive environment.

....

Cause for concern D. In December 2013 in Bute House late in the evening when Ms A was alone in FFM's company on official business, and when FFM had been drinking alcohol, FFM: instructed her to move from a public room to FFM's bedroom; repeatedly offered her alcohol, which she declined; instructed her to take off her boots; instructed her to lie on the bed; lay on top of her on the bed; kissed her; touched her sexually on the breasts and bottom through her clothes; continued this conduct for several minutes and only stopped when asked repeatedly by her to do so. FFM later apologised to her for this conduct.

Conclusion: Well founded. The conduct was unwanted and of a sexual nature. It had the purpose or effect of violating Ms A's dignity and creating an intimidating, degrading, humiliating and offensive environment. In addition, this conduct, when taken with other incidents at A, B and C, forms parts of a course of conduct which would appear to a reasonable person to amount to harassment.

Complainer B (Causes for concern E, F, G, H and I)

Cause for concern E. On [redacted] in a government car FFM said to Ms B accompanying him on official business, 'don't you think I'm so sexy'.

Conclusion: Not well founded.

Cause for concern F. In [redacted] in Bute House FFM said to Ms B: 'stand there and give me a twirl'.

Conclusion: Not well founded in itself. However, when taken with other incidents it may demonstrate a course of conduct which would appear to a reasonable person to amount to harassment. Therefore I consider this again in cause for concern I.

....

Cause for concern G. In [redacted] at a dinner, FFM, while quite drunk and in front of other attendees, put his hand on Ms B's face and under her chin and pulled her hair.

Conclusion: Well founded. The conduct was unwanted and had the effect of violating Ms B's dignity and occurred because of her sex.

....

Cause for concern H. In [redacted] in a government car on an official business FFM: shouted aggressively at Ms B, pointed his finger directly in her face, called her a 'disgrace' and accused her of letting her colleagues down over a trivial matter.

Conclusion: No finding has been made.

....

Cause for concern I. In November 2014 at a dinner at Stirling Castle following a meeting and after FFM had been drinking, FFM: instructed Ms B to have her photograph taken with him and others which she did with reluctance; reached his arm around her when the photograph was being taken; grabbed her bottom; did not stop when she looked directly at FFM to make him stop; and then squeezed her bottom harder.

Conclusion: Well founded. The conduct was unwanted and of a sexual nature. It had the purpose or effect of violating Ms B's dignity and creating an intimidating, degrading, humiliating and offensive environment. In addition, this conduct, when taken with other incidents at F and G forms parts of a course of conduct which would appear to a reasonable person to amount to harassment.

ACKNOWLEDGEMENTS

This book was produced under considerable time pressure by two people who for a large part of the writing process were legally not allowed to be in the same room. Under the unusual circumstances of Covid restrictions, we were even more dependent on the goodwill, help and support of numerous friends and colleagues without whom *Break-Up* would not have been possible.

The authors would like to thank the team at Biteback for their time and patience – especially our editor, Olivia Beattie, whose advice, suggestions and eye for detail vastly improved the text. Martin Redfern, of Northbank Talent Management, believed in the project from the minute we pitched it to him and has been a brilliant guide through the unfamiliar world of book publishing. We hope to meet both Olivia and Martin in the flesh sometime when the fates allow. Patrick Maguire introduced us to Martin and was an enthusiastic supporter of the book. The unflappable Campbell Deane once again proved himself a fantastic media lawyer. This was not an easy book to legal, but he made it as painless as possible.

Several journalistic colleagues also helped with advice, support and encouragement during the gruelling process of making *Break-Up* a reality. Particular thanks must go to Andy Philip, Lindsay McIntosh and Andrew Picken for their time, insight and counsel.

The author David Torrance did an excellent job of cataloguing the early days of Alex Salmond and Nicola Sturgeon's political partnership in his respective biographies of the two politicians. Both those books were invaluable in preparation for this one. If you enjoyed this, you'll enjoy them. The court reporting of Kieran's colleagues at *The Times* and the *Scottish Sun* was also drawn on heavily in the section of the book that deals with Salmond's criminal trial.

David Clegg would like to thank all his colleagues at *The Courier*, especially Richard Neville and Graham Huband, for their help and encouragement – and allowing me to take annual leave when it suited the book schedule. My former colleagues at the *Daily Record* also played a crucial role in the early part of this story, especially Kevin Mansi. Having the best news desk operator in the business to work with that night was the only reason the story got over the line. Severin Carrell of *The Guardian* was also particularly supportive during the high-pressure moments of the past three years. His passion for journalism kept me pulling on the thread.

My parents, Lorna and Leslie, provided immense help and encouragement throughout, as they always do. They even had me stay for a writing week, which involved my mum plying me with bacon and reading early drafts. My greatest debt of gratitude, however, undoubtedly goes to my wife, Suzanne, and our two brilliant boys for putting up with me working so much this year despite rarely leaving the house. I promise to spend more time downstairs with them from now on.

Kieran Andrews would like to thank his colleagues at *The Times* for their support, especially Magnus Llewellin and David McCann for the leeway given when required and Mike Wade for being the ideal reporting partner during the trial and its aftermath. Rachel Watson of the *Scottish Daily Mail* and Paul Hutcheon of the *Daily Record* were the two reporters I worried about most when opening the papers in the morning while covering the Holyrood committee, but their friendship, insight and wisdom – alongside that competition – meant my reporting was vastly improved. The late, great Steve Mitchell taught me that people are the most important thing when reporting the news, while Campbell Gunn and Steve Bargeton, alongside David Clegg, looked after me when I started working in Holyrood. My parents, Carol and Peter, believed in me before I did and showed it through both encouragement and Sunday night chats. I will always be grateful to them and my brother, Mike, for being there when I have most needed them. Most of all, I am indebted to my partner, Rachel, for putting up with so much while simultaneously being incredibly supportive – I have now unchained myself from the laptop.